THE MIDAS TOUCH

D0166911

Other Books by John Train

The Money Masters

Preserving Capital and Making It Grow

Famous Financial Fiascos

John Train's Most Remarkable Names

Remarkable Occurrences

Remarkable Words

Remarkable Relatives

THE MIDAS TOUCH

*The Strategies That Have Made
Warren Buffett America's
Pre-eminent Investor*

JOHN TRAIN

Harper & Row, Publishers, New York
Cambridge, Philadelphia, San Francisco, Washington
London, Mexico City, São Paulo, Singapore, Sydney

Copyright acknowledgments follow the index.

A hardcover edition of this book is published by Harper & Row Publishers.

THE MIDAS TOUCH. Copyright © 1987 by John Train. All rights reserved. Printed in the United States of America. No part of this book may be used or reproduced in any manner whatsoever without written permission except in the case of brief quotations embodied in critical articles and reviews. For information address Harper & Row, Publishers, Inc., 10 East 53rd Street, New York, N.Y. 10022. Published simultaneously in Canada by Fitzhenry & Whiteside Limited, Toronto.

Copyeditor: Ann Finlayson
Designer: Sidney Feinberg
Indexer: Auralie Logan

Library of Congress Cataloging-in-Publication Data

Train, John
    The midas touch.
    "Perennial Library."
    Includes index.
    1. Buffet, Warren.   2. Capitalists and financiers—United States—Biography.
3. Investments—United States.   I. Title.
HQ172.B84T72   1988   332.6'092'4   [B]   86-45157
ISBN 0-06-091500-5(pbk.)

88 89 90 91 92 FG 10 9 8 7 6 5 4 3 2 1

Contents

III. Buffett's Methods

IV. How to Invest Like Buffett

Conclusion

Acknowledgments

I am grateful to Virginia Armat for her editorial wisdom and dedication; to Alexandra Ourusoff, research assistant; to Andrew Sidoti for summarizing Berkshire transactions; to Kiril Sokoloff and Piers Dixon for reviewing the text, and to Claudette Teen for her usual skill and patience. Also to Street Smart Investing and Standard & Poor's for material in Appendix I.

Introduction

Warren Buffett has been one of the most successful of today's portfolio investors. He is convenient to study, since he has written and spoken extensively on the subject. Indeed, there was for years a brisk samizdat circulation of the annual reports, which include his "Letters to the Shareholders," of the company Buffett controls, Berkshire Hathaway. Berkshire finally coped with this demand by collecting and republishing the series.

Buffett started out as a disciple of Benjamin Graham, the most eminent theoretician of the "value" (as distinct from "growth") technique of investing. He has edited and introduced successive editions of Graham's *The Intelligent Investor,* one of the most useful books for the nonprofessional reader, and remains generally close to Graham's thinking—which is, however, only one of many valid techniques. But when a disciple becomes in turn a master himself and comprehends the reasons behind his former mentor's formulations, he rises above the previous orthodoxy and breaks new ground. As we will see, Buffett is no exception.

One hopes that Warren Buffett will one day write his own book about investing; in the meantime, I trust this modest summary will be found helpful. It is based on his writings, interviews, addresses, and informal observations. Some of his views have evolved since they were first put forward and others will in the future. Nobody is right all the time, and one goes on learning. Times change and so must we.

THE MIDAS TOUCH

I

A Master Investor

"I'll Take the Money"

If you had put $10,000 in Buffett's original investing partnership at its inception in 1956, you would have collected about $293,738 by the time he dissolved it at the end of 1969, minus, however, his 25 percent general partner's share of the profits above a 6 percent return to the limited partners, or $267,691 net. He had never suffered a down year, even in the severe bear markets of 1957, 1962, 1966, and 1969. When the partnership was wound up, you could have elected to stay with Buffett as a shareholder of Berkshire Hathaway, Inc., which was spun off from the partnership and became Buffett's investing vehicle. In that event, your $10,000 would by the end of 1986 have turned into well over $5 million.

His neighbor in Omaha, Donald Keough, once mentioned in an interview that when he was a young executive with Beech-Nut, he went off to work every day while Buffett ran his investment operation from his house. "He had a marvelous hobby, model trains, and my kids used to troop over there and play with them. One day, Warren popped over and asked if I'd thought about how I was going to educate these kids. In truth, I hadn't given it much thought. But I told him I planned to work hard and see what happened. Warren said that if I gave him $5,000 to invest, he'd probably be able to do better. My wife and I talked it over, but we figured we didn't know what this guy even did for a living—how could we give him $5,000? We've been kicking ourselves ever since. I mean, if we had given him the dough, we could have *owned* a college by now."[1]

For all his wealth—roughly $1.5 billion—Buffett's manner has been called corn-fed; it is straightforward and genial. Professionally, he is in the vulture business, but he is a cheerful sort of vulture. He has a round face with a wide mouth, bracketed by deep smile-wrinkles. His quizzical eyes peer from behind large, horn-rimmed glasses. From a high hairline, surmounted by a somewhat unruly thatch, run heavy vertical frown lines. Buffett's clothes are rumpled Middle West, although his good friend *Washington Post* chairman Katharine Graham sometimes sends him colored shirts, in the hope of pushing him toward a snappier turnout.[2] He loves junk food, including hamburgers and fudge, and was formerly devoted to Pepsi-Cola laced with cherry syrup; he has switched to the new Cherry Coke variation. He has even been known to decline a proffered glass of wine at dinner, saying, "No, thanks, I'll take the money."[3] In short, Warren Buffett doesn't act rich. In 1986, he acquired a corporate jet, but it's a fairly elderly, modest corporate jet. Few plutocrats today can manage the marble palace in town and the magnificent country seat, the 200-foot yacht and the bloodstock breeding establishment, each tended by hundreds of retainers, the vast art collections and wide benefactions of the old-time tycoon. Buffett isn't rich in that sense.

Of course, as Buffett well knows, being immensely rich (as distinct from just being rich) objectively does you more harm than good. It isn't logical, any more than endless body building or an oversized chair. From the conspicuously rich everybody wants something. Buffett's wife Susan, once a nightclub singer, has moved to San Francisco, in part to escape the unending demands of worthy causes in Omaha. (The two remain on amicable terms, but Buffett now lives with housekeeper-companion Astrid Menks, a former hostess at the same French Café in Omaha that Susan once sang in.[4]) If you get hugely rich, most or even all of the people around you are, beneath their flattery, envious and resentful. Instead of companions they become courtiers. Wealth is a form of power, and the very powerful have few intimates. (The French say that the Rothschilds have no friends, only clients.)

Even worse than the loss of real friends is the probable ruin of one's children. Privilege without responsibility is a formula for decadence, and enjoying rewards without having earned them, for insatiability and discontent. Buffett, who doesn't want to subject his children to such dangers, has created trusts for each worth a few hundred thousand dollars, but does not want to give them more for fear of corrupting them. He says: "My kids are going to carve out their own place in this world, and they know I'm for them whatever they do." But he refuses to bequeath them "a lifetime supply of food stamps just because they came out of the right womb. . . ."[5]

Buffett's family are not altogether delighted by this delicate solicitude, however. Peter Buffett has gone to San Francisco to make musical commercials; son Howard works for an Omaha land development firm, is in the business of removing snow, with which Omaha is copiously supplied, and farms on the side. "If I was rich I would help [my kids] out more than my dad did," he grumbles.[6] Daughter Susan, who sold real estate in California before moving to work on the business side of magazine publishing in Washington, recounts that when she asked for a loan her father sent her to the bank. On the subject of inheritance, she says, "My dad is one of the most honest, principled, good guys I know, and I basically agree with him. But it's sort of strange when you know most parents want to buy things for their kids and all you need is a small sum of money. . . . He won't give it to us on principle. All my life my father has been teaching us. Well, I feel I've learned the lesson. At a certain point you can stop."[7]

Buffett's father, Omaha stockbroker Howard Homan Buffett, was also frugal. In 1942, when Warren was twelve, his father, running on the Republican ticket, was elected to the first of his four terms as a Congressman. An ardent, old-fashioned conservative, he had little interest in money beyond what he needed to live on. So when Congressmen's salaries were raised from $10,000 to $12,500, Congressman Buffett, to illustrate his belief in government economy, returned the increase to the Treasury.

The bulk of Buffett's fortune is going into foundations to grapple with his two main concerns: population control and avoiding nuclear conflict. He points out, though, that it is very hard to create a foundation and be confident that the money will be well spent. As he says, "The secret of making money is to avoid risks; you *have* to take risks when you spend it."

That's certainly true. Many foundations end up working against the objectives of the creators, as Henry Ford pointed out when he resigned from the Ford Foundation. Many more do things that someone else would do anyway, or that need not be done at all, and, like the pyramids, essentially exist to glorify the founder's name.

So what makes men like Buffett run? Not the prize of high living or helping your neighbor, but winning the game. Most of the greatest investors are, to use an old-fashioned word, misers.

Starting Early

Even before he was a teenager, Warren had held a job marking prices on the slate in the boardroom of his father's office in Harris, Upham while studying the technical analysis of the market (in which he later lost faith) on his own. He took a few flyers. When only eleven years old, he induced his sister, aged fourteen, to buy three shares of Cities Service Preferred at 38. The stock sagged to 27. His sister, seeing her life's savings going up in smoke, badgered him daily about this reverse. Finally the stock staggered back to 40. To be rid of the nuisance he bailed out, clearing $5 after commissions, feeling relieved though embittered. Cities Service Preferred then soared right on up to 200. The budding tycoon, scarred by this experience, had an early lesson in two principles that he followed thereafter: First, don't be guided by what other people say; second, if you accept clients, don't tell them what you are doing at the time you are doing it.

After his father's election to Congress, the family established itself in Fredericksburg, Virginia. Although his two sisters were happy enough, Warren didn't like it there, and returned to Omaha to live with his grandfather. Then the Buffetts moved into Washington itself, to 49th Street near Massachusetts Avenue. Warren joined them again, attending Alice Deal Junior High School. He was still unhappy and rebellious, and his grades showed it. But, Eureka! As Mozart discovered music, as Casanova discovered women, and as Jane Austen discovered literature, Warren Buffett discovered money.

He embarked on a series of enterprises. He retrieved lost golf balls from the rough bordering a local course, and sold them. He ran paper routes, distributing just under 500 copies a day in all, for both the *Washington Post* and the *Washington Times-Herald,* which Eugene Meyer later merged into the *Post.* While he was at it, he sold magazine subscriptions to his newspaper customers. He turned two of his interests, math and publishing, to commercial account by handicapping horses and publishing a tip sheet called *Stable Boy Selections.**

Congressman Buffett, who had hoped that Warren would share his fervent dedication to principle and become a clergyman, found this preoccupation with material things distressing. He was also dismayed by Warren's poor grades, and eventually told him he would either have to get them up or abandon his paper routes. Warren, shaken, pulled himself together, although he never did well in his Washington schools.

At fifteen, now a student at Woodrow Wilson High School, Buffett moved into high gear, commercially speaking. With another student he bought a $25 pinball machine, which they put in a barbershop on Wisconsin Avenue that they frequented. After its first day of operation, the youthful entrepreneurs returned to milk the device of its revenue and retrieved no less than $4. As Buffett says, for a glorious moment he thought he had discovered the wheel. They started the Wilson Coin-Operated Machine Company, placing pinball machines in barbershops. The heavies who controlled the pinball business in the area were indifferent to barbershops, and the barbers liked the machines. When the barbers clamored for more of them, Buffett and his little colleague would reply that they'd take it up with the boss: "We pretended like we were these hired hands."[8] In time, the Wilson Coin-Operated Machine Company was netting $50 a week: "I hadn't dreamed life could be so good," declares Buffett.[9] While still in high school he was able to save enough from his take to lay out $1,200 for an unimproved farm of forty acres in the northeastern part of Nebraska.

His total earnings from these various commercial endeavors reached $9,000 plus the farm. With the money he was able to cover his college tuition. (For a student to make and keep $10,000-odd in the late 1940s was quite a stunt. The sum would be worth some ten times as much in today's money.)

Buffett attended the University of Pennsylvania's Wharton School during 1947–49 and, transferring in his junior year, graduated from the University of Nebraska in 1950. He had always been intrigued by the stock market, but initially, like so many others, had approached it looking for easy solutions. He collected hot tips from brokers and

* A Congressman is entitled to free information from the Library of Congress, and Representative Buffett was prevailed upon by his son to bend his principles sufficiently to request everything the Library had on handicapping and betting on horse races. One wonders what the librarians made of his straitlaced father's request.

published services, and tried ineffective technical analysis, the McGee point and figure charting system, and other variations of market alchemy. He was ready to try almost any investment device that looked as though it might work. Finally, however, when it came out in 1949, he read Benjamin Graham's *Intelligent Investor.** Greatly impressed, he headed East to study under Graham—and David Dodd, the coauthor of their monumental *Security Analysis*—at Columbia University. After receiving an M.B.A. there in 1951, he offered to work free for Benjamin Graham's New York investment company, Graham-Newman Corporation. Graham wasn't interested, so Buffett went back to Omaha to join his father's brokerage firm, Buffett-Falk & Company.

While working for his father in Omaha, from time to time Buffett tried to sell Benjamin Graham one stock or another. Graham was perfectly willing to hear from him and commented freely on his ideas. Finally, Graham suggested that Buffett visit him in New York. Buffett didn't hesitate, and went East. Graham-Newman Corporation hired him, and he spent two years there as an analyst.

After those two years in New York, Buffett returned yet again to Omaha. This time he and his wife, a Nebraskan whom he had married in 1952, bought a comfortable house on a wooded corner for $32,500 and settled down for good. Buffett has never moved, although he has added rooms to the house in the subsequent thirty-odd years. (He even put in a handball court, but hasn't played the game since he hurt his back some years ago.)

"Warren's kept his perspective clear by living in Omaha, away from it all, and looking at what's important rather than what's urgent or fashionable," says William Phillips, chairman of Ogilvy & Mather International, in which Berkshire had a sizable holding until recently. "He's been able to separate the wheat from the chaff, and he's been right."[10] Phillips is of course speaking in business terms. Omaha is not the Athens of the West, and Buffett is not Bertrand Russell.

Buffett's own view of Omaha is that "I can be anywhere in three hours—New York or Los Angeles. . . . This is a good place to bring up children and a good place to live. You can think here. You can think better about the market; you don't hear so many stories, and you can

---

* "Reading it," according to Buffett, "was like seeing the light." See "How Omaha Beats Wall Street," *Forbes* Magazine, November 1, 1969, p. 86. He has called Benjamin Graham his "intellectual patriarch."

just sit and look at the stock on the desk in front of you. You can think about a lot of things."[11]

In 1956, at twenty-five, Buffett formed a $100,000 investing partnership. He managed it as the general partner, with the investors, who were limited partners, having no say in the business. The deal was that each year the limited partners could have a 6 percent return with, as stated previously, Buffett receiving 25 percent of all profits earned above that figure. In time, he added all his own money to the partnership.

The initial limited partners were family members, but one day a friend and associate of Benjamin Graham's, Homer Dodge, who was both a physicist and a retired college president, came by on a canoe trip, the canoe itself reposing on the roof of his car. Homer Dodge had done extremely well picking stockpickers, and already knew about Buffett through Graham. After a brief conversation, he wrote out a check to subscribe, and thus became Buffett's first outside limited partner.

Buffett had no office or staff at this time, just a small room in his house. So it took a lot of confidence to sign up, particularly since he didn't tell his investors what was going on. (Given the same opportunity, I held back.) Those who dared, however, were well rewarded. By recent count, Omaha had fifty-two "Buffett millionaires."

Buffett Partnership, Ltd., bought securities it considered undervalued, generally by Grahamite criteria. It also engaged in merger arbitrage and in a few cases acquired controlling interests in public companies or took over private businesses. In the fifth year of the partnership Buffett acquired a controlling interest in Dempster Mill Manufacturing Company of Beatrice, Nebraska, which made farm equipment. It never did well, and two years later he resolved to sell it if he could. Since it was the biggest employer in Beatrice, the town pitched in to help finance a new group who bought Buffett out.

Two years later, in 1965, he acquired Berkshire Hathaway, a New Bedford, Massachusetts, textile company. As with Dempster, the price was cheap, although the company's operations were unimpressive. Buffett hoped to turn Berkshire around and improve its profits. He put in new management, but in fact has never been able to get very far with the operation. The experience convinced him that he should never attempt another "turnaround" in an operating company. Running a company is a completely different art from buying and selling stocks. (For some details regarding Buffett's lack of success in textiles, see Appendix III, pp. 184–87.)

Buffett made a practice of writing his limited partners annually to remind them of his cardinal principles:

> I cannot promise results to partners, but I can and do promise this:
> (a) Our investments will be chosen on the basis of value, not popularity.
> (b) Our patterns of operations will attempt to reduce permanent capital loss (not short-term quotational loss) to a minimum.[12]

He has certainly remained true to that principle, which might be described as the essence of "business" investment: buying a stock at the largest possible discount from true value, rather than chasing it up because it is supposed to be headed even higher.

In running Buffett Partnership, Warren declined to inform his investors as to what they had their money in. He was confident that if he did, then—like his sister many years before in their flutter in Cities Service Preferred—they would pass on their concerns, send him suggestions, and take up his time in other ways. Since time was his chief resource, he sought above all to avoid being put in that position.

In 1969, after thirteen years of highly successful operations, Buffett found himself in a dilemma. The stock market was booming, even the cats and dogs were selling for way over their value as businesses, and he found scarcely anything he felt he could buy in the spirit of his annual declaration to his partners. What to do? Since by now his share of the profits had earned him a substantial personal fortune, he made the courageous decision and simply wound the whole thing up. The results had been extraordinary. The partnership had grown thirty times in its value per unit or a pretax compound gain per unit of 30 percent a year. Having added ninety nonfamily members, it had reached a total value of $100 million. Buffett's own capital and share of the profits had reached $25 million.

He sent a letter to his limited partners:

> I am out of step with present conditions. When the game is no longer played your way, it is only human to say the new approach is all wrong, bound to lead to trouble, and so on. . . . On one point, however, I am clear. I will not abandon a previous approach whose logic I understand (although I find it difficult to apply) even though it may mean forgoing large, and apparently easy, profits to embrace an ap-

proach which I don't fully understand, have not practiced successfully, and which possibly could lead to substantial permanent loss of
capital.[13]

So he distributed to each investor his capital plus profits, together
with his pro rata interest in Berkshire Hathaway, which was illiquid
and constituted a large part of the whole. Buffett, who became chairman, now owns 44 percent of Berkshire, and his wife owns 3 percent.
Other former partners of Buffett Partnership own 35 percent, and
outside investors have 18 percent. There is low turnover in the stock,
and many of the shareholders have most of their savings in it.

The departing limited partners were given several choices: They
could go off on their own, or Buffett would buy them a spread of
municipal bonds with their money, or he would refer them to other
investment advisers. If they followed the latter course, he generally
recommended his old colleague at Graham-Newman, William Ruane,
who formed a mutual fund to handle their investments, Sequoia Fund.
Sequoia has in the subsequent years stuck close to Buffett's own investment philosophy, and historically its portfolio has been quite similar to Berkshire Hathaway's. (See Appendix IV, pp. 188–89.)

A factor that militated in favor of liquidating the partnership was
that Buffett had grown fond of some of his operating businesses; he did
not want to sell them even though to maximize capital this might have
been expedient. Another factor may have been that when he reached
100 limited partners he would have had to register as an investment
company, which would have greatly hampered his operating style. He
would have had to reveal his transactions publicly, quarter by quarter,
which would attract attention to his moves and create baying
competition.

Still another factor was that, as he said, "my idea quota used to be
like Niagara Falls—I'd have many more than I could use. Now it's as
though someone had dammed up the water and was letting it flow with
an eyedropper."[14] He also pointed out that there were too many
players of his game: The conglomerates were glad to buy anything that
seemed cheap. In a word, it was a typical bull market—everything was
overpriced.

Buffett felt better not having to be responsible for managing his
partnership day by day. "It's a tremendous relief being out of money
management, he said. "I'm not constantly thinking about business

anymore. During the partnership my ego was on the line, and I was trying to lead the league in hitting every year."[15]

In any event, the one thing one knows about markets is that they are cyclical. Three years after the partnership was liquidated, the market had the severest drop in decades, the 1973–74 collapse, during which Buffett was able to put his capital to work again, taking advantage of the extraordinary bargains that became available. "I'm like a sex-starved guy in a harem," he announced.[16] In the media area, which he understands particularly well, he bought 8 percent of Ogilvy & Mather at $5, 15 percent of Interpublic at $3, 11 percent of the *Washington Post* at $3, 8 percent of Affiliated Publishing, the parent of the *Boston Globe*, at $2, .7 percent of Knight-Ridder newspapers at $8, and 5 percent of Media General at $16, among others. He also bought, through a subsidiary, Blue Chip Stamps, 37 percent of Pinkerton's, the private detective agency, at $33 for $23.4 million, and a number of banks and insurance companies.* Many of these investments subsequently enjoyed prodigious market advances. Some have been cut back or sold.

Influences: 85 Percent Ben Graham

Buffett has described himself as "85 percent Benjamin Graham and 15 percent Phil Fisher."[17] He is referring to two of the most notable practitioners of portfolio investment, and in the case of Graham also the most eminent writer on the subject. Graham and Dodd's *Security Analysis* is usually considered the Bible of the profession and Graham's *The Intelligent Investor,* written late in his career, encapsulates his thinking. For that matter, Fisher's *Common Stocks and Uncommon Profits* and *Conservative Investors Sleep Well* are well worth studying. In this section I will sum up some of Graham's ideas and compare them with Buffett's, and in the next I will do the same for Fisher.

Graham's thinking evolved considerably during his long career. Not only did the markets themselves change, but he continued to develop his ideas, both through experience and study. In *Security Analysis* he examines dozens of different industries. He offers criteria, chiefly

---

* As these purchases were made over a period of time, these are average prices per share.

through the examination of such ratios as inventories to sales, debt to equity, depreciation to plant value, and the like, that can guide the investor in determining the quality and value of a company. By his latter years, two things had happened. First, a large population of analysts had begun applying Graham's methods, or similar ones, so that the advantage that his disciples once enjoyed was gradually dissipated as it became more widely shared. Second, by trial and error Graham had discovered much simpler criteria that seemed to indicate when a stock was attractively priced. Using a team of assistants, he tested one formula after another, conducting "playbacks" through the previous decades to see how the various methods would have worked out.

The simplest and most famous of these was his dictum that you can safely buy a stock for a price that represents not more than two-thirds of the company's net quick assets, deducting all prior charges, and giving no weight to its other assets—the factory buildings, offices, machinery, goodwill, and so forth. In other words, you buy a hotel for two-thirds of the cash in the till and equivalents, including immediately salable inventory, minus current debt. You pay nothing for the hotel structure itself or the customer list. Graham suggested that you should always hold a wide diversification of any stocks bought on these principles, since any one could go wrong. You should even buy odd lots, if necessary.

Graham recommended selling when a stock so bought has advanced to the equivalent of one times net quick assets, less all prior charges as before. This would ordinarily imply an advance of 50 percent. Graham found that from the end of World War II to 1976 this method, rigidly applied, produced returns in excess of 19 percent per annum compounded.

Graham's second best-known criterion was slightly more complicated. To explain it, let me introduce the English term "earnings yield." If a stock is selling for ten times earnings, the English say that it has a 10 percent "earnings yield." If it is selling for five times earnings, it has a 20 percent earnings yield. (This is not the *dividend* yield, which is the amount paid out to the shareholders in cash, often expressed as a percentage of the market price.)

Anyway, Graham's second criterion has two parts. *First,* one should buy a stock whose "earnings yield" is not less than twice the then yield of Moody's AAA bonds. Thus, if bonds are yielding, let us say, 6 percent, one doubles this amount, giving 12 percent. To be attractive, a stock should have an earnings yield of no less than 12 percent; that is, should sell for no more than eight times earnings. Suppose that AAA bonds are yielding 5 percent. Twice that makes 10 percent, justifying a 10 percent earnings yield for a stock, the same thing as ten times earnings. Clearly, the less bonds are yielding, the higher a price/earnings ratio one can afford to pay. This is a common-sense observation, since investors are in fact always comparing the dividend yield or "total return" they can get from stocks with the yields available from various categories of bonds.

The *second* part of Graham's second criterion is that total debt of the company must not exceed its tangible net worth. In other words, it should not owe more than it is worth.

This second criterion, carried back for thirty years from the time of Graham's study, also produced a compound annual rate of return of about 19 percent.

Graham's third criterion is straightforward: Again, the company's debt must not exceed its net worth. In addition, the dividend yield of the stock must be no less than two thirds of the AAA bond yield. In other words, if bonds are yielding 9 percent, then the stock's dividend yield on its then market price must be no less than 6 percent. This method was found to produce a compound annual rate of return of about 18.5 percent.

In all three techniques, every qualifying stock in both the Moody's and Standard and Poor's manuals is assumed to be bought. One must not exclude companies that one dislikes, or that are under a cloud, such as those that have recently experienced some catastrophe, or where management is considered incompetent, selfish, or dishonest. After all, it's more likely that something drastic will happen to the bad company, such as sale or liquidation—thus realizing its potential—than to the good company.

As to all three criteria, Graham proposed selling either if the stock rose 50 percent or after two years had passed, whichever came first; or if the dividend was omitted, or earnings declined so far that the current market price was 50 percent over the hypothetical purchase price.

Graham never stopped studying, and in a work published posthumously in 1977 he came up with still another approach that seemed to work equally well and offered more opportunities. It involves five different tests for value and five for safety. A stock can be bought if it satisfies any one of the value criteria plus any one of the safety criteria.

The *five value criteria*—of which any one will suffice—are the following:

1. The earnings yield should be at least twice the AAA bond yield.
2. The stock's price/earnings ratio should be less than 40 percent of its highest price/earnings ratio of the previous five years. (This simply quantifies the extent to which a stock has been knocked down.)
3. This familiar criterion requires that a stock's dividend yield should be at least two thirds of the AAA bond yield.
4. The stock's price should be no more than two thirds of the company's tangible book value per share.
5. The company should be selling in the market for no more than two thirds of its net current assets.

The *five safety criteria* are the following:

1. Graham's familiar one that the company should owe no more than it is worth: Total debt should not exceed book value. (In accounting terms, it should have a debt/equity ratio of less than 1.0.)
2. Current assets should be at least twice current liabilities. (That is, the current ratio should be more than 2.0.)
3. Total debt should be less than twice net current assets.
4. Earnings growth should have been at least 7 percent per annum compounded over the previous decade.
5. As an indication of stability of earnings, there should have been no more than two annual earnings declines of 5 percent or more during the previous decade.

Graham believed that if an investment satisfied at least one of the five value criteria and one of the safety criteria, you would do very well. He particularly favored the first within each section, namely a low price/earnings ratio and a favorable debt/equity ratio.

Professor Harry Oppenheimer of Texas Christian University studied those two criteria (the first in each section) for 1973 through 1981 by developing a hypothetical stock portfolio starting March 31, 1973, for all New York Stock and American Stock Exchange stocks that satisfied them. On each anniversary date new holdings were bought in accordance with the preceding year's financial data. A stock was sold if it no longer qualified, or it had risen 50 percent from purchase.

Over the period, Professor Oppenheimer's hypothetical portfolio would have given an investor a total return of about 25 percent compounded. Although there are believed to be certain flaws in this study, the least one can say is that it shows that Graham was basically right. An obvious question is this: Can one find stocks to buy that fill these rigorous criteria? The answer is that you may have to wait, but if you are patient, you will. For instance, there were more than 100 qualifying stocks each year between 1973 and 1978. The peak year was 1974, with over 300 stocks. In a strong bull market, the number of selections will dwindle, but a Grahamite would say that under those circumstances one should simply retire from the market and hold liquid assets. Buffett's liquidation of his own partnership in 1969 was an example. It set the stage for his bargain-hunting spree in 1974.*

Influences: 15 Percent Phil Fisher

But what does Buffett mean by saying that he's "fifteen percent Phil Fisher"? Fisher is the most famous of the older generation of investment advisers in California. His trademark is remorseless thoroughness and concentration on a few things, two principles that obviously go hand in hand. One man can't be as knowledgeable about many subjects as he can about a few, so great investors usually concentrate, either on an industry or on a category of investment—e.g., convertibles—or on a geographical area. Since Silicon Valley is in Fisher's backyard, in recent decades he has tended to stick to the high-tech world. Some of his famous picks were Food Machinery Corporation (FMC) in 1931, created through the merger of several Bay area companies, and Texas Instruments, which he bought, after careful investigation, on the original Morgan, Stanley private placement in the mid-fifties. Two others were Dow Chemical right after World War II and Motorola, both of whose superior growth continued, with occasional interruptions, for decades. I doubt, though, that Buffett would have bought any of these stocks, since none had a unique, defensible niche in a particular market.

Fisher avoids insurance companies or banks. In that he differs from Buffett. Why is this? I see two reasons. First, Buffett, who enjoys numbers, has quite liked the mathematical quality of banks and insur-

* There are incidentally several services available that provide lists of stocks fulfilling Graham's criteria.

ance companies. If one is careful, both are a license to coin money, slowly but steadily. Those decades after decades of 15 percent compounded provide huge gains in the end. Second, from time to time one can buy both banks and insurance companies at a discount from their net cash in the till, a reassuring framework in which to put your money to work. Recently, however, Buffett has stated that he no longer cares much for banking and savings and loan businesses because of government guarantees of deposits, which make for sloppy banking.[18]

Fisher does resemble Buffett in being wary of consumer companies. One reason is that his taste is not that of the everyday buyer. He likes good old clothes and good old cars, not the latest productions, and observes that if he particularly enjoys a TV show, it's likely to be taken off the air because of a lack of audience.

Fisher is basically a growth investor. But that doesn't necessarily mean the high flyer that everybody's talking about at any given time, usually because it dominates some currently exploding business area —biogenetics, let's say. The "star" company often has exceptionally high profit margins; but those comfortable margins and high growth rates are often a honey pot for competition—two, four, and then eight vultures descend to share your dinner. Fisher generally feels most comfortable with the leading company in a settled-down fully competitive area. Years of tough competition will have invigorated and fortified the leader, which may indeed have barely higher margins than the number two company, but perhaps will turn over inventory more rapidly. Fisher would certainly want to see that a company he bought had the best research effort in its industry, a vigorous forward-looking management of high integrity, a continuous, effective cost-cutting program, and the other hallmarks of a superior enterprise. Another one of his beliefs is that management should be trying continuously to make the company a better place for the employees to work. Most important of all, though, is that management should be authentically—not just in words—dedicated to long-term growth, and to that end should plow back most of the company's earnings into research, new products, modern plant, and the other ingredients of higher earnings in the future. If management knows what it's doing, growth in earnings will in time produce a corresponding growth in share prices, which is what investing is all about.

Buffett cites with approval an analogy devised by Philip Fisher for the long-term investment process. Suppose, says Fisher (and Buffett echoes), you could buy 10 percent of the earning power of any ten members of the graduating class for $75,000 a head. Suppose further that after ten years you have a chance to make substitutions among your picks. A few would be doing outstandingly well, and a few, perhaps "because their personalities had gotten in the way of their intellect" would be failing to make the grade. You might well decide to sell off some of your losers for less than you paid. But what about offers you might get to double your money for your 10 percent interest in some of the rising stars—executives with large unexercised stock options, or whatever?[19]

Buffett points out that to sell off a big winner in order to buy a large collection of losers, even if losers came cheaper, would probably be a big mistake.[20] It's hard to identify winners, hard to develop enough of a conviction to invest in them, and unusual to have things work out according to plan. To abandon all that for a collection of new uncertainties would probably not be a winning strategy. Asked once when one should sell one's great growth investments, Fisher replied, "Almost never."

So, what parts of Philip Fisher's investment philosophy, as distinguished from Graham's, does Buffett share? I can see a few:

1. Only buy a company that is first-class in its way. (Graham, on the contrary, favored the statistically cheap company.)

2. Insist on management of the utmost competence. Buffett has been an enthusiastic backer of such dedicated managers as Tom Murphy, chairman of Capital Cities/ABC, John Byrne, head of Fireman's Fund (formerly of GEICO), the late Gene Abegg, founder and chairman of Illinois National Bank & Trust Company, and Rose Blumkin of Nebraska Furniture Mart. Buffett would, I think, agree with Fisher's observation that the first thing to look for in the management of a technology company is *business* skill. (Graham overlooked poor management in an underpriced company.)

3. Don't touch a company whose management is not honest, or one that takes advantage of its position to profit unreasonably at the expense of the shareholders. It should also be straightforward and truthful in its reports to shareholders, and both Buffett and Fisher deplore the hype in most annual reports. As Fisher says, a divisional vice-president would be fired if he reported to the president that way.

Why can't the president be equally candid with the shareholders, who are, after all, his employers? (Graham also abominated deceptive company reporting, but would tolerate it in a purchase candidate if the company were statistically cheap.)

4. Fisher only buys a company that he is willing to hold for a long time, the way you buy a house. You may in practice sell it again when it realizes its market potential, but that shouldn't be your original objective. (Graham's method encourages turnover.)

Both Buffett and Fisher generally stick to industries they're already familiar with, where the knowledge they acquire as a stockholder of one company can give them insights into other, similar companies.

Both, unlike Benjamin Graham, believe in sizing up management personally—although Buffett sometimes seems to make exceptions, I assume for companies whose business franchises he considers so strong that they could if necessary find other managers without losing too much ground. The most notable example is the *Buffalo Evening News,* which (through Blue Chip Stamps) he bought in toto sight unseen. Fisher would never have done that! But Buffett knows newspapers backward and forward, and doubtless felt that an examination of the product and the financials told him what he needed to know about the people behind them.

So, in sum, is it true that Buffett is 85 percent Graham and 15 percent Fisher? While he may have been once, he seems less so now. Of course, Buffett, like every good investor, talks about buying a stock for less than it is worth. (Graham hopes that his purchase is selling for less than it is worth, and Fisher, for less than it will be worth in the future.) But Graham's method is based on analysis of the whole company on the basis of financial ratios, assembling the larger picture from many specific signs. Since this is an inexact procedure, Graham insists on wide diversification of his holdings. As the amounts of money he is handling have increased, Buffett, who does not want to add the staff that would enable him to acquire and follow a large number of small positions, feels most comfortable buying larger and larger pieces of companies, and indeed whole companies. Buffett's purchase of media companies, what he is by far best known for, would almost certainly not have suited Graham: They are based on a qualitative and indeed juridic franchise that will have to pay off in the future. It is not a case of buying hard assets at a discount, Graham's usual game.

Buffett's 1977 purchase of the *Buffalo Evening News* would have troubled Graham. For the transaction to work out, it was extremely important that the paper should launch a Sunday edition. Buffett knew enough about the business to be able to judge that possibility, but the knowledge cannot be said to have originated from the *News*'s own financial statements.* Buffett has admitted that Graham would not have liked his 1985 investment in Capital Cities (discussed in detail on pp. 30–32) either: "I doubt if Ben's up there applauding me on this one," he said.[21]†

Is Buffett then a practitioner of Philip Fisher's investment style? As suggested, Fisher is at home with high-tech companies, since so many of them are in nearby Silicon Valley. He also holds that a highly competitive company that has successfully fought off rivals for decades and been fortified thereby may well be a stronger bet than the companies with unique business franchises (discussed in the next section) that Buffett feels most comfortable with. Fisher is also a remorseless digger. He isn't happy unless he has talked to a company's management at all levels, the competition, disgruntled ex-employees, suppliers, representative consumers of its products, industry association executives, and other standard sources. He also likes to hold his investments for very long periods of time—twenty or thirty years, sometimes. One does indeed see many resemblances between Buffett and Graham. Those between him and Fisher are less apparent.

"Commodity" and "Franchise"

At this point it is important to consider the concepts of "commodity" and "franchise." A commodity as the word is ordinarily used refers to some material that is generally available, such as iron ore, gravel, potatoes, or whatever. At a price, you can always get it. If the price rises, more will be produced. In the potato business, for instance, you can count on never having high prices over three years in a row.

* The Sunday edition was launched and the rival morning *Courier-Express* folded in 1982, leaving the monopoly position to the *News*.

† An understandable doubt: If the eminent unbeliever has reached heaven, one hopes he is concerned with larger questions.

After the third year, the farmers "plant the sidewalks," the supply increases, and prices fall.

So a "commodity" business is one in which higher prices will attract more competition almost without limit. If, for example, there is a highly successful gas station at one corner of a busy crossroad, you can be reasonably confident that another will appear, and if it in turn does well, then another and another. The same for fast food emporia, real estate agencies, dress shops, gift boutiques, and small restaurants. They are easy enough to start and seem so attractive that few will do really well; four out five new restaurants fail in their first year.

In contrast to the "commodity" business, you have what can be called the impregnable business franchise. I am not talking about the familiar use of the word "franchise" in the sense of a McDonald's franchise, but rather a business that is almost impossible to compete with.

Who, for instance, would have supposed that moist snuff should be a virtual monopoly? And yet it is. U.S. Tobacco's Skoal and Copenhagen brands dominate the field, and it turns out to be a wretched task to compete with them. Since moist snuff has a short shelf life before it dries out, and is disagreeable after it ceases to be moist (you might as well have cellophane in your mouth), the tobacconist has to sell it fast; this means limiting himself to small orders that are uneconomical for a new competitor to supply. (Moist snuff is not a minor business, either; U.S. Tobacco's sales are well over $250 million.) Another odd franchise is Bandag, which dominates the business of retreading radial tires. Another is demulsification, the process of taking water bubbles out of oil on its way from the well to the refinery; Lubrizol dominates the business. Another is high school class rings, a huge part of which are sold by a single company called Josten's.

Anyway, Buffett loves companies (not necessarily these ones) with strong business franchises. He seeks the impregnable but unrecognized franchise, when it is available at a reasonable price. The best example may be the monopoly daily newspaper (discussed in detail later on), but there are many others tucked here and there in the economy that people are often almost unconscious of.

Asked about his concept of franchise in 1985, Buffett explained:

> The test of a franchise is what a smart guy with a lot of money could

do to it if he tried. If you gave me a billion dollars, and you gave me first draft pick of fifty business managers throughout the United States, I could absolutely cream both the business world and the journalistic world. If you said, "Go take the *Wall Street Journal* apart," I would hand you back the billion dollars. Reluctantly, but I would hand it back to you.

Now, incidentally, if you gave me a similar amount of money and you told me to make a dent in the profitability or change the market position of the Omaha National Bank or the leading department store in Omaha, I could give them a very hard time. I might not do much for you in the process, but I could cause them a lot of trouble. The real test of a business is how much damage a competitor can do, even if he is stupid about returns.

There are some businesses that have very large moats around them and they have crocodiles and sharks and piranhas swimming around them. Those are the kind of businesses you want. You want some business that, going back to my day, Johnny Weissmuller in a suit of armor could not make across the moat [sic]. There are businesses like that. Sometimes they're regulated. If I had the only water company in Omaha, I'd do fine if I didn't have a regulator. What you are looking for is an unregulated water company. The trick is to find the ones that haven't been identified by someone else. What you want is a disguised television station or a newspaper.[22]

The Advertising Oligopoly and Other Favorites

Among companies with strong franchises, Buffett has done extremely well by investing in advertising agencies. He observes that the big seven or so agencies—Interpublic, Ted Bates, J. Walter Thompson, Ogilvy Group, Doyle Dane, and the rest—have what has sometimes been called a shared monopoly, or more properly an oligopoly. The reason is that for the very largest corporations—Ford, Coca-Cola, IBM, Campbell's Soup, or whatever—the agency must be able to conduct campaigns on a worldwide basis. If Mobil changes its logo or Coke changes its formula, for instance, it usually happens simultaneously all over the world, in a hundred or more countries. To coordinate this operation the company's agency should have branches in most of the places where it does business. To handle it through correspondents would be chaotic. So the number of possible agencies for a big multinational is extremely limited. Thus, if a multinational quits one agency, it will probably have to go to another of about the same size, and as a result there is little leakage out of the whole family of top agencies. Indeed, as more multinationals come into being, the ad business gradually tends to improve. In theory, a new worldwide agency could be created, but in practice the task grows more difficult all the time, since a number of years ago the major ones went on buying sprees, soaking up the qualified local companies in Spain, Thailand, and so forth; now there aren't enough left to be assembled into a first-class worldwide operation.

Because of the amount of business it controls, a big international agency can pay any reasonable price for the best remaining local shop, and by diverting business to it justify the acquisition.*

A further curious problem is that unlike, for example, architects, where in pure theory one firm could get business from every major bank in the country, advertising agencies, since they advise on competitive strategy, can't accept accounts from competing companies. Citibank and Chase would scarcely both employ the same outfit. Thus, there must perforce be enough business for each of the handful of major international ad agencies. (Some have started quasi-independent subsidiaries to try to get around this problem, particularly for purely domestic business, but that may not satisfy a major multinational client.)

As mentioned, Buffett's plunge into advertising took place in the 1974 stock market washout. In that year he was able to become the largest outside shareholder of Interpublic, paying less than twice pretax earnings per share, and less than half the value of its tangible assets. Considering that Interpublic's primary asset isn't its tangible assets at all but rather its reputation, skill, and its membership in the oligopoly, this was an astonishingly good buy, which should never have come about except for the irrationality of the public during bear markets. Indeed, even small, wobbly agencies were being acquired by knowledgeable larger ones for triple the ratio of tangible assets, or earnings per share, that Buffett was paying for his share of Interpublic. Can you lose money on that basis? Very difficult! While he was at it, he scooped up a big piece of Ogilvy & Mather. At his peak, Buffett owned 15 percent of Interpublic and 9 percent of Ogilvy. In 1985, he cut back on these holdings, feeling they had become well understood and thus fully priced.

---

* A few businesses are in essence royalties on the sales of other businesses. Advertising agencies share this characteristic with newspapers.

GEICO

Buffett has also prospered with insurance companies he has bought for investment, notably Geico. While still a student at Columbia, Warren had noticed that Benjamin Graham was a director of Government Employees Insurance Company. GEICO developed an unusual specialty, selling car insurance through the mail, which means it doesn't need to pay commissions to agents.

One Saturday Buffett visited GEICO's office in Washington. It was closed. He banged on the door until a janitor appeared, whom Buffett asked if there was anybody at work. As it happens, there was: an executive, Lorimar A. Davidson, who later became chairman. Buffett introduced himself and asked Davidson about the company. He grew more and more interested, and since Davidson was willing to talk, he spent five hours learning about how it all worked. He became excited about the company and its stock, and bought a few shares. He then tried the idea out on a couple of brokers who specialized in analyzing and dealing in insurance company issues. Neither liked it, since the standard analytical methods didn't show it as cheap. However, the tables did not focus on the essence of GEICO: that since it sold directly to its customers, it short-circuited the insurance agents, and thus could make a 20 percent profit on its underwriting activities, as compared to a normal underwriter's profit of about 5 percent. The whole company then had a market value of only $7 million. Years later, when it had become a Wall Street favorite, the value rose to $2 billion.

Back in Omaha again, where he entered his father's brokerage firm, Buffett tried to sell GEICO stock to the customers, but no one wanted it. Indeed, some of the insurance brokers around town were indignant that Buffett-Falk should be pushing the stock of a company that didn't have any agents, and urged Buffett, Sr., to discourage his son from handling the stock.

Finally, it occurred to Warren that although he didn't seem able to sell GEICO specifically, he ought to be able to sell stock in a sound and attractively priced insurance company to the people who actually worked for it. (His customers were never quite sure that GEICO was authentic.) Kansas City Life, on the other hand, which had an agent in Omaha, was only selling for three times its statutory earnings. Buffett reasoned that the local Kansas City Life agent ought to be willing to buy the company's stock on the basis of a 33 percent "earnings yield," particularly since he was aware that the rate at which the policy-holders' savings grew under their policies was only 2.5 percent. In other words, thanks to the bad deal given to the policyholders, the company's stock itself was about thirteen times better a deal—although not as safe, to be sure—than the investment component of its own insurance policies. Buffett felt that the general agent couldn't help knowing that Kansas City Life was solid, since he was constantly selling new policies and indeed mailing in the premiums. Alas, the agent proved to be as blind as everyone else. He went on buying life insurance for himself, apparently prepared to settle for the 2.5 percent growth of value, and could not be induced to take advantage of the 33 percent value buildup rate in his company's stock.

Describing the state of things when he bought into GEICO for the second time, Buffett explains:

It wasn't essentially bankrupt but it was heading there. It was 1976. It had a lot of great business franchise which had not been destroyed by a lot of errors that had been made in terms of exploiting that franchise. And it had a manager who I met the night before I bought the first 500 and some thousand shares who I felt had the ability to get through an extraordinarily tough period there and to re-establish the value of that franchise. They still were a low-cost operator. They made all kinds of mistakes. They still didn't know their cost[s] because they didn't know what their loss reserves should be and they got captivated by growth; they did all kinds of things wrong but they still had the franchise.

It was similar to American Express in late 1963 when the salad oil scandal hit it. It did not hurt the franchise of the travellers check or the credit card. It could have ruined the balance sheet of American Express but the answer of course was that American Express with no net worth was worth a tremendous amount of money.

And GEICO with no net worth was worth a tremendous amount of money too except it might get closed up the next day because it had no net worth, but I was satisfied that the net worth would be there. The truth is a lot of insurance companies for the ownership of it would have put up the net worth. We would have put it up. But they were trying to save it for the old shareholders, which is what they should have done. It had a very valuable franchise. Take away all the net worth. Let's just say that GEICO paid out a $500 million dividend right now which would eliminate the net worth of GEICO, would it still have a lot of value? Of course, it would have a lot of value. You'd have to do something, you'd have to be part of another entity that kept insurance regulators happy, but the franchise value is the big value in something like that. . . .[23]

Berkshire Hathaway now owns 40 percent of GEICO. Current results in Berkshire Hathaway's property and casualty insurance business have been favorable, he reported at the 1986 annual meeting, but the insurance industry has added large amounts of capacity in the last year from capital raised in the capital markets. Traditionally, he said, when capital has been available, pricing and profitability in the industry have declined. Some softening, he said, is already evident, and the period of prosperity in property and casualty underwriting may not be long-lived.[24]

Buffett's Big Idea

Warren Buffett has observed that there is no need—indeed it is positively deleterious—for an investor to try constantly to come up with new ideas. He has said that it would be better if the newly minted graduate of a course on investments were issued a punch card with twenty holes in it, or even fewer, which would represent all the investment concepts he would ever be entitled to try.[25] This would underline for him the importance of the occasional big idea, rather than lots of small ideas. In Tolstoy's famous analogy, he should be a hedgehog rather than a fox: the fox knows lots of things, but the hedgehog knows one big thing. Anyway, it would have sufficed for Buffett to have had only one hole in his punch card.

Buffett's great conception can be summed up as follows: *A monopoly daily newspaper is the most perfect business franchise in America.* There are something over 1,700 dailies in America, of which something over 1,500 are monopolies. Such a paper is what Buffett likes to call a "gross profits royalty," a toll bridge that almost all the businesses in town have to use, a business surrounded by the kind of moat that not even Johnny Weissmuller could cross. Thus, although business may be poor, the K-Mart has to advertise its specials through an ad in the newspaper or a brochure distributed by the paper. Even the local TV station has to advertise its weekly programming in print. In fact, some businesses have to advertise more when times are bad, to keep the merchandise moving. Newspaper advertising gets results, and newspapers without competitors usually prosper.*

You can say that printer's ink was in Buffett's blood. His grandfather on his mother's side was once owner and editor of a weekly newspaper in West Point, Nebraska, called the *Cuming County Democrat.* His mother, Leila Stahl, set type in the family printshop and worked for the paper. His father edited the *Daily Nebraskan* at the University of Nebraska, where he met Buffett's mother, who came looking for a job. Buffett himself was around newspapers as a child—when he was a delivery boy for both the *Washington Times-Herald* (now gone) and the *Washington Post.* Indeed, if one takes things back to his horseracing tip sheet, *Stable Boy Selections,* which he published at the age of twelve, one can trace his career as a press lord back nearly fifty years. Later, while still a student at the University of Nebraska, Buffett became a regional circulation manager for the *Lincoln Journal.* So the least one can say is that Buffett is a veteran of the newspaper business.

The first newspaper Buffett actually bought was the *Omaha Sun* in 1969, along with a string of weeklies. He sold it in 1981, two years before it folded. In 1973–74 he bought a major stake in the *Washington Post,* ending up as the largest outside investor, with 1.9 million shares of the Class B common stock, now representing about a 13 percent interest, or about half as much as the Graham family, which controls the paper.

When Affiliated Publications, which publishes the *Boston Globe,* first went public in 1973, Buffett acquired over a million shares through Berkshire Hathaway. He did not become a director of Affiliated, since he was a director of the *Washington Post.* In addition, Buffett has had substantial holdings in Knight-Ridder Newspapers, Media General, and Multimedia. Another media company in which he has had a substantial interest is Time, Inc.—since sold—of which Berkshire Hathaway once owned 4 percent.

* Some others who have made this discovery have done even better than Buffett. For instance, Sam Newhouse, a penniless assistant to a Staten Island magistrate, was assigned by his boss to chase up ads for a tiny newspaper, at the princely compensation of $2 a week. In time, Newhouse was able to acquire the paper from the magistrate's estate, and gradually parlayed it into an enormous newspaper empire. When he died, the amount *in dispute* with the Internal Revenue Service over the estate tax (not the tax itself) was $560 million! Similarly, Walter Annenberg has profited enormously from his ownership of *TV Guide* and *The Racing Form,* two virtual monopolies in their respective sections, and two of the most valuable media properties in the country.

In 1977 Buffett, through Blue Chip Stamp Company, paid nearly $35 million to the estate of Mrs. Edward H. Butler, Jr., for the entire Buffalo Evening News Company. At the time, the city had two newspapers. The other was the *Courier-Express,* owned by the Conners family. The *News* had a weekly circulation of about 280,000 and a Saturday circulation of 295,000. The *Courier* sold 125,000 copies during the week and 270,000 on Sunday. Buffett has always felt that a daily paper without a Sunday edition could not succeed and so he sank additional money into the *News* to start one, which began with the free distribution of three sample Sunday papers. The *Courier* brought suit, claiming that the giveaway program "could possibly be the catalyst to put us out of business."[26]

Buffett testified that if the *News* became a monopoly newspaper, it would be worth three times what he had paid for it, but when asked if the possibility of killing off the *Courier-Express* was in his mind when he resolved to publish a Sunday edition, he replied, "No, sir. I think the *Courier-Express* is going to be around a long time." However, in fact the *Courier-Express* did fold, and today the *News* is worth close to ten times Buffett's cost.[27]

Newspaper monopolies exist because of the First Amendment. Rather than have government "trust-busting" involved in the newspaper industry, Congress decreed, in the 1970 Newspaper Preservation Act, that the last surviving paper in a given territory can buy the penultimate publication if it goes under, without—as would happen in many other industries—being forced under the antitrust principle to split itself in two to re-create competition. There has never in recent generations been a monopoly newspaper territory where a well-entrenched daily either went out of business or saw a successful rival become implanted. It takes a long time for a new paper to displace an existing one, whose readership has gotten used to its particular columnists, cartoon strips, sports section, the layout of its stock exchange columns and personal ads, and the general feel of it. As a result, the rival paper finds itself in the painful necessity of printing copies every day and taking them back, printing and taking back, printing and taking back. It is a most expensive and discouraging process, the more so when one knows that in recent generations, at least, attempts to start a new paper have rarely paid off financially.

Furthermore, a monopoly paper can safely challenge the unions, which almost every paper has to do sooner or later. In a multipaper city, the first daily to attempt this incurs a severe risk of going out of business altogether in the ensuing strike. A monopoly paper, on the contrary, can expect to see a rather feeble competitor spring up during the strike, published usually by the strikers themselves, but the monopolist always wins sooner or later, knocks out the ad hoc competitor, and recovers its former position.

Thus, says Buffett:

> The economics of a dominant newspaper are excellent, among the very best in the business world. . . . While first-class newspapers make excellent profits, the profits of third-rate papers are as good or better —as long as either class of paper is dominant within its community . . . even a poor newspaper is a bargain to most citizens simply because of its "bulletin board" value. Other things being equal, a poor product will not achieve quite the level of readership achieved by a first-class product. A poor product, however, will still remain essential to most citizens, and what commands their attention will command the attention of advertisers.[28]

For his part, Buffett simply likes newspapers: "Let's face it, newspapers are a hell of a lot more interesting a business than, say, making couplers for rail cars. While I don't get involved in the editorial operations of the papers I own, I really enjoy being part of the institutions that help shape society."[29]

The Other Graham

In 1971, the *Washington Post* had its first public issue of Class B common stock at $6.50 a share; Class A stock was held by the Graham family. There were at that time about 14 million shares outstanding, of which the 2.7 million-odd Class A shares, which had voting control of the company, were owned by Katharine Graham, daughter of Eugene Meyer, Jr., a Wall Street financier who bought the paper in 1933. The 11.3 million Class B shares participated fully in earnings. This price per share implied about a $100 million evaluation for the whole company.

In 1973, the beginning of the 1973–74 market slump, the price per share had dropped to below $4, so that Buffett was able to buy 10 percent of the *Post* for $10.6 million. At that time, the revenues of the company were about $200 million, including sales of its subsidiaries, *Newsweek,* the Times Herald Company, four television stations, and the paper company that provided most of its newsprint. Good newspapers seem to sell in the market at about two and a half times their revenues: thus, even when he bought into it, the entire Washington Post Company was probably worth comfortably four times its market price. In 1981, the *Post*'s rival newspaper, the *Washington Star,* ceased operations; now the *Post* has acquired most of its rival's readership, in spite of the arrival on the scene of the *Washington Times,* published by the Reverend Sun Myung Moon's Unification Church with many former *Star* staffers.

In the usual fashion of companies in which Buffett has a substantial interest, the *Post* has been buying back its own shares. From about 19 million shares outstanding when he bought his interest, the capitalization has now fallen below 13 million shares, raising his percentage interest to 13 percent.

The market price of *Washington Post* stock did not move solidly above Buffett's cost price until 1976, five years after his acquisition. From then on, however, it has never looked back. By 1985 the stock had climbed to twenty times his cost. His near $11 million block was worth about a quarter of a billion dollars.

After buying the stock, Buffett wrote Katharine Graham, stating that he was a passive investor and represented no threat to her position, which was assured anyway by her 100 percent ownership of the Class A stock, which had voting control. They had been in touch before, when Buffett asked her to help him buy the *New Yorker* (she declined), but they had never met. She arranged to meet him in Los Angeles, at the office of the *Los Angeles Times.* Partially reassured by this encounter, she asked him to come to dinner in Washington and inspect the *Post.* At dinner, Buffett sat between Barbara Bush and Jane Muskie, and everything went swimmingly.[30] Over at the *Post,* though, the pressmen were on strike—an intimation of future troubles. Buffett joined the *Post* board in 1975, and became chairman of its finance committee. In October of that year a bitter labor dispute erupted. Mrs. Graham was uneasy about the risk involved in holding out, in view of the threat represented by the *Star,* but Buffett encouraged her. On occasion he joined Mrs. Graham and other executives at work in the plant, replacing striking laborers. Eventually the strike collapsed. The *Post* hired nonunion pressmen.

Buffett, who has always loved TV as a business, in 1985 urged Mrs. Graham to pay Capital Cities $350 million for fifty-three cable TV systems. This had become possible because of the enormous increase in the *Post*'s earnings over the period: from about $7 million in 1981 to about $100 million in 1985.

With the passage of time Buffett and Mrs. Graham have become good friends, exchanging visits in Washington and the Buffett family's Laguna Beach vacation home. Over the years he has acted as a financial mentor to Mrs. Graham, who after the suicide of her husband, who had been running the company, found herself with great responsibilities. Buffett would bring a stack of corporate annual reports and lead her through them. Her friends soon noticed the change in her way of speaking about business questions. She says, "I've had two great professors—one is Warren Buffett, and the other is experience."[31]

Mrs. Graham's son Donald, already publisher, is being prepared for the succession, and apparently consults Buffett as an adviser as well. According to Donald Graham, Buffett has "a truly formidable mind. . . . He has a recall of numbers I've rarely seen, and he has a sense of their order of magnitude. . . . He's always thinking, always watching."[32]

In Washington, Buffett has joined the Urban Institute, a liberal think tank, and the all-male Alfalfa Club. He has put some money into the *Washington Monthly,* a journal of opinion. He likes getting to know the D.C. establishment. According to one acquaintance, Buffett "loves moving in the circle of politicians and other luminaries that Kay Graham has introduced him to. He plays tennis with [*Post* Executive Editor] Ben Bradlee. He gets to sit in the VIP area at the political conventions and presidential debates. He really revels in the whole scene."[33]

A College Goes into the Television Business

Buffett became a trustee of Grinnell College in 1968, at the urging of his friend Joseph F. Rosenfield of Des Moines, a lawyer, investor, and retired chairman of Younker department stores.

In 1967 Rosenfield, a member of the investment committee of Grinnell's board, had the endowment buy 300 shares of Berkshire Hathaway at $17.50 per share. That was scarcely a significant investment, but it worked out well, since each share is now worth over $3,000. Buffett has rarely attended the all-day meetings of the trustees, which take place three times a year in the college library, preferring to talk about investment strategy directly with Rosenfield and, if necessary, the finance committee.

In 1976, attending a conference in New Orleans on the economics of newspapers, Buffett discovered that Avco Corporation had decided to sell its television stations. Under FCC rules Buffett couldn't buy the stations for Berkshire Hathaway, because of the TV holdings of the *Washington Post*. So he proposed to Rosenfield that Grinnell College try to buy one of them, if it could be gotten at a bargain price. His first choice was the station in Cincinnati. Unfortunately, the Grinnell board spent so much time discussing how to finance the transaction that Multimedia, not Grinnell, bought the station, for $16 million. (Grinnell responded by buying $315,000 worth of Multimedia stock, which subsequently soared.)

Buffett's second try was Avco's TV station in Dayton. This time he decided simply to make a bid and only later to arrange financing. He offered $12.9 million in 1976, representing two and a half times the gross revenues of the station. He won. Late in 1984 Grinnell sold the station again, to Hearst Corporation for $50 million. This transaction doubled Grinnell's endowment, which now represents $127,000 per student, compared to $180,000 per student for Harvard and $121,000 for Yale. Having done his bit, Buffett turned the active management of the endowment over to Bill Ruane of the Sequoia Fund and to James Gipson of Pacific Financial Management. Both have done well.[34]

Buffett's Great Throw of the Dice

His earlier media deals are overshadowed by Buffett's latest transaction. In January 1986, he put up $517.5 million in cash—about a quarter of Berkshire Hathaway's liquid assets—to buy three million shares of Capital Cities/ABC at $172.50 a share, in order to provide Cap Cities with additional funds for the $3.5 billion acquisition of ABC. Buffett thus picked up 18.7 percent of the Capital Cities/ABC equity and a place on the board as its largest shareholder. This represented by far the largest investment Buffett has ever made.

Buffett has struck an unusual arrangement with Capital Cities/
ABC: He becomes a director, but has agreed to vote with management
for eleven years, as long as Chairman Tom Murphy, now sixty-one, or
President Daniel Burke, now fifty-eight, is in charge. So Buffett has the
access inherent in a directorship but not the power. Since he does not
want an operating role in a company he invests in—he buys management as well as the business—this isn't too much of a sacrifice. In
essence the arrangement increases the strength of Murphy's and
Burke's positions, which is Buffett's goal:

> With them in place, the first-class managers with whom we have
> aligned ourselves can focus their efforts entirely upon running the
> businesses and maximizing long-term values for owners. Certainly this
> is much better than having those managers distracted by "revolving-
> door capitalists" hoping to put the company "in play." (Of course,
> some managers place their own interests above those of the company
> and its owners and deserve to be shaken up—but, in making invest-
> ments we try to steer clear of this type.)
>
> Today, corporate instability is an inevitable consequence of widely-
> diffused ownership of voting stock. At any time a major holder can
> surface, usually mouthing reassuring rhetoric but frequently harboring
> uncivil intentions. By circumscribing our blocks of stock as we often
> do, we intend to promote stability where it otherwise might be lacking.
> That kind of certainty, combined with a good manager and a good
> business, provides excellent soil for a rich financial harvest. That's the
> economic case for our arrangements. The human side is just as im-
> portant. We don't want managers we like and admire—and who have
> welcomed a major financial commitment by us—to ever lose any
> sleep wondering whether surprises might occur because of our large
> ownership. I have told them there will be no surprises, and these
> agreements put Berkshire's signature where my mouth is. That signa-
> ture also means the managers have a corporate commitment and
> therefore need not worry if my personal participation in Berkshire's
> affairs ends prematurely (a term I define as any age short of three
> digits).[35]

Having bought Capital Cities, Buffett is understandably rueful over
his decision to sell the same stock in the late seventies:

> Of course some of you probably wonder why we are now buying
> Capital Cities at $172.50 per share given that this author, in a charac-
> teristic burst of brilliance, sold Berkshire's holdings in the same com-
> pany at $43 per share in 1978–80. Anticipating your question, I spent

a lot of time working on a snappy answer that would reconcile these acts.

A little more time please.[36]

Buffett had to resign his *Washington Post* directorship to go on Capital Cities/ABC's board, but there again, since it is firmly controlled by the Graham family, his role was in reality limited to that of a respected adviser.

"Warren adores Tom Murphy," says John J. Byrne, also a longtime friend of Buffett's and CEO of GEICO, one of Berkshire's major positions, until mid-1985, when he took over management of the Fireman's Fund. (See Appendix I, pp. 160–65.) "Just to be partners with him is attractive to Warren, no matter what it is they're up to."[37] In a June 1986 meeting with the ABC affiliates, Murphy introduced Buffett as the parent company's "400-pound gorilla," needed to deter unfriendly acquisitors. Buffett, in turn, compared Murphy and Burke to having Babe Ruth and Lou Gehrig as numbers three and four in the batting order. They used to vote a full player's share of the World Series proceeds to the bat boy. He added, "The key in life is to figure out who to be the bat boy for."[38]

Murphy is famous for his corporate fat trimming. For instance, the Kansas City *Star-Times*'s profit rose sixfold after Capital Cities bought it from its own employees, who had managed it sloppily. Buffett expects Chairman Tom Murphy to improve the profitability of ABC's TV stations, but there are uncertainties in the situation. That is why Walter Schloss, Buffett's fellow apprentice in Graham-Newman Corporation, said of the transaction, "It's right for Warren, but it's not right for me."[39] In a 1985 interview with *Business Week,* Buffett agreed that the Capital Cities/ABC investment does not have the "huge margin of safety" between a stock's intrinsic value and its market price that Graham demanded.[40] Still, by the end of 1986, Buffett had made a $300 million paper profit on the deal, since Cap Cities/ABC's price per share had risen from $172.50 to over $275.

II

Some Favorite Investing Principles

Good Businesses

Buffett only buys good businesses. Sometimes he has departed from this rule, and it has almost always cost him money. Many substantial and enterprising investors buy a bad business if it's cheap enough, and then, if necessary, help management straighten things out. Buffett finds that he is much better off as a passive investor, and does not want to complicate his life by venturing into troubled situations. Aside from anything else, wonderful businesses, although they are rare, from time to time sell as cheaply in the market as bad ones, and once you own one, you are far better off.

How, then, does one recognize an outstanding business? Here are some of the signs:

1. It has a high return on invested capital. Buffett finds that this indicator, rather than the more familiar one of earnings growth, is the safest, since earnings are often manipulated.

2. Related to this, a good business should create its profits in cash, not merely accounting profits.

3. A good business will have rapid turnover of inventory, have a high rate of return on the total of plant plus inventory, and have predictable earnings.

4. In the annual reports Buffett writes for Berkshire Hathaway (see Appendix III) he repeatedly stresses the importance of one indispensable quality for the manager of any business in which he proposes to

buy stock: The manager thinks like an owner. This is the basis for his admiration for Tom Murphy of Cap Cities/ABC, Jack Byrne of GEICO and Fireman's Fund, and those who run Berkshire companies —whom he often compliments lavishly in the company's annual reports.

5. It should enjoy a strong "business franchise," so that as costs rise, it can pass on the increase to its customers.

6. A very satisfactory type of business is what Buffett calls a toll bridge or gross profits royalty on the sales of other businesses. Ideally, it will be a monopoly or a "shared monopoly"—an oligopoly. Four of his favorites are television stations, monopoly daily newspapers, the handful of outstanding multinational advertising agencies, and, at times, the outstanding insurance brokerage firms. In each instance, the economic base—the business community in the area where the TV station or newspaper operates, or the businesses that the advertising agency serves, or those with which the insurance broker deals—do the work of building the market, and the "gross profits royalty" company merely tags along.

7. A good business should have a definable character. Conglomerates, for example, or businesses in high-technology areas where the very character of the enterprise changes periodically as the technology changes, are hard to run and hard to invest in.

8. A corollary of this is that the business should not present such complex management problems as to narrow inordinately the choice of possible managers.

Bad Businesses

There are far more bad businesses than good ones. Most of the characteristics of a bad business are the reverse of those of the good business:

1. (a) It makes money in accounting profits rather than in cash, or (b) it requires more and more investment as sales grow: a "chain letter" business. This can easily cause working capital asphyxiation, the entrepreneurial equivalent of crib death.

2. It has dishonest or grasping managers, who do not consider

themselves faithful stewards of their shareholders' savings. Buffett scorns executives who work themselves into high positions in companies and then abuse, or indeed manipulate their position for personal advantage. And he detests management that expands the size of the company through overpriced acquisitions without considering the effects on the old shareholders. Sometimes one company will buy another in the same industry at a premium over book value per share, and then issue its own shares at a discount from book value to pay for that acquisition. This may well leave the shareholders of the first company worse off, while enhancing the glory of its president. Buffett also detests management that fails to consult shareholders on major philosophical issues relating to the future of the company, such as a massive divestiture.

Another atrocity Buffett laments is insiders selling their stock for much more than it is worth in the midst of great market excitement over their particular industry. Then things degenerate, there is a period of disillusionment, and the stock collapses to what it is worth—or even substantially below what it is worth. With that, the insiders solicit tenders from the exasperated shareholders and buy their company back again. All they have done for the investors who put their faith in them is to bilk them of their savings.*

Here, incidentally, is where the ordinary retail buyer of stocks is at a particular disadvantage over the large-scale buyer. It can be quite hard for the small investor to determine the moral qualities of management—brokers don't emphasize it in their writings—and yet almost nothing could be more important to the future of his investment.

3. It profoundly changes character from time to time. For instance, defense contractors often have to come up with vast new programs to stay in business, programs where the company has to assume so much risk that, if something goes wrong, it may not even survive. Buffett calls this the "bet your company" situation. Federal Express, Polaroid, Lockheed and IBM have had to make huge commitments which, had they failed to work, would have meant the companies'

---

* A notorious example was Wells, Rich, Greene, a hot agency of the day. It sold a substantial part of its stock to the public at about $20 a share, which in due course drifted down to $6. Mrs. Wells et al. then bought all the stock back for about $9 per share. So the trusting investors ended up having transferred half their money to the insiders. Well-known greenmailers have done the same thing elsewhere. It is silly to confide your money to managers who may not act in your interest.

ruin. Many extractive industries are also in this position, a famous (and disastrous) case being Dome Petroleum.

4. Businesses heavily burdened with debt should be avoided. A rising debt load often indicates that things are going the wrong way; if they don't get better, the company may some day collapse, or have to refinance on unfavorable terms that dilute the interest of the old shareholders.

5. A business that is committed to provide a service or a commodity a long time in the future, and isn't able to protect it against inflation, may be subject to a grave risk. Westinghouse, for example, was brought to its knees by its promises to provide uranium under long-term contracts; some casualty insurance companies have been shattered by "long-tail" liabilities (those whose results do not surface until years after the event), notably asbestosis.

6. Perhaps because he lives in an agricultural area, Buffett is gloomy about businesses that serve the farmer and about farming itself. Farm-related businesses have a very slow—one year—turnover of a very high "inventory," the expense of planting and cultivating. If there is a crop failure, the farmer may not have a chance to bail himself out with a quick new cycle. By the same token, the supplier who sells equipment or seed to the farmer and the bank that lends to both of them often have trouble collecting when the farmer himself gets into trouble. And the farmer's difficulties can be completely beyond his control: Higher oil prices damage farmers, who depend on oil or oil-derived chemicals for fuel, fertilizer, refrigeration, and so forth; likewise a boom in the dollar, which can render many farm exports uneconomic but is not the farmers' fault.

Today most people are aware of the troubles of the farmer. Buffett, however, held this opinion years ago, when Europeans were buying farms so enthusiastically that some Congressmen got worried that our farms would be largely foreign-owned.

7. Buffett has had bad luck with retailing companies, apart from a few exceptions. He has said he does not really understand them.

8. Nor does Buffett like life insurance—which he says usually works out as a much less interesting business than one expects—or reinsurance, which presents the same problem. Life insurance, he says, doesn't give you enough profit to justify the trouble of selling the

policies. In reinsurance, there is often a long delay before the long-tail risks emerge clearly and the costs of future claims are known.

9. Buffett finds large, capital-intensive companies generally unattractive for investment. The available cash flow often cannot pay a satisfactory dividend and maintain plant at the level required for such a company to stay competitive. As a result, over very long periods of time, most steel companies, most automobile companies, some utility companies, most heavy chemical companies, most appliance companies and most oil companies need to float new issues of equity or debt capital in the market just to maintain their position, without necessarily increasing their profits.

As an example, for years the major petroleum companies had been paying more to find a new barrel of oil and get it ready to sell than they had been collecting at the pump. So as their old, low-cost inventory of oil was depleted, they showed declining real profits.

Mining companies are often an even worse case. The deeper you get into the ground, the higher costs rise. And often the demands of local governments in Latin America and elsewhere get more and more insistent as the size of the project increases. Cash flow then has to be reinvested to expand production and cope with these increasing difficulties. But in the end it often turns out that the company has been working for the benefit of its customers and a greedy host government, which finally deprives it of its property, either directly or indirectly, under the guise of confiscatory taxes or intolerable regulation. The owners end up with paper.

In 1985, Buffett finally closed down the textile business of Berkshire Hathaway, which he had bought in 1965 and with which he had begun his holding company. The operation had lost money for years, and all his efforts could not turn it around. As he admits himself, with the textile mills, he ignored Comte's advice that "intellect should be the servant of the heart, not its slave."[41]

In explaining his decision, Buffett noted what had happened to Burlington Industries, the largest textile company in America. He observed that over a two-decade period Burlington invested in capital expenditures an amount equal to three times its price per share at the outset. It more than doubled its sales as a result, but at the end of the period sold at the same price per share as it did at the beginning, since margins had declined. Thus, net of inflation, a share was worth only a third as much at the end of two decades as at the beginning. In other words, by not diversifying out of textiles, management had cost its shareholders two thirds of their money in real terms. Buffett cites Samuel Johnson: "A horse that can count to ten is a remarkable horse—not a remarkable mathematician," and adds that "a textile company that allocates capital brilliantly within its industry is a remarkable textile company—not a remarkable business."[42]

Buffett goes on to quote his own statement of some years previously: "When a management with a reputation for brilliance tackles a business with a reputation for poor fundamental economics, it is the reputation of the business that remains intact."[43]

10. This leads into the problem of government regulation for businesses in general. Natural targets, such as utility companies, usually make unsatisfactory, long-term investments because of the high cost of stringent government regulations.

The Market and Fair Value

Of all Buffett's ideas perhaps the simplest and most important for a nonprofessional to grasp is just this: *Value will in time be reflected in market price.* (It certainly is not so reflected continuously.)

It's just a question of time, and not always very much time. Most investors don't have the profound feeling professionals acquire that market anomalies are perforce ephemeral. If a bond is selling out of line with other bonds of similar tenor and quality, it *will* move to its correct value in time. If a stock that really does represent a dollar's worth of solid assets is selling for 60 cents, it *will,* sooner or later, not only go back to a dollar but quite likely more than a dollar. Prices of stocks, and of the market as a whole, in time not only reflect fair value but sooner or later excessive valuation.

Further, it's improbable that from the low point this recognition will take more than a few years, and it's likely that the period will in fact be about three. In studying the records of great investors I've often been struck by this three-year phenomenon. What's the reason? Good investment is quantified fussiness: When you buy, you want to hold out for the lowest price you really can buy for, and when you sell, you want to hold out for the highest price you really can receive. There are dozens of criteria for bargains and for excess prices. If they work, you'll find yourself buying around the bottom of the usual four-year market cycle, and selling near the peak about three years later, before the dive in the fourth year. (*Value Line* periodically publishes a list of stocks available for less than net working capital. The roster declined over the five-year period ending in mid-1985 from fifty-five companies to only five.)

So by the nature of that cycle, it would be surprising if a really good buy—presumably bought near the lows of the cycle—would not show a good profit later in the same cycle. (Of course, if you buy before the low, then it could take an extra year, or even two.)

This was not always so. Thirty years ago, most trading was done by the public, there were relatively few mutual funds and security analysis was done by hand on accounting spreadsheets, the computer and such not being available. Under those circumstances it was theoretically possible—although unlikely—for a bargain to go unperceived for years. Not that this was Graham's experience. (It's still true in Japan, but changing.) Today, however, with analysts constantly combing their data base for bargains, like an airport tower searching the skies with radar, a bargain rarely continues unperceived for long, so in the effervescence of a market boom, it is almost certain to have its move.

There are some ways of improving on this procedure. One is to try to wait until the *relative* performance of a given stock to the whole market shows that it is no longer collapsing but is beginning to find support from courageous buyers. If you are not a large institution, this approach can save you money. If you are an institution, then it's better to buy right into the weakness.*

Another, practiced by, among others, Robert Wilson, for years a highly aggressive and successful speculator, consists of taking a large position and then talking about it to all and sundry—preferably Wall Street columnists.†

---

* The Vikings liked to say, "We set sail into the teeth of the gale, that when we arrive all may be in sunder."

† "I am always trying to get my longs up and my shorts down, so I am constantly using people. I feel perfectly free to tell Alan [Abelson of *Barron's*] anything I have in my mind as long as it isn't insider information." See *The Money Masters* (New York: Harper & Row, 1980), p. 205.

Disasters

The stock market reacts in a manic-depressive way to news, and when disillusionment strikes, things will probably go too far the other way. That, in turn, may create the very opportunity that the skillful investor waits for. If a stock, fallen from favor, is now selling at $100 a share, and a piece of very bad news *should* push it down to $90, the chances are good that it will in fact drop to $80 or $70, thus creating a buying opportunity. Sometimes it will even go to $60 or $50.

One of Buffett's purchases that people still talk about was when the 1963 Tino de Angelis* salad oil scandal hit American Express. Briefly, an American Express subsidiary found itself possibly liable for hundreds of millions of dollars of damage claims arising from the sale of salad oil that did not exist, and the stock dropped sharply in the market. Buffett was able to establish that the "franchise" value of the company's basic business, notably its credit card and the traveler's checks with their huge "float," were intact. When you buy an American Express traveler's check, you in essence make the company a free loan in exchange for a piece of printed paper. The total of those free loans—the "float"—amounts to a couple of billion dollars at all times. Anyway, Buffett bought 5 percent of American Express, and it paid off handsomely. The stock quintupled in five years.

More recent examples of disasters: the Bhopal explosion, which collapsed Union Carbide, giving the Bass Brothers a chance to make an immense profit in a matter of months as the stock rebounded almost to its old price; the Chrysler near-bankruptcy, which Magellan Fund cashed in on; Disney, during the gas lines; and the cigarette companies back in the 1970s, after they were banned from advertising on TV. The succeeding years produced enormous gains in their stock prices.

Most illogical of all, incidentally, is to sell on a war scare. The experienced investor does the opposite. Herbert Allen bought a mining company in the Philippines in 1942. War always means a debauching of the currency, as the country incurs huge deficits to finance the military buildup and then the fighting. As the currency fades away,

---

* In Italy foundlings abandoned at the church door used to be given such surnames as "Innocenti," "de Angelis," "de Santis," or "Esposito."

investors flee to things, including things represented by stocks. The things themselves are denominated in larger and larger numbers of depreciating currency units. So in fact one should sell bonds and buy stocks on a war scare, particularly if the scare pushes stock prices down, as it usually does.

Nothing Exceeds Like Success

When, however, an outstanding business franchise is finally recognized, often after a number of years of neglect, all too probably the public, having finally understood, will bid it up to an excessive valuation, not recognizing that everything has its price, and that a popular concept is more likely than anything else to get overpriced.

This is an extremely important conception for the nonprofessional investor to think about and grasp profoundly; the greater the truth, the greater the overvaluation.

Pricing the Whole House

Most analysts appraise an asset from a Lilliputian viewpoint; they peer up at the company, as it were. If you were a Lilliputian who had succeeded in fastening Gulliver to the ground with thousands of pieces of string, and if you wanted an appraisal of your captive, you would send surveyors around the structure to contemplate the size of the legs, the worth of the silver buckles on the shoes, the ivory in the teeth, and how many carpets the coat, trousers, and shirt could be cut up into. You would be calculating the salvage value of the material. This is a variation of the "value" approach.

If, on the contrary, you were an executive recruiter, you would ask yourself how much Gulliver could be expected to earn over the coming years. This is a "growth" approach.

Closely allied to the "growth" approach would be what you might call the slave market analysis: If Gulliver were standing in a line beside a number of other men, all of whom were being sold into slavery, there would be an active supply and demand price structure, so that after a few minutes you might be able to form an impression of what Gulliver was worth as is, on the block.

A much more familiar example is what happens when you call in a real estate agent to advise you on the value of your house. He asks to see the floor plan, counts the number of rooms, considers how much it would cost to get the kitchen into shape, goes downstairs to see if the cellar is damp, investigates the attic to make sure that the roof is tight, asks how many acres you have, and in a few minutes comes up with a range of fair values and a suggested asking price, based on what other comparable houses are selling for. He would also take note that your house included a decrepit separate cottage and space over the garage, along with some acres over by the property line that could be developed. Certainly, in selling it he would not fail to point out to a prospective buyer that the property might command a much higher price if sold as four lots—house, cottage, garage-apartment, and developable acreage—than if it were sold as one parcel.

Still another (and essentially misleading) way to appraise a house is how it is measured for property taxes. An assessor arrives and calculates the cubic feet of each room, which when added give the volume of the whole structure. He then multiplies by a coefficient that has been established for that area, and gives you an assessed valuation. No one claims that the assessed valuation of a house appraised in this way corresponds to what you could actually sell it for.

Now, most investors, and many security analysts, evaluate companies in the style of the Lilliputians or the tax assessor. They contemplate a series of measurements and try to develop a theory of value for the whole: earnings per share, return on capital, profit margin, price-earnings ratio, compound growth rate of earnings, dividends, book value, and so forth. From such elements they try to construct a mathematical conception of what the whole property might be worth in terms of discounted cash flow or earning power.

An investment banker, however, will typically ask himself, What would the whole company sell for if I had to break it up? How much would it cost to reproduce it? Who would buy it as is, and what would he pay? In other words, the investment banker contemplates whole companies as though they were standing there in the slave market, or as though he were a real estate dealer trying to come up with a suggested asking price for a house: he looks at it in the round, not from the bottom up.

When you buy an entire company, you end up in the "valuing the whole house" situation. You can't do better than to find out from people familiar with that industry what entire companies of a given type are selling for between private buyers. At that point, however, you are essentially a bargain-hunting wheeler-dealer, not necessarily a Grahamite or anything else. Your success is likely to be based on your understanding of large factors that may or may not emerge from the figures.

In order to determine the value of a whole media company, for example, one seeks out the milieu that deals in it and talks to men who buy and sell newspapers and TV stations. A Buffett, for instance, does not need to do a mathematical discount model of the projected future revenues of a package of television stations. He simply knows what the whole kit is worth and could be worth.

Over and over again, we see Buffett buying a company in its entirety or, via share purchases, in part, that he knows is worth more to a private buyer than it is selling for at the moment, particularly if a few changes are made.

As he says, "When we bought 8 percent or 9 percent of the *Washington Post* in one month, not one person who was selling stock to us was thinking: I'm selling $400 million [worth of stock] for $80 million. They don't think that way. They had all these nonsensical reasons [for selling]: Communications stocks were going down ... other people were selling. . . ."[44]

Buffett himself once said that growth investing and value investing are aspects of the same thing.[45] They are indeed different elements of a single larger subject, but the analytical techniques are in practice different, for most investors. One need only look at the record: Individual great value investors—Max Heine of Mutual Shares, for example, whose record is superb—almost never have growth stocks in portfolios, and the great growth investors do not ordinarily bother with the dull although sure techniques of the artists in busted railroad bonds and floundering rust-belt industries, who seek realizable assets at a price way below the current market. Growth is often fueled by technology, and if one does not understand the technology, one is not likely to be too successful in that sector. Most value investors would not touch computer software, biogenetics, or long-range fiber optic plays. Neither would Warren Buffett. As he says:

> I have a limited area. It may cover 5% or 10% or 20% of businesses that I think I can probably evaluate. If any of those are interesting, fine. If somebody tells me something is interesting outside that field, I don't care. I mean, if I wanted him to run my money I'd give it to him. So I'm not interested in anything I can't value and most people are going to have trouble valuing most businesses. Anybody who tells you they can value, you know, all the stocks in Value Line, and on the board, must have a very inflated idea of their own ability because it's not that easy.
>
> But if you spend your time focusing on some industries you'll learn a lot about valuation. People can value oil or gas reserves, they can value television stations, you can see when you agree with those valuations and only when the game kind of shouts at you do you play and you don't worry about ways to make money.[46]

So as a footnote to Buffett's comment about the similarity of growth and value investing, one can well agree at the philosophical level, but there are often differences in analytical technique.

The Part Is Better Than the Whole

Despite his recent big flyer in Capital Cities/ABC, one of Buffett's long-held ideas, which large-scale investors would be well advised to consider, is that one has a much easier time putting large amounts of money to work in a number of minority situations than in a few controlling positions. This runs contrary to the instinct of most tycoons, whose preference is to buy control, then elect themselves chairman and put their friends and relations in as directors and officers. However, Buffett observes, this is in fact a much harder game to play. As he told stockholders in 1986, whole companies, complete with control, are rarely priced attractively. Berkshire Hathaway has done best buying minority stock positions in the market when stocks sell at large discounts to the worth of the underlying companies.

Buffett explains: "When I buy a stock, I think of it in terms of buying a whole company, just as if I were buying the store down the street.* If I were buying the store, I'd want to know all about it. I mean, look at what Walt Disney was worth on the stock market in the first half of 1966. The price per share was $53 and this didn't look especially cheap, but on that basis you could buy the whole company for $80 million when *Snow White, Swiss Family Robinson,* and some other cartoons, which had been written off the books, were worth that much [by themselves]. And then [in addition] you had Disneyland and Walt Disney, a genius, as a partner."[47]

In a market washout you can buy blocks of stock at extraordinary discounts from true value. When you buy a whole company, however, everybody has a chance to look carefully at the price being offered, and it is management's duty to try to get a better bid from another buyer. The company will thus usually hire an investment banker, who scours the marketplace to generate interest. Often a veritable auction will begin, with prices rising every few days. To be sure, if you succeed in buying a fair amount of stock at a very low price before this process begins, you may have a chance to sell out at a higher price.

At the same time, that approach precludes the very large gain that comes from staying with a good situation for a number of years. You can make 20 percent or 30 percent, or even 50 percent, by buying a block of stock that is then bought out in a tender solicitation of the whole company; but you are unlikely to make 300 percent or 500 percent on your investment.

There is, of course, another variation, which is to buy a block of stock and then make such a nuisance of yourself, or have such a bad reputation, that management buys out your particular block at a premium over market price—what is politely called greenmail but is really blackmail. This process is technically legal in the U.S., but an honorable person would not contemplate it: certainly not Buffett.

The other disadvantage of buying a whole company is that its management may not be able to do the job. In recent years, Buffett has always underlined, in spelling out the kinds of businesses he is interested in, that they must have good management in place, since he is not able to supply it. It is certain, for instance, that if he didn't have high esteem for Capital Cities' Tom Murphy and his team, he would not have helped Cap Cities buy ABC.

* Later on, he did buy Mrs. Rose Blumkin's (furniture) store down the street. See below, pp. 70–71.

Risk and Reward

It is the noninvestor who will most often say that there is a close relationship between investment risk and investment reward. This is generally so in gambling and certainly in speculation. The gambler, to a greater extent than the aggressive speculator, will take a leap into the unknown, trusting that his experience and intuition will give him a big winner. It would be true if the efficient market theory were correct. It is not true in skillful, value-oriented investment.

The value or quasi-scientific investor, such as Buffett, is more in the situation of the casino than of the gambler. He will normally make a series of bets, always with the odds (apparently) on his side. As long as he never departs from these two principles—favorable odds and many bets—he is in fact reducing risk, and indeed transferring the risk to whoever is opposite him in the transaction.*

As Buffett says, "The market, like the Lord, helps those who help themselves. But, unlike the Lord, the market does not forgive those who know not what they do."[48]

The Margin of Safety

Buffett likes to repeat an idea of Benjamin Graham's, which is that if you buy $1 worth of assets for 90 cents, you are giving yourself some coverage for the risk of the transaction, but if you buy it for 80 cents or 70 cents or 60 cents or 50 cents, your margin of safety improves correspondingly. You have every incentive to give yourself the biggest margin of safety possible, within reason.

As his sometime professor David Dodd observed, "You don't try to buy something for $80 million that you think is worth $83,400,000." Instead, "you build a bridge that 30,000-pound trucks

* Buffett, in fact, doesn't like everyday wagers. Once, when his golfing companions urged him to double their dollar-a-hole stake, he replied, "Based on the way we're playing today, it wouldn't be a good bet." Joseph Rosenfield has mentioned that Buffett and he sometimes bet on football games, but that Buffett won't go over a few dollars a throw: "Warren's not a betting man." See "Aw, Shucks, It's Warren Buffett," *New York* magazine, April 22, 1985, p. 56.

can go across and then you drive 10,000-pound trucks across it. That is the way I like to go across bridges."[49]

Similarly, Buffett has said that if you have stock worth a dollar that is now selling at 80 cents, you should sell and lose the 20 cents, in order to buy something about which you are equally confident that is selling at 60 cents.[50]

On the other hand, he says now, "I'm willing to pay more for a good business and for good management than I would twenty years ago. Ben tended to look at the statistics alone. I've looked at the intangibles."[51]

Also, he is finding it harder to locate acceptable bargains these days, while the number of bargain hunters has grown. "Everybody and his brother is a value-added investor these days," he mourns.[52]

In April 1985, he told the *Wall Street Journal,* for example, that he was revising his investment philosophy, hitherto rooted in Graham and Dodd, to accord with today's investing climate. Besides the growing scarcity of bargains, he foresees more inflation, making investing even more difficult. He forecast that Berkshire Hathaway would have to earn $3.9 billion over the next decade to maintain 15 percent annual earnings. And, he explained:

> Accomplishing this will require a few big ideas—small ones just won't do. Charlie Munger, my partner in general management, and I do not have any such ideas at present, but our experience has been that they pop up occasionally. (How's that for a strategic plan?)[53]

Not a week after the report had gone to the typographer came news of the deal with Capital Cities—a big idea that, surely, did not just "pop up." This illustrated Buffett's characteristic secrecy about investment plans, as against his openness about his investment principles, as well as how Buffett's Grahamite caution has evolved in response to changed conditions for investing.

Zigging When You Ought to Zag

In an article in the August 6, 1979, *Forbes,* Buffett presents an admirably rational (and, in the event, correct) argument for buying stocks at that time.[54] He begins by pointing out that in the year 1971 the managers of American corporate pension funds put 122 percent of the investment funds available to them into stocks rather than bonds. That is, they bought stocks with all the money they had coming in and in addition sold bonds to buy still more stocks.

The following year, 1972, they applied 105 percent of their funds available to buying stocks. The result of these two years was to boost the equity component of pension assets from 61 percent to 74 percent, which remains the highest proportion ever reached.

In 1972 the Dow earned $67, representing an 11 percent return on its opening book value of 607. The Dow closed the year at 1020, so this $67 meant a meager return of less than 7 percent on its market value.

Sure enough, in 1973–74 the market collapsed. In 1974 the Dow earned $99, representing a 14 percent return on its opening book value of $690, and 16 percent on its closing market value of 616. That was a vastly more attractive deal than less than 7 percent at the end of 1972. Nevertheless, pension managers only put 21 percent of their incoming investment funds into stocks in 1974, an extraordinarily low figure. The proportion of private noninsured pension plans represented by stocks fell to 54 percent of net assets, or exactly twenty percentage points lower than what had been considered reasonable two years earlier.

The Dow sold below book value for most of the year 1978, but during that year a new all-time low of 9 percent of incoming investment money was invested by pension fund managers in stocks.

In this article, Buffett points out that at the time of writing the latest figures indicated that in 1979 pension fund managers were still putting almost all their money into bonds, not into stocks.

He implies that this is an absurd arrangement, since prevailing bond interest rates at the time were only 9–10 percent, whereas in buying stocks the pension fund manager could get the usual 13 percent return on book value at a discount.

He characterizes as "schizophrenia" the attitude of corporate managers who are willing to pay 150–200 percent of book value to acquire run-of-the-mill outside businesses but, in their role as the person ultimately responsible for the pension fund assets, hesitate to put their money to work at a discount from book.

In trying to explain this bit of inanity, he notes that for some time previously stocks had been unsatisfactory investments. However, this was not because the businesses whose ownership the stocks represented had performed badly, but rather simply that the stocks had declined in the market. But prices cannot decline forever. At some point the stocks will rise to reflect the underlying value of the businesses in question, just as stocks could not outperform their underlying value forever—the phenomenon that had coaxed pension fund managers into equities at the top of the market.

At that time, pension fund managers rationalized this—their avoidance of stocks with an implied return of 13 percent in favor of bonds with a return of 8–9 percent—by putting forward two arguments (really, rationalizations of groupthink), both of which Buffett demolishes. The first argument was that earnings were overstated, since after realistic depreciation the true earnings of many companies would be substantially less than the reported earnings. To this Buffett replies that there were many areas, including service businesses, banking, life insurance, fire and casualty insurance, and finance companies, where the results if reported using replacement-cost accounting would be about the same as actual results.

The second argument, or excuse, that pension managers were putting forward to justify avoiding stocks in favor of bonds in mid-1979 was, according to Buffett, that the future was uncertain. But, he answers, the future is always uncertain. Sometimes, to be sure, you have a "cheery consensus" in Wall Street, but all that means is that at those times you pay more for everything.

Further, Buffett continues, pension fund managers more than almost anyone else can afford to take the long view. They are certainly doing so in buying twenty and thirty-year bonds, as they were at the time he was writing, and by the very nature of pensions they not only have no need to take a short view, but on the contrary have to take the long view.

Managers buying bonds instead of stocks were really betting that they were going to be able to switch back into stocks at exactly the right moment in the future; but, Buffett concludes, "you can be sure that at such a time the future will seem neither predictable nor pleasant. Those now awaiting a 'better time' for equity investing are highly likely to maintain that posture until well into the next bull market."[55] That, of course, was exactly what happened.

The Efficient Market Hypothesis

Buffett has had much to say about a voguish heresy, the efficient market hypothesis. This theory holds that at all times the level of the stock market and the prices of each stock tend to reflect whatever is known about both the companies and the economy. So it's no use trying to beat the market.

There has been a vast outpouring of argument about the efficient market hypothesis, two of whose principal advocates are Dean Burton G. Malkiel of the Yale Graduate School of Management and economist Eugene F. Fama of the University of Chicago; Professors Fischer Black and Paul Samuelson of MIT and others have also been intrigued by it. It has become so fully accepted in academia that, as Michael C. Jensen of the University of Rochester has said, we are dangerously close to the point where no graduate student would dare send off a paper criticizing it. Nonetheless, many of the best investment practitioners, including Buffett, regard it as absurd.

There would be two ways one could attack a theory of this sort. The first would be by showing that some investors do regularly beat the market. The second would be by demolishing the theoretical underpinnings of the hypothesis. Showing that some investors regularly do beat the market presents the same problems as trying to show that some persons can perceive the future or observe things taking place at a great distance. It is not enough to show that various individuals who are thought to have these powers do *not;* it is, however, sufficient to show that any person *does.* Thus, for example, a number of studies have shown how hard it is to predict the future performance of a mutual fund on the basis of its performance in the recent past. Dean Malkiel likes to cite the Mates Investment Fund, which after the top record in 1968 had one of the worst in subsequent years. (Fred Mates was eventually driven out of the fund business entirely and started a New York singles bar, called, as one might have hoped, "Mates.")

To this one might reply that, to be sure, some funds with outstanding records in one year will have poor records in a later year. But it is almost unheard-of for a given market sector, such as pharmaceuticals, food, or housing, to have three good years in a row. After two years, the concept is likely to be overworked, and a reaction can be expected. So if, for instance, a given fund is very heavy in over-the-counter high-growth stocks and does well for two or three years, the inevitable reaction will come along, and then you can expect it to do badly. The correct approach is therefore to find a mutual fund that enjoys outstanding success in its own category and then buy it when the category itself has fallen out of favor.

For some reason, the efficient market hypothesis protagonists have tended to ignore the thinking of the Aristotle of academic students of investing, Benjamin Graham himself. By rigidly applying his various criteria, he and a number of his followers, including Buffett, have enjoyed consistent investment performance records vastly superior to the records of investors in general. The reason is simply that the Graham approach sets objective measures of when common stocks are as cheap as they are likely to get, so that you can buy them with confidence, and sets further standards of when they are reaching a full valuation, so that you are well advised to sell them again. This type of gradual buy-and-sell strategy, which tends to produce a round trip every three years or so, is, if consistently applied, substantially more profitable—although, of course, more trouble—than a buy-and-hold strategy, which ordinarily gives you simply the performance of the averages.

What a Good Boy Am I

In the February 23, 1985, issue of *Barron's,* Warren Buffett presented his own evidence against the efficient market hypothesis by setting forth and discussing the investment records of his own partnership, which ran from 1957 to 1969, and the records of three fellow employees of his in the Graham-Newman Corporation between 1954 and 1956.[56] From the table, it will be observed that all of these managers significantly outperformed the averages.[53]

At that time, the entire Graham-Newman staff, in addition to Graham and his partners, consisted of four assistants, including Buffett. The older three were Thomas Knapp, William Ruane, and Walter

Subsequent performance records of Graham's four assistants in 1954–56.

	1. Fund's annual percent compound rate of return including dividends	2. Percent return to investor after management costs	3. S&P 500 percent annual return	4. Percent achievement (2 minus 3)
Warren Buffett: *Buffett Partnership, Ltd.* 1959–1969	29.5	23.8	7.4	16.4
Thomas Knapp: *Tweedy, Browne, Inc.* 1968 (9 months)–1983	20.0	16.0	7.0	9.0
William Ruane: *Sequoia Fund, Inc.* 1970 (from July 15)– 1984 (1st quarter)	18.2	17.2	10.0	7.2
Walter J. Schloss: *Walter J. Schloss Associates* 1956–1984 (1st quarter)	21.3	16.1	8.4	7.7

Schloss, whose careers, like Buffett's, have all been highly successful as well as instructive.

Knapp majored in chemistry at Princeton before World War II; after the war he audited David Dodd's investment course at Columbia, and then obtained an MBA at the Columbia Business School, taking Dodd's course over again, for credit this time, as well as Benjamin Graham's course. With fellow Grahamite Ed Anderson and others, he joined in forming Tweedy, Browne Partners in 1968. Tweedy, Browne, Inc., is a curious firm run, as old Mr. Browne used to say, like a pawnshop. It stands ready to buy, and, once they are bought, to sell, several thousand different little-traded stocks, always bidding or offering on strict Ben Graham lines. It often has a thousand or so items in its inventory. I do not consider its operations a fair test of Graham's method, however, since an individual could as a practical matter scarcely invest in this way. Tweedy, Browne requires an expensive staff to function, so it is really a business run in the spirit of Graham but quite unlike anything Graham did. Still, the results for the partners, net of costs, have been quite satisfactory.

Tweedy, Browne's total investment return from inception through 1983 has been 936 percent, compared to 238 percent for the Standard & Poor's Average. The average annual compound growth rate was 16 percent, compared to the 7 percent Standard and Poor's Average annual compound return.

The next instance Buffett cites is that of his former Graham-Newman colleague William Ruane. William Ruane and Warren Buffett met in Benjamin Graham's course at Columbia in 1951. When Buffett wound up Buffett Partnership, he asked Ruane to set up a fund for the partners' money, which, under the name of Sequoia Fund, Ruane did. Sequoia has usually owned many of the same stocks as Buffett, including major holdings in media companies, advertising agencies, banks, and insurance companies. The total investment return for Ruane's Sequoia Fund through 1985 was 775 percent, compared to 270 percent for Standard & Poor's. Sequoia Fund's average annual compound growth rate of 17 percent from inception through 1985 compares with 10 percent for Standard & Poor's.

Walter Schloss had studied under Graham at night at the New York Institute of Finance, but he did not go to college. In 1958 he set up his own investing partnership. He likes to work much as Graham did, finding opportunities in the standard manuals and then sending for the companies' annual reports, on the basis of which he makes up his mind. He talks to very few people. He often owns over 100 different stocks and has almost no interest in the underlying nature of the business. See table, p. 52.

Buffett goes on to mention some other Grahamite investors who have consistently done much better than the averages: His partner Charles Munger, Rick Guerin, and Stan Perlmeter, whose long-term records have all been outstanding.[57]

In a talk given at Columbia in 1985, Buffett said all of these investors have done as well as they have by clinging to a single tenet. It is that of always buying parts of a business—that is, shares of its common stock selling in the market—at a price proportionately far less than what an informed individual investor would pay for the whole company—what I call the "part is better than the whole" strategy.[58]

Buffett does not bother with a general theoretical attack on the efficient market hypothesis, but here are some thoughts on this subject.

Academic students of investment are always of mathematical bent. In their pantheon Athena always sits higher than, say, Mars or Venus. However, the ancients understood life and gave the other gods preeminence in turn. The world is not an orderly affair, whose conduct follows logical principles. Quite the contrary. My point is that from time to time sentiment, not mathematics, rules. When, every four years or so, Pan takes charge, and "panic" fears sweep the marketplace, then rationality goes by the board, and even though there may not be any current news to justify it, prices drop hour by hour, day by day, week by week, and month by month, fear feeding fear, so fast and so far that nobody can believe it. A severe bear market can cut your portfolio by half in a few months. And at the other end of the cycle, when the divinity of greed moves to temporary supremacy, prices are bid up to levels that nobody could have conceived of a year or two before. The study of market behavior belongs to anthropology as much as it does to economics.

A familiar demonstration is house prices. In theory, since much is known about the factors bearing on their value, prices should be quite stable. In practice, however, they lurch about astonishingly. Many apartments lost half their market value from 1972 to 1974, and have advanced fivefold in the following decade. Which was the correct, "efficient" price?

To parody the efficient market hypothesis somewhat, should we not also presume that there might be an efficient skirt hypothesis, under which an optimum length of women's skirt could be determined for all time? And should there not be an efficient art hypothesis, so that the squabbles, century after century, of the romantics against the classicists, the innovators against the conservators, the realists against the magicians, might finally be concluded?

Here I would also like to offer the "efficient professor hypothesis." According to it, all that need be known—about such subjects as politics, religion, ethics, aesthetics, epistemology, literary theory, and historiography—is available in the books. So any day now disputes between the learned in these areas will cease once and for all, and a settled consensus will emerge. A short volume can be prepared by a committee which will state the definitive few ideas on these matters. The professors need rage no more.

On that blessed day Lenin will embrace J. P. Morgan and the lion lie down with the lamb; the bull and the bear will also curl up with each other. The Dow will forever sell at fifteen times earnings and 1.3 times book value, the brokers will burn their chart books, and all equity mutual funds will, every decade, have the same performance.

In the meanwhile, however, the arguments—in market terms, the inefficiencies—will continue.

Beta

Besides debunking the efficient marketeers, Buffett dismisses the "modern portfolio theory" idea of avoiding high "beta" stocks—essentially, stocks whose historic volatility is high compared to the market—as an absurd oversimplification of good investment practice. He offers the hypothesis of being able to buy $1 worth of assets in the market for 75 cents. Suppose that the market declines so that the same $1 worth of assets can be had for 50 cents. In such a case the beta has increased, but so has the opportunity. To reject this opportunity because of an increasingly alarming beta would be absurd.

Nor do such notions as capital asset pricing models or covariance, so beloved of the theorists attracted by modern portfolio theory, interest Graham and Dodd investors—who, however, unlike the professors, actually make money. Indeed, one supposes that most successful investors would have difficulty even stating what those terms meant. They concentrate instead on the true concerns of the investor: *price and value.*

Consider Buffett's purchase of stock in the Washington Post Company in 1973. Its market capitalization was then $80 million. The underlying assets could have been sold to any one of a number of buyers for at least $400 million. Indeed, the value of these underlying assets would today be $2 billion.

Anyway, what if the 1973 market capitalization had declined further, from $80 million to $40 million? Should a real investor have been frightened off by this adverse volatility—that is, by the higher beta? Obviously not. He should have bought more.

The Out of My League *Dilemma*

In his book of that title, George Plimpton, "professional amateur" sportsman, describes a pickle he got himself into while writing on baseball. Proposing to describe what it was like to be a major league ballplayer, he arranged to pitch to the Yankee lineup as part of an exhibition game. However, in negotiating the deal, he had neglected to cross one of the Ts. It had not been specified that the batters were out after three called strikes, only if they missed on three swings. They could just wait and wait and wait! The catcher knew what sort of pitch each batter *didn't* like—an inside fast ball, for instance—but that knowledge, usually so handy, did George no good, since the batter, on the contrary, knew what he *did* like, and had the option of holding out all day for it.

As the afternoon wore on, George, getting more and more exhausted in a baking sun, perforce occasionally lost control enough so that each Yankee in turn sooner or later got his dream pitch. All the batter had to do was stand there. Time was on his side.

For Buffett, this tale would be a parable of the investment process. Plimpton's batters knew what they wanted and could wait as long as it took to get it. Similarly, a good investor knows what *he* wants and what price he's prepared to pay. How low a price is that? Low enough so that he knows he has a fabulous bargain. As Buffett says, sometimes when an opportunity appears you can almost hear the cash register.

Buffett once described this predicament of most professional money managers as the "Swing, you bum!" syndrome.[59] The experienced and patient individual investor can take his time ad infinitum waiting for the sweetheart pitch. If the whole market is too high, or there's so much optimism it makes you nervous, you can just go to Europe or to Mexico for a while until things come back into range. The hotshot go-go portfolio manager, on the other hand, from whom continuous activity is expected, is in the predicament of a dangerous hitter going to the plate and finding that the pitcher has decided to walk him. All the pitches are out of reach, or nearly so. The batter knows that his best tactic is to accept the walk, but thousands of fans, who want to see some action, are shouting, "Swing, you bum!" Not to disappoint them, the batter feels he has to take a cut, and so risks an unnecessary putout.

Stockbrokers, of course, who live on turnover, sometimes push the customer into this position. Even if you have a sound holding and are at home with the underlying business, which you understand well, a broker may call up with a new story to draw you into unnecessary and, indeed, harmful hyperactivity. To that extent a discount broker can be preferable to a full-service broker: The discount broker will leave you alone.

It is worth noting that the Sequoia Fund, run by Bill Ruane, Buffett's friend and fellow student in Benjamin Graham's course, has almost no turnover at all. The same rather tiresome holdings sit there year after year, and year after year Sequoia has had one of the best records in the business.

For this approach to work, however, you must truly *know*. That means doing your homework very thoroughly indeed. When you really have done it, you should have confidence enough to make a solid bet, so that if things work out, the result can bring a significant

benefit to your fortunes. Most people don't take the trouble to establish the facts about companies for sure and thus quite rightly don't
dare concentrate their holdings, preferring instead to diversify widely.
But monitoring many holdings means that the investor has a difficult
time maintaining superior knowledge about most of them.*

Getting back to the topic, how easy a pitch should the skilled investor insist on? One answer is simply the best pitch—or investment opportunity—that he's likely to find in a reasonable time, within a few
years, let's say. Benjamin Graham, for instance, offers a number of easy
tests (yes, they really are easy!) for an authentic investment opportunity.
One that we have been seeing in this day of leveraged management
buyouts is simply that a bank will agree to lend you the entire market
value of the company just on the security of the company's own assets. I
have found this one of the most useful of Graham's value tests, simply
because it is not as widely followed, except by corporate raiders, as some
of his other ones. Graham never got around to doing a playback of how
this method would have worked out over a long period of time and
calculating its rate of return, as he did with some of his other methods.
But in my own work, I find it rarely fails to work out very well indeed.

For Buffett, then, "investing is the greatest business in the world
because you never have to swing. You stand at the plate; the pitcher
throws you General Motors at 47! U.S. Steel at 39! And nobody calls a
strike on you. There's no penalty except opportunity cost. All day you
wait for the pitch you like; then when the fielders are asleep, you step
up and hit it."[60]

The Leverage in Insurance Companies

If you own shares in a mutual fund that enjoys a superior record,
then your own capital will grow at the same rate that the portfolio
grows.

* Buffett's idea of diversification is to own perhaps a dozen different holdings. He
calls the traditional notion (shared by Benjamin Graham) of diversifying one's assets
among a very large number of companies the Noah's Ark technique: One buys two of
everything and in the end owns a zoo. See the author's "Warren Buffett: The Investor's
Investor," *Financial World,* December 12, 1979. Buffett is less of a generalist than one
might suppose. By his own account, he does not understand high-tech or consumer
companies. Indeed, the very essence of his method is that he only moves when he is
certain. And there are not many things one can be certain about without a broader
experience than is possible in one lifetime.

Suppose, however, an investment company has $100 million of equity outstanding, as well as $100 million of bonds, on which must be paid interest of, let us say, 7 percent. Suppose further, that the resulting $200 million of portfolio assets grow at 20 percent per annum. In this case, as to the first $100 million the shareholders will make 20 percent, or $20 million. As to the second $100 million (represented by the bonds) they again make 20 percent, or $20 million, minus the $7 million paid out in interest, or $13 million. The total net earnings on the entire $200 million will thus be $33 million (20 plus 13), which for the common stock of the company is a 33 percent annual return. Essentially, one has thus created a margin account: fine if it works and disastrous if it doesn't. (The disaster in fact occurred in the 1930s, when many of the old leveraged trusts collapsed.)

Now, an insurance company provides an even more exciting possibility. Insurance companies have two possible sources of income. First, you hope to make money in the basic business, underwriting risks in return for premiums. Second, however, you have the use of the premium dollars between the time they are paid in to you and you have to pay out to satisfy the claims.

Let's say that we start an insurance company with $100 million of capital. We write $400 million of annual premium income. Suppose that we break even on the underwriting business, but every year make 10 percent on the premium dollars that we are holding until paid out, as well as on our original capital. That would represent 10 percent × $500 million, or $50 million, which, translated back to our original capital of $100 million, is a 50 percent annual return, before costs and taxes.

In other words, an insurance company is a sort of super margin account. Most investors do worse than the Dow Jones Industrial Average, and in a rising stock market this is particularly true of insurance companies, since they feel they should maintain most of their assets in bonds, their obligations being reasonably predictable. They must above all invest safely, and need not try to offset inflation like the rest of us, since as to life insurance, inflation strips away the value of the benefits to be paid, along with the company's own portfolio, and as to property/casualty, the periods of time involved are short, typically a year at a time, so inflation can be allowed for. (This is not true of long-tail liability insurance, which can be extremely dangerous and which Buffett avoids as much as possible.)

Anyway, when managed by a master investor, who does not bother to hedge his bets by putting most of his reserves in fixed-income instruments and instead makes large bets in the stock market, an insurance company can turn into a prodigous margin account, with extraordinary investment results. This is what Buffett has in fact done with the insurance subsidiaries of Berkshire Hathaway. When one reads that "Warren Buffett" has bought, e.g., an interest in General Foods, it usually means that an insurance subsidiary of Berkshire Hathaway—using its reserves built up against future claims—has made the investment, which can cost more than Berkshire Hathaway, the parent company, could readily afford. Nonetheless, the gains (and losses) of this investment are eventually translated back to Berkshire's equity and thus to Buffett himself. The same maneuver, using insurance companies, is performed by such operators as Henry Singleton, Larry Tisch, Carl Lindner and Saul Steinberg, among others.

The Cash Magnification Effect

One of Buffett's favorite techniques, then, is to buy companies—not just in the insurance business—with free (disposable) cash and use the cash to buy the next company with free cash, and so on. For instance, when Buffett began buying Blue Chip Stamps in 1968, the company had a "float" of over $60 million in outstanding, unredeemed stamps. With $25 million of this money Berkshire bought See's Candies, whose annual sales were then $35 million. See's annual sales volume is now over four times that, and its pretax earnings surpass Buffett's original purchase price.

Similarly, Buffett made his purchase of 100 percent of the *Buffalo Evening News* through Blue Chip Stamps.* Blue Chip also bought 80.1 percent of Wesco Financial Corporation, which was then able to buy 100 percent of Precision Steel and Mutual Savings & Loan. Wesco, an extremely successful investment, recently bought 2 percent of Fire-

---

* Lord Thomson, the late Canadian magnate who owned fifty-seven American newspapers, had much the same idea. He once said, "I buy newspapers to make money to buy more newspapers to make more money. As for editorial content, that's the stuff you separate the ads with."

man's Fund (headed since mid-1985 by Jack Byrne); Berkshire bought another 5 percent at the same time.

To understand the leverage in this process, which might be called the cash magnification effect, think of the growth of an empire: Prussia, then a relatively small country, added the military and economic strength of its dozens of neighboring principalities to its own, and created Greater Germany, with its formidable military apparatus. This larger entity next looked around for further victims. In due course the Wehrmacht fell upon Austria, Czechoslovakia, Poland, Holland, Belgium, and France.

In the same way, Russia grew from a small nucleus around Moscow to the present vast conglomeration of people and countries, with its tremendous military might. Russia has been steadily expanding its power by conquest for centuries now. The earlier conquests barely remember that they were once sovereign states. Likewise, the British Empire increased its dominion from a small base in England until it ruled a large part of the globe, before, like Germany, shrinking again.

In these examples soldiers acquire more soldiers, and those soldiers acquire still more soldiers until the original ruler and his successors dispose of a far larger army.

In just this way, corporate acquisitors, including Warren Buffett, target a cash-rich company, which they buy. The most energetic acquisitors start with a relatively small amount of cash, and borrow what is required to complete the acquisition. The name for this process today is the "leveraged buy-out." Investment bankers may lend enough so that with, say, $10 million in cash you can take control of a company worth $50 million. If that company has another $5 million in cash in available reserves, you can sell off enough of its assets to add the cash reserves, plus however much more the assets are worth than you paid for them, to your original hoard. The money does not even need to be entirely in cash: If you can borrow on the assets you've acquired, it comes to much the same thing. Armed now with $20 million of cash, you can attack a $100 million company, and perhaps double your hoard again. In a few years the skilled and aggressive acquisitor can attack a billion dollar company, then a multibillion dollar company.

In greenmail, as mentioned earlier, the acquisitor does not even have to go to all this trouble. The greenmailer uses his cash, which indeed he may in part borrow, to buy enough of a victim company so that the managers, in order to get rid of him and protect their jobs—but using the company's own assets—will buy him out again at a profit. In effect, he joins a club and, with the ink barely dry, demands a much better deal than the other members get. This should be illegal here, as it is in many countries.

Buffett does not ordinarily use borrowed money, and he is far too scrupulous to stoop to such a maneuver.*

The 12 Percent Equity Bond

One of Warren Buffett's most interesting ideas is his conception that all stocks as a class can best be understood as a kind of bond, thus being subject to destruction by inflation like any other bond.[61] Since traditionally investors have regarded things, including things owned through the medium of shares, as intrinsically inflation-resistant, Buffett's contention is very important. If it is correct, then in a highly inflationary environment, rather than avoiding bonds altogether one should be willing to own either stocks or bonds depending on how each is priced.

His thesis applies less to growth companies that have the freedom to reprice their products constantly to offset inflation than to large, capital-intensive companies, and those that operate in a highly competitive or heavily unionized environment. Buffett begins his argument by noting that, in the thirty years following the end of World War II, large companies tended to have a return on book value of about 12 percent or 13 percent. This has been true regardless of the inflation rate during the different periods.

At some times the 12 percent coupon is exceedingly attractive. For instance, during the 1950s and the early 1960s, bond yields ran around 4 percent. So not only was the 12 percent total return available in stocks a highly satisfactory deal relative to bonds, but the reinvestment

---

* These two approaches, expanding one's military strength through conquest and one's wealth through acquisition, are parallel strategies. Money is a form of power. Soldiers are a form of power. With money you can hire soldiers, and with soldiers you can extract money. Mao said, "Power grows out of the barrel of a gun," while Racine said, "No money, no Swiss [guards]."

characteristic of some stocks represented a valuable privilege. At a time when a shareholder can only reinvest his bond interest in other bonds yielding 4 percent, a company's ability to earn 12 percent or 13 percent on retained earnings makes those retained earnings more useful than dividends, particularly after taxes. Under such circumstances investors can have a great time with "plowback" stocks, which is why at one time growth utilities were so desirable.

On the other hand, utilities occasionally offer the shareholder a very poor life, particularly if the company constantly needs more capital to stay in business. In this situation a utility company may, by way of illustration, earn $8 a share, and pay $4 of tax on it. Of the remaining $4 a share, $2 may be distributed to the shareholder, who in turn may pay 70¢ in tax, and thus be left with just $1.30 to spend out of the original $8.

Further, however, the company may urge a dividend reinvestment plan upon the shareholder, so that his $2 a share of earnings will be reinvested in additional shares. That would leave him liable for $1 of tax, but give him no cash to pay it with. Worse, the whole $8 of earnings may be required for new plant so the company can stay in business. Worse yet, the $8 might not be authentic, being based on inadequate depreciation, so in reality there might be no earnings at all. By the 1970s many utility companies, including AT&T, were in this position. As their shareholders realized what was happening, the companies' shares fell in the market below book value. As new equity capital was raised, the old stockholders saw their share of the business shrinking. Thus the poor fish who subscribed to the dividend reinvestment plan was essentially paying annual dues (tax) in order to hold a depreciating asset.

And over the thirty years, inflation, and thus prevailing interest rates, gradually rose, to the point where by 1974 one could also buy bonds yielding 12 percent. So, which investment, the utility or the bond, was more attractive? It can well be argued, says Buffett, that by then the bond was preferable. In a manner of speaking the 12 percent common stock "coupon" never matures. There is no time when you can be sure of getting your capital back at some designated face value. The market is unwilling to accept hundred-year bonds, or perpetual bonds, and yet it does accept the perpetual 12 percent equity coupon.

Also, bondholders are served first, ahead of stockholders, whether in the distribution of earnings or the division of the company's assets in liquidation. To that extent, a 10 percent bond, being more secure, is preferable to a stock with a 10 percent earnings yield. So as they see bond yields rising above the earnings yield in the stock, stockholders start trying to get out of their "perpetual-coupon" shares. But for the whole class of such stockholders that's impossible. They have no place to go.

After years of happily getting 12 percent on their money in stocks while the bondholders got 4 percent, or whatever, equity investors began to think they had found nirvana, and started bidding up the price of these stocks, which thus advanced from a modest premium over book value at the end of World War II to over twice book value. During this period investors thus received not only the intrinsic 12 percent return but a capital gain. Financial institutions and market pundits began discovering the glories of common stock investing. A famous Ford Foundation report exhorted educational institutions to be more enterprising with their endowments, and excoriated those who failed to take advantage of the marvelous opportunities that equities represented. They were encouraged to spend not only the income on their portfolios but also the anticipated capital gain—that is, a projection of the capital gains achieved during the boom years.

Many colleges discovered that they had geared up their budgets to an expectation of returns that, far from rising as hoped, declined. Many endowments, including that of the Ford Foundation itself, which believed its own propaganda, suffered crippling losses during this period.

[McGeorge] Bundy urged the same policy on his own trustees and the foundation's finance committee, of which he was a member, with the same results. Between 1966 and 1974, shocking losses were suffered. At the time of his arrival, its portfolio had a value of some $3.7 billion. By 1970 that had slumped to $2.8 billion and then fell further to $1.7 billion in 1974. . . . Ford has dissipated almost three fourths of the real value of its assets over the past fifteen years, a loss of something on the order of $6 billion of philanthropic resources measured in current dollars. No disaster of comparable magnitude has ever been recorded.[62]

Alas, the timing was fatal. If you buy the 12 percent equity coupon at twice book value, you are really only getting 6 percent. Further, however, inflation began to accelerate. Bond yields rose rapidly to match, in due course moving up to 10 percent. So the enthusiasts who thought that sound investing meant buying common stocks at any price discovered that by looking at the trend instead of the underlying values they were designing their own ruin.

Soon came the 1974 decline, in which many stocks lost three quarters of their value. An important market recovery started later that year, but the inflation-created impairment of earnings became, if anything, worse. So by the time Buffett started propounding his 12 percent perpetual bond thesis, a high degree of caution seemed appropriate. Many investors, he pointed out, hoped to beat the law of the 12 percent perpetual coupon by outtrading the market. However, as a group they obviously can't do that. The crowd can't outtrade itself.

In his noteworthy analysis of the 12 percent coupon conception, Buffett asks whether this is an unchanging principle: Can equity returns never rise higher than their traditional levels? Unlikely, he says. It would mean that all corporations as a class would have to achieve either (a) a sudden increase in their sales, (b) lowered borrowing costs, (c) more leverage, (d) lower income taxes, or (e) more profitable operations.

Buffett observes that in an inflationary era none of these is likely to be achieved. Higher sales will call for more capital; inflation means higher, not lower, borrowing costs; American companies had already increased their borrowings substantially during the midseventies period; there seemed little reason to expect tax cuts, and rising levels of labor, materials, energy, and other costs meant that profit margins had been tending to erode rather than rise.

Only in recent years have we seen a fall in inflation produce a corresponding decline in bond rates, although not a fully corresponding decline, since the market hasn't believed that inflation has been cured.

Buffett, in fact, has stated that there is a 95 percent chance that inflation over the next ten to fifteen years will average about 7 percent, that is, somewhat over the consensus view. This rate, he believes, is made inevitable by the magnitude of the federal deficits. He has also stated that there is a 5 percent chance of runaway inflation, which would turn bonds into "a total disaster." Stocks would suffer from "an enormous shrinkage in real purchasing power, but you would have something left."[63] He says that this view is based on how America functions politically. When politicians can choose between a tax for which the electorate can hold them responsible and an anonymous one, they choose the second. Expenditures, in turn, determine the level of taxation; whatever cannot be raised through direct taxation has to be raised through implicit taxation—that is, inflation.

> Essentially, we've learned that when politicians have a choice between an explicit tax and an implicit tax, to some extent they opt for an implicit tax. No one passes it. No one's name is on the bill. Expenditures determine the level of taxation. Direct taxation determines how much of that taxation shall be explicit and how much shall be implicit, in effect through inflation. . . .
>
> What has happened in the last four or five years is an administration that you would feel was as sensitive to that whole problem as one you could have, and one that has strong feelings on it. When you see the inability to tax explicitly or to lower expenditures to the level of explicit taxes you have to say this is a culture that may not be able to handle a situation where essentially the policy cycle is longer than the electoral cycle.* I could eliminate inflation or reduce it very easily, if you had a constitutional amendment that said that no congressman or senator was eligible for re-election in a year in which the CPI increased more than over 3%. You would change the priorities. It's simply a question of what your priorities are.[64]

To be sure, Buffett's opinions on inflation are less significant than his calculation of the values of specific stocks. He is not a macroeconomist or futurologist. The Graham method discourages grand conceptions about the future. Indeed, the United States is at the moment experiencing a period of disinflation. Such investors as Larry Tisch, fully as eminent as Buffett, are basing their investment strategy on the presumption that disinflation will continue.

In 1985, Buffett indicated that he thought that an assumed 13 percent return on book value for American industry "or a trifle better" might be feasible.[65] But in February 1987, paying approximately 200 percent of book value, that is, at a premium of about 100 percent, instead of getting a return of 13 percent, one is down to less than 6.5 percent. With safe bonds offering returns of, let us say, 7 percent, the ordinary investor is receiving no premium for the risks of equity ownership. (Of course, when interest rates decline, this justifies a correspondingly higher valuation for equities.) He reminds us again that the optimist who observes that stocks have been better investments than

---

* To use a sinister expression I once heard from Professor C. Northcote Parkinson: "Democracy equals inflation."

bonds over the last thirty years may not be giving due weight to generally lower bond interest rates during the same period.

In spite of this, Buffett has said he will in no event buy a *long*-term bond unless he can find some pronounced anomaly, such as the Washington Public Power Supply System. He is too afraid of accelerated inflation. So only cash or short-term bonds are left as prudent fixed-interest alternatives.

Goodwill—the Gift That Keeps Giving

For Buffett, a more or less impregnable business franchise—related to what accountants call goodwill—is a far more reassuring asset, especially during inflationary periods, than extensive tangible assets, notably machinery and buildings.[66] He calls goodwill "the gift that keeps giving" during periods of inflation.[67]

This is a departure from a traditional investment idea, the "plant in place" thesis, which holds that the machinery or raw materials needed to produce something in short supply will increase in value to match inflation: If, to satisfy a shortage, a company builds a new plant, and if the new plant costs more than existing ones, then the earlier plants should also be worth more, just as existing houses tend to rise in value to match the rising cost of new ones. This can be called the "in goods we trust" doctrine.

When Berkshire Hathaway sold its equipment in New Bedford, Massachusetts, it received $163,000 for machinery with a book value of $866,000, an original cost of $13,000, and a new replacement value of $30–50 million. In other words, there was no relation between the sales proceeds and either the book value, the original cost, or the replacement value. Looms bought a few years before at $5,000 apiece were sold for scrap for $26 each, less than the cost of taking them away.

Buffett points out that, unlike his textile mills, three of his other businesses, Nebraska Furniture Mart, See's Candies, and *Buffalo Evening News,* had a contrary experience. Fifteen years previously, the three companies together earned $8 million pretax, whereas in 1985 they earned together $72 million pretax. Only $40 million of additional investment had been required to bring about this increase. That is, each dollar of increased investment produced more than $1.50 of increase in pretax earnings. Buffett compares this result with the general position of American industry, which has required some $5 of increased investment per $1 of additional pretax earnings.

What is the difference between these three and the general run of American business, not to speak of the textile business? Simply the superior business franchise enjoyed by those three companies, Buffett says.

Buffett argues that, on the contrary, during inflation a company without goodwill, or franchise, *must* get rising prices for what it sells, in order to replace its plant and inventory at higher prices as they are used up. If it can't get those price rises, it will be squeezed. That is, the "plant in place" price readjustment is a one-time thing. Suppose, for example, that you own and operate a taxi in a city that like most cities regulates how much you can charge for a ride. But suppose that the cost of fuel starts rising sharply. Here is what happens: First, you collect the same old fares, while the price of fuel soars. Then, when your taxi wears out, the new one, instead of costing $8,000, costs $14,000. You can't pay for the replacement taxi out of the depreciation the tax collector let you put aside for that purpose. So the best thing you could have done with your taxi at the beginning of this model would have been to have sold it at once.

Suppose, on the other hand, that you are the only taxi in a village that does not regulate the fares you can charge and where there isn't enough business to support a second taxi. In this situation you can raise fares to reflect the higher cost of fuel, of the replacement taxi, and with luck even something more. In other words, during inflation, the intangible goodwill arising from your position as the only taxi operator in the village (even if you do not own your vehicle but lease it) is more valuable than the physical vehicle in a big city that has lots of them.

A superb example of the "goodwill" business, for Buffett, is a television station, which has a negligible plant value but a wonderful business franchise. It can often carry 50 percent or so of its revenues into the profit column, and use its cash flow to buy other good businesses, even during inflation.

III

Buffett's Methods

Keep It Simple

Despite his far-flung investment interests, Buffett avoids the apparatus of conventional corporate life. His staff is tiny, he shuns meetings, he has no acquisition team. Buffett is on the whole against corporate acquisition departments, whose very existence, like an aggressive military general staff, constitutes an incentive to buy and whose recommendations are frequently designed to reflect the CEO's dreams of glory rather than a hard-nosed strategy.*

For Buffett, a good manager should be a dedicated cost-cutter. He does not need a budget; he should *know* how much he is spending on everything, right down to the office supplies. He once cited the example of Omaha's leading business, Peter Kiewit's construction firm, and pointed out that the top executives worked on Saturday, and their offices had no carpets.

In recent years, Buffett has operated from a five-room office on the top floor of Kiewit Plaza on Farnam Street in Omaha, which is roughly at the midpoint between his house and the heart of the city. On the walls are framed headlines describing remarkable days in Wall Street, the usual Wall Street prints, and a notice that "A Fool and His Money Are Soon Invited Everywhere."[68]

Buffett works an extremely long day, reading financial publications

---

* Buffett has often expressed disapproval of what he calls the Fortune 500 syndrome. See *The Money Masters*, p, 31. He says that all too frequently the chief executive of a large company primarily wants to move higher on the lists of the largest enterprises in the country, rather than improve his profit margin.

and talking to his chief partner, attorney-investor Charles Munger, who lives in California, and such associates as Tom Murphy and Katharine Graham. He works directly with his staff, rather than through intermediate layers of management. His principal office colleagues are Jay Verne McKenzie, who is secretary-treasurer of Berkshire Hathaway; William J. Scott, who used to be manager of the Buffett Partnership; Michael Goldberg, and two secretaries. Recently he has also hired management consultants from McKinsey and Company.

Scott runs the municipal bond holdings of Berkshire's bank and insurance subsidiaries, worth hundreds of millions of dollars. "Most companies would have at least half a dozen full-time people running a bond fund of that size, but Bill illustrates the fact that money management doesn't take a lot of feverish effort. He spends most of his day playing handball and rehearsing his polka band," says Buffett.[69]

Munger is one of Buffett's oldest friends. He once had a job in Buffett's grandfather's grocery store, which did not survive the arrival of supermarkets. He and Buffett joined forces early in the 1960s. "Charlie Munger and I can handle a four-page memo over the phone with three grunts," Buffett has said. "Charlie and I are interchangeable on business decisions. Distance impedes us not at all; we've always found a telephone call to be more productive than a half-day meeting."[70] ("My idea of a group decision is to look in the mirror," he maintains.)[71]

Their talks have led Buffett to buy Blue Chip Stamps (100 percent)—a trading stamp company that in turn bought See's Candy (100 percent), Wesco Financial Insurance Corporation (80.1 percent) (100 percent owner in turn of Precision Steel, a steel service center), Mutual Savings (100 percent), and the *Buffalo Evening News* (100 percent). Blue Chip was merged with Berkshire Hathaway in 1983. Berkshire meanwhile bought GEICO (40 percent) and Safeco insurance companies, Diversified Retailing (100 percent), and Nebraska Furniture Mart (90 percent), a furniture store. (The comings and goings of such investments can be followed in Appendix I, pp. 103–65.)

Buffett's somewhat unorthodox approach to purchasing the Nebraska Furniture Mart tells much about his belief in keeping things simple. Rose Blumkin, at ninety-four, still runs the Mart, which she founded in 1937 in a cellar, using a $500 loan. It today occupies three city blocks—some forty acres—and 1985 sales were $125 million.

Born one of eight children of a rabbi, at the age of sixteen she was managing a dry goods store in Russia that employed six men. She emigrated from Russia at age twenty-three, having had no formal education; in America, her elder daughter coached her in English at night.

A four-foot-ten-inch dynamo, Mrs. Blumkin continues to work every day and three nights a week. To get around the vast expanse of her store, she uses a three-wheeled motorized golf cart. Her motto is "sell cheap, tell the truth, don't cheat nobody and don't take kickbacks." She adds, "God blessed me just like my mother wished me. I lived a very normal life. I never had parties. I never had a vacation. I stuck to my family and my business. That was my only interest in life. My strongest quality is ambitious [sic]." And she says, "I don't care how many hours it'll take, I'm going to do it. I use common sense. Some people, they go to college eighteen years, they stupid as a post."[72] A competitor once sued Mrs. Blumkin for violating Nebraska's fair-trade laws, which prohibited selling below cost. The judge in the case accepted her argument that there was nothing wrong with giving a customer a good deal. The day after the trial the judge came to the store and bought $1,400 worth of carpeting.[73]

Early in her career she found herself overextended and had to raise money suddenly. While her children were out, she sold off all the furniture and appliances in the house, which enabled her to pay off her creditors. Her oldest daughter, now sixty-nine, reports that even in later years, her mother sometimes sold her own furniture if she didn't have a particular item left in the store.

In 1983, when Mrs. B., as he calls her, was ninety, Buffett appeared. As she tells the story, "One day, he walks in and says to me, 'You want to sell me your store?' And I say, 'Yeah.' He says, 'How much do you want?' I say, 'Sixty million.' He goes to the office and brings back a check. I say, 'You are crazy. Where are your lawyers? Where are your accountants?' He says, 'I trust you more.' "[74]

When Buffett finally did take an inventory of the Nebraska Furniture Mart, it revealed that the enterprise was in fact worth $85 million, not $60 million. Mrs. Blumkin commented, "I wouldn't go back on my word, but I was surprised. He never thought a minute. But he studies. I bet you he knew."[75]

Even more surprising, far from having a computer, Buffett doesn't even have a calculator. He hates computer printouts and "number-crunching." As far as Buffett is concerned, either you know something in your head or you don't know it at all. He says, in fact, that in working out the Capital Cities/ABC transaction he did not write down one figure.[76]

His mentor Benjamin Graham distrusted complicated calculations in the investment business, but not to that point!

Networking

Every other year, Buffett organizes a gathering of some of his investment friends to discuss things: the media business, world events, or whatever. Regular participants have been Tom Murphy, Carol Loomis of *Fortune,* Loews' chairman Larry Tisch, Joseph Rosenfield, chairman of Younkers, a Midwestern department store chain, and a number of others.

Normally, the group goes to a resort and meets in the mornings to discuss matters of global concern, each making a presentation in turn to the others. These gatherings have been held in Nassau, in Aspen, Colorado, and even, in 1983, aboard the *Queen Elizabeth 2.*[77]

In addition, Buffett reads incessantly: corporate reports, business publications, and also nonfiction books. And now that he's become a media magnate, he goes regularly to Washington where, as noted earlier, he has access to well-placed sources.

Buffett often has friends to visit at his vacation house in Laguna Beach, California, a hundred feet from the ocean. His family gathers there from time to time as well.

Characteristically, even when relaxing, his thoughts frequently turn to business. Jack Byrne has described a golf game with Buffett at the Burning Tree Country Club just outside Washington. Byrne, intent on his game, barely noticed a question from Buffett about GEICO's huge holding of thirty-year bonds, worth some $800 million. Buffett did not get a satisfactory answer. So, said Byrne, "His backswing kept getting faster and faster each hole, until finally, on the eighteenth, he swung so fast, he missed the ball and blurted out, 'Anyone who loans long now is a fool!' " Byrne heard Buffett this time, and did indeed shorten the maturity of his bond portfolios.[78]*

Gold Is Where You Find It

A great many banks and pension fund managers practice what is called in the jargon of Wall Street top-down or thesis investing. You will get a letter from your bank's investment department saying that the firm's economics department has decided that oil prices will go up (or down) and therefore that they want to buy (or sell) "energy-sensitives"—motels, trucking companies, and so on. In other words, they start by determining some general truth and then try to reduce it to the specific, usually by choosing the better-known companies in the categories they select.

Buffett would not ordinarily do that. There are lots of categories he will *avoid* because they just aren't good businesses or he doesn't feel he can understand them. But there are few if any that he will buy on the grounds that the economic situation or life in general will change in their favor in some way he can take advantage of.

The Graham-Buffett modus operandi resembles that of a New York antique dealer visiting London. The dealer takes a taxi to the Portobello Road and strolls through the shops there with his eyes peeled. He knows quite well what he can sell any object for in New York. If he can buy it for half that price in London, then he probably has a deal. It's unlikely that he will buy only one class of object: Louis XVI furniture, Meissen ceramics, Kazak rugs, or whatever. Rather, he will contemplate the objects one by one, and if he finds something outstanding, he will—very likely ignoring the price tag—just make a bid that he knows will yield a profit if it is accepted. If not, too bad! There are always more fish in the sea.

---

* Buffett does not believe in bonds in general, but he will buy them under special circumstances. For instance, after the Washington Public Power Supply System defaulted, Berkshire Hathaway bought $139 million of the system's bonds at a steep discount. (The WPPSS bonds offer a fixed 16.3 percent, tax-free current yield—and a $22.7 million annual return on Buffett's investment.) Similarly, after Penn Central went bust, he bought the company's bonds at about 50 cents on the dollar, and similarly the bonds of Chrysler Financial Corporation when Chrysler itself was close to collapsing.

The amateur, on the contrary, often collects a class of charming object—Wedgwood bowls or books illustrated by Arthur Rackham—and, having unearthed some prize in his area, will fall in love with it, paying more than the going market price without concern. He's not in it for the money. Many stock buyers are in the same category. They become intrigued by a particular investment conception and are willing to pay too much for it. Of course, for the investor who is not too well informed, the philosophy of buying what you know and sticking to it may well work better than hopping around at random like a bird on a tree.

But the professional approach is not to hop around, except for good reason; Buffett and his ilk usually buy what they know, at the right price, intending to hold on to it. "Finding great businesses," he says, "is not easy to do. Really having the conviction about them, and having the conviction that the people are going to behave in a high-grade manner, I'd be really slow to sell if I really had strong feelings about the business and management. . . ."*[79]

Res Ipsa Loquitur

If you have a particular mentality, or are looking for a particular target and only that target, it is often possible to overlook something right before your eyes that does not fit your preconceptions or your technique of looking.

Most professional investors "play the surprises," that is, seek a situation in which the reality differs from the appearance. Indeed, investment opportunity can be defined as the difference between reality and perception. If you can see things that other people miss, you can make a profit.

Most of Buffett's best investments, however, seem to be the opposite. He is able to satisfy himself that the reality *is* what it seems. So his

---

* As mentioned earlier, Buffett momentarily lost sight of this wisdom when he bought Capital Cities stock in 1976 and sold it two years later, only to buy it back in 1986 at a much higher price. "Temporary insanity," he says now. See "Aw Shucks, It's Warren Buffett," p. 65.

investment opportunity is generated by the market's skepticism about that reality.*

When he first began buying a major stake in General Foods in the mid-30s per share during 1979, most investors found the idea so boring that they couldn't summon up enough interest to investigate. Then in 1981 General Foods bought the Oscar Mayer Company for $469 million, which seemed a huge sum for yet another pedestrian business. Well, that's how it was. The giant, dull, reasonably priced General Foods was no better and no worse than it looked. But the values were there! Without changing much, General Foods slowly advanced from Buffett's cost in the $30s to $120 a share in 1985, at which price Philip Morris, searching for a hedge against the tobacco business, bought the whole company. Buffett's 4.3 million shares were worth over $500 million by the end of 1986, up from his purchase price of $163 million. Res ipsa loquitur!

Corporate Stock Repurchase Programs

Buffett has for years argued energetically that companies that do not have a good return on reinvested capital should pay out all they can to their shareholders. One way is to declare dividends. Another way is to repurchase stock from the shareholders. Indeed, it is a hallmark of Buffett's influence in companies of which he becomes a director that they start buying back their own stock.

Some managements of mature companies in mature industries prefer to keep as much control as possible of the cash generated, rather than pay it out to the shareholders. Buffett considers this an abuse, the more so if the money is then used for unsatisfactory acquisitions. Of course, if the company uses the cash to diversify out of a declining industry into a flourishing one, then he would be all for it. An example is his own diversification out of the original businesses in which Berkshire Hathaway was involved. (See Appendix I, pp. 103–65.)

---

* One thinks of the old Jewish joke about the two merchants meeting in the railway station. "Where are you going?" asks the first. "To Minsk," replies the second. "Aha!" replies the first, "you tell me you are going to Minsk because you want me to think you must be going to Pinsk. But I happen to know you really *are* going to Minsk!"

Buffett particularly objects to companies in dull industries employing their excess earnings to expand in the same industry, or perhaps to buy a company in another dull industry, at a higher premium over book value than their own stock is selling for. Many companies have in fact lost their profitability in the course of being built up to an excessively large size. W. R. Grace, for instance, has conducted literally hundreds of purchases and sales of divisions since its original migration out of South America. CEO Peter Grace seems to sell one unsatisfactory division and buy another in a supposedly more "exciting" industry as a matter of routine. When that industry becomes overly competitive in its turn, the new division is sold to chase the next fad. But the total return per share has grown far less than the S&P 500. For his part, as noted, Buffett dislikes corporate acquisition departments in general, believing that they push activity for its own sake.

Furthermore, it is important to define excess earnings. Quite often, real earnings are less than what is reported. For instance, the government may only permit a depreciation rate that is inadequate in an inflationary environment; stated earnings must be reduced correspondingly to find real earnings. Then, in a changing world one often has to reinvest part—or indeed all—of one's earnings just to maintain one's competitive position. Again the company is earning less than it seems. If, however, there really are excess earnings after making allowances for all such factors, and if the company has no good use for the money, then, says Buffett, the shareholders are entitled to the cash.

What is the best way to do that? If dividends are increased, the extra payments are taxable to the recipient, at his highest income tax rate. So it has often been better for the company to repurchase its own stock. By selling his proportionate share of the repurchase program back to the company and thus maintaining his percentage interest in the enterprise, the shareholder can get cash out to live on. And he only pays a capital gains tax. Historically, capital gains taxes have been much lower than ordinary income taxes. Under the 1986 Tax Act, this will no longer be so, but it is likely to become true again in the future.

One demonstration of the value of this approach is found in the fortunes of the *Washington Post.* Since 1972 the company has bought back about a third of its outstanding stock at a cost of some $234 million. About 6 million of the 7.5 million shares repurchased were bought at an average price of $14, for a total cost of $84 million. Today, they are worth $930 million. Buffett, as a major Post Company stockholder, has been a prime beneficiary of that policy. He wrote Katharine Graham in 1984:

> Berkshire Hathaway bought its shares in [the] *Washington Post* in the spring and summer of 1973. The cost of these shares was $10.6 million, and the present market value is about $140 million. . . . If we had spent this same $10.6 million at the same time in the shares of . . . other [media] companies . . . we now would have either $60 million worth of Dow Jones, $30 million worth of Gannett, $75 million worth of Knight-Ridder, $60 million worth of *New York Times,* or $40 million of *Times Mirror.*
>
> So—instead of thanks a million—make it thanks anywhere from $65 to $110 million.[80]

Some commentators deplore share repurchase programs, calling them "deindustrialization." Actually, it is healthy that capital no longer required in mature industries should be returned to its owners, who can reinvest it in high-growth sectors where it is needed more and will provide a higher return.*

Alternatively, the capital in such businesses can be reinvested by management for higher growth—if they will really do that and can do it well. Indeed, as Buffett regularly stresses in his annual reports, his personal empire would scarcely exist if he had not vigorously followed this policy.

Special Distributions

Sometimes a company buys back its own stock from a number of shareholders in such a way as to leave each shareholder with the same percentage of the company's thus shrunken equity base as before the transaction. The IRS regards this transaction as essentially a dividend,

---

* In the United States the judgment of the marketplace slowly drains capital out of mature industries that no longer need it and allots it to new and growing ones. In Japan the government fosters the process, obliging old and inefficient producers in, for example, the steel business to shut down, and helping retrain the workers for jobs in industries where they are needed. Politicized economic decision makers in countries with populist governments—Italy and Mexico, for example—often do just the opposite, using public money to prop up obsolete enterprises in order to protect the jobs. It's as though an orchard manager never pulled out dying trees and replanted with new ones. Eventually your orchard consists mostly of dying trees—uncompetitive companies—creating a wasteland of stagflation, increasingly heavy taxes . . . and structural unemployment.

since the shareholders receive cash while ending up with the same percentage share of ownership as before. Buffett has been amenable to these transactions as they have come along. In 1985 they were conducted with both the *Washington Post* and General Foods. Such transactions are of unusual benefit to Berkshire Hathaway, since as a corporation, it pays lower taxes on income it receives as dividends than income it receives from operations or, heretofore, funds received as long-term capital gains.

Stock Options

In an April 1986 article published in *Barron's*, Buffett underscored his criticism of another American business practice. When an enterprise is controlled by its executives, and these executives are not overly scrupulous, they will often reward themselves with lush option plans based on the performance of the company's common stock.[81]

However, as Buffett says, the stock may rise even though the executive has *not* done a good job. This can create an injustice, especially for an executive in a single division of a company, whose good performance may go unrewarded, or whose bad performance may be richly rewarded.

Buffett noted that in Berkshire Hathaway some executives stood to make as much as $2 million a year in performance bonuses, but only on the results of their division, not in the stock of the parent company.

Some other injustices of the option technique of rewarding shareholders, notes Buffett, are that:

1. By the simple compounding of retained profits, a share of stock in a mediocre business where management makes little contribution can enormously increase in value over the years, rewarding the manager in a princely fashion for doing very little.

2. It is often said that giving the manager an option on the stock puts him and the other shareholders in the same boat. In fact, however, the shareholders participate in all the risks, whereas the optionholder participates only in profits. This is not a fair deal.

Corporate Philanthropy

Most American corporations today make charitable donations to worthy causes in the regions where they operate and to causes that attract top management. The chief executive will often use corporate philanthropy to advance company or personal goals, e.g., having himself named a trustee of a museum or symphony orchestra, or having the corporation listed as a benefactor.

Buffett's contribution to the theory of corporate philanthropy flows from his concept of shareholders as partners, which is truer of investment companies—which Berkshire essentially is—than industrial companies, where capital is often considered a cost of the business. In 1983 Buffett announced that each shareholder of Berkshire Hathaway could designate $2 of corporate donations for each share owned. If every shareholder took advantage of this opportunity, the total of all donations would come to $2 million, compared with Berkshire's typical total giving of $200,000 in previous years. Since Buffett and his wife own almost half the company, their own share was $1 million, to go to the Buffett Foundation, established in 1966, and to organizations promoting birth control. In 1984 Berkshire Hathaway donated some $3 for each of its own shares held, or a total of over $3 million, and in 1985 and again in 1986 $4 a share, or $4 million.

On the one hand this is obviously fair and offers a pleasant possibility for the outside shareholders; on the other, by focusing such a high proportion of a corporation's largesse upon the chief stockholder's favorite vehicle, it does more for that vehicle than would have been likely if the decision were made in the usual way by management.

IV

How to Invest Like Buffett

Understand the Figures

In training yourself to be a first-class investor, the first step is to learn basic accounting. Like a chess player, the investor is playing a competitive game. By the nature of any competitive game, the number of top players must be limited. So if you lack a crucial skill that the best players have, you greatly diminish your chances.

Without an adequate knowledge of accounting, the investor cannot even understand the subject being discussed, let alone determine where the truth lies. Without it, the investor is at the same disadvantage as an aspiring orchestra conductor who cannot read music. Musical notation is the language of music and figures the language of business. Great musicians may have existed who couldn't read music, and there may be some skillful investors who are baffled by accounting, but they are very, very few.

We all understand instinctively what it means when in baseball the Little League announces that it is excluding Japanese teams from competition: The Japanese have been winning too many of the games. The investor, similarly, needs to notice changes in the accounting system of a company he is interested in and be able to interpret the significance of that change. Why has management switched from LIFO to FIFO? Is it in order to manufacture inventory profits to offset a lack of operating profits? Why, in the investment portfolio of one conglomerate's insurance subsidiary, were capital gains being realized and recognized as ordinary income—much more heavily taxed at that time—at the parent company level? An owner of a company should try to minimize taxes, so why does the conglomerate suddenly develop a craving to pay them? Is it because operating earnings are faltering elsewhere in the system and the parent company wants to keep up appearances, even at the price of unnecessary tax? And if so, what does that say about its management as curator of our assets? Questions of this sort emerge from a careful study of the figures.

Thanks to the SEC, most public companies divulge an extraordinary amount of information, not only in annual reports, proxy statements, and quarterly earnings reports, but also in the 10K, which is a treasure house of insight into a company's affairs. The skillful investor as a matter of course works his way through all the figures in each of these reports. He uses them as a starting point for more detailed inquiries, which he conducts directly with the company, its competition, and other sources.

Many investors hope to make more than their share of money in the stock market, but have neither the energy nor the skill to extract or interpret all this information. In an information contest their situation is hopeless, like pygmies playing basketball against Watusis. They are reduced to flair and exciting impressions, being seduced by intriguing images—exactly how you *lose* money in the market.

The worst of it is that often the investor who cannot read figures well is flattered by stockbrokers into thinking that he actually does have a hope of competing in this game. The stockbroker will be delighted to do your work for you. However, the successful investor should in due course become more skillful at his craft than most of the stockbrokers he talks to.

And alas, very often the stockbrokers themselves do not read the figures closely. Stockbroking is a difficult trade, and to survive the broker can't afford to spend great amounts of time overengineering the solution to his problem, which is simply to trade stock. He needs to know enough about a company's prospects to get a customer sufficiently excited to buy, but he has little need for answers to questions that the customer will never ask. Furthermore, the selling personality is different from the analytical personality.

Two further points on this subject: The customer always hopes that the stockbroker's research department will do the necessary work and then give him the answers, but perforce the brokerage house will share those answers with all its other customers—often in the tens of thousands—and then, involuntarily with all the customers of the other stockbrokers who read its reports. The good investor, however, should be almost alone when he is buying stock in a company whose merits he has discovered ahead of the pack.

There are services that will do the job of analyzing a company's financial reports for you and tell you what they find. However, the good ones have a large number of subscribers, usually institutional investors running large amounts of capital. So, once again, the subscriber is sharing the news with a great many of his competitors. And if the publishers of such reports were skillful enough to do what Buffett does, they would very likely go out of the market-letter business and become great investors themselves. The man who discovers how to turn lead into gold isn't going to give you the secret for $100 a year.*

An adviser who really has the Midas touch won't share it with you for any modest emolument. He will want what he's worth, which is nearly everything. So you must develop the touch yourself. And in business that means understanding figures.

Buffett goes further. "When managers want to get across the facts of the business to you, it can be done within the rules of accounting. Unfortunately, when they want to play games, in at least some industries, it can also be done within the rules of accounting. If you can't recognize the differences, you shouldn't be in the equity-picking business."[82] The equity investor needs to understand the *nuances* of accounting, he stresses.

Apply Your Own Business Experience

Buffett generally sticks to investing in businesses that he believes he can understand: financial enterprises, such as banks and casualty insurance companies; companies with extremely strong "business franchises," where unexpected competition is unlikely to appear, such as

---

* One is reminded of a charming anecdote recounted by Baldwin Bane, once the SEC's New York chief, in Martin Mayer's *Wall Street—Men and Money* (New York: Harper, 1955). Bane was being bedeviled by a promoter who wanted his approval to register stock in a gold mine. Every day, Bane, who smelled a rat, found a reason to turn away the promoter, always demanding more information. One day Bane, opening his mail, mistakenly read a telegram for the promoter from his partner out west. It read, "CANCEL REGISTRATION. HAVE FOUND GOLD."

media enterprises, and so forth. You do not ordinarily find Buffett in the shifting world of consumer preferences (See's and Nebraska Furniture Mart being exceptions) or the extractive industries and never in high technology. Other investors have done extremely well in those areas. But in high technology, for instance, they usually live close enough to Silicon Valley or Route 128 to get to know those companies and their executives; they breathe that air. The same holds true for other investment areas.

The reader of this book who wants to become a great investor has a better chance of doing so if he places his bets on sound companies whose nature, along with their industries, he fully understands. Managerial experience in the industry helps. He is unlikely to succeed by placing bets on companies about which he does not know the facts, in industries with which he has little experience.

Go and Look

A good investor in many ways resembles a good detective or newspaper reporter. He should enjoy expending shoe leather in his quest. In this he differs from the academic, often reluctant to leave his study, preferring to rely on whatever data he can absorb from books and papers. You wouldn't solve crimes or break news stories that way, and you can't expect to become a good investor that way. You have to be ready to go to a company, meet its management, inspect the plant, and understand what you are seeing.

Particularly, however, a good investor—and Buffett specifically—wants to know the people. And of all the human qualities to seek in the management of a company you propose to buy stock in, perhaps the most important is intellectual honesty and good character—trustworthiness, in short. The insiders have a thousand ways of taking advantage of the shareholders. If you think they're likely to do that, you don't want them as partners. The next is dedication to the job—fanaticism, as Buffett says. Then you can learn a lot by looking around and talking to the employees you meet—what might be called the sniff test. If you know what a plant should look like, so much the better.

The investor may be deceived by management when he investigates these qualities, although the more experienced he is as a student of mankind the less likely that becomes. However, he certainly has no hope of finding out whether management passes these tests if he doesn't get to know the people involved. Then, you should go through the steps followed by Philip Fisher, talking to the competition, and so on. This takes time, but it's important.

Venture Capital

Here we enter an area of high potential value to society, but also grave risk and uncertain reward—not Buffett's game at all. He hasn't written or talked too much about ventures, but he has, as they say, voted with his feet. Of course, the entrepreneurial and risk-taking spirit is how a country is built. The homesteader goes out to a new territory and dedicates his life to clearing the land and making it produce. After him comes the entrepreneur, who, discovering the need for a flour mill, say, dams a stream, builds a mill wheel, sets up his gears and grindstones, and goes into business. He charges enough to make a profit and keep his machinery in order, but enough less than it costs the farmer to perform the same function so that he can attract business and make a satisfactory livelihood.

If a project is too big for the entrepreneur to build himself, though, then he has to call on the savings of others—accumulated economic power—to build it. Those savings will require a satisfactory return to coax them out of safer stores of value into a risky endeavor. The most logical entrepreneurs are companies investing their own surplus cash flow in new products or new markets. However, since innovation moves faster than existing companies can keep up with it, a place arises for the entrepreneur allied to the venture capitalist.

In a typical venture capital deal, the limited partners frequently get a half interest in the company for their investment, the rest going to the investor, the promoters, the earliest backers, and management. But the enterprise will probably fail. It takes less intelligence, although some patience, for the investor to wait for the next severe stock market washout, when he can buy interests in fine companies for fractions of the money that has been put into them.

In venture capital you hope that one or two deals out of ten will work out well enough to pay off your losses or frustrations in the others. Few people outside that business realize how difficult it is. The usual sequence in successful venture capital is that of a hundred ideas maybe one is worth trying, and of ten ideas you try, maybe one will strike it rich.

The worst way to approach venture capital is to sit at a desk with a fat checkbook and take pieces of all sorts of deals that come along: electronic companies, biotechnology companies, TV deals, agricultural deals, process innovations in standard manufacturing industries, foreign propositions, and so forth. If the venture capitalist survives long enough, he will probably concentrate on a very few areas, end up backing innovations in some narrow area, and rarely lose money. At that point he may well have a good life, having become in essence a specialized merchant banker, not too different in function, indeed, from the comparable department of a large corporation.

One often forgets that a venture capitalist is not a passive investor. He will probably become involved in the workings of the company that he is backing: resisting the original investor's megalomania in favor of hiring a professional manager when the time comes; helping develop marketing policy; acting as an unpaid executive recruiter; finding additional capital when needed; dealing with banks. A venture capitalist without these skills can scarcely do his job.

So when we are talking about return on venture capital, we really mean the return to the limited partner of a venture capitalist who in turn receives a general partnership compensation. What return can such a passive venture capitalist reasonably expect? A 15 percent rate of return before tax would be highly satisfactory for the mass of all venture capital deals. By this I mean 15 percent when the deal is run out to the bitter end, not assuming a public issue at just the right time and bailing out in a bubbling stock market. One can't assume that the bubbling stock market will be there just when you want to sell. (If you are that good at market timing, incidentally, you can again do more than well enough in the easier world of listed securities.) I mean, that is, a 15 percent "internal rate of return" from the first outside money to the time when the company can list its stock under normal conditions.

One must focus carefully on the heavy promotional bite to which the passive venture capitalist is subject. In the first place, the original inventor always wants too much: 20 percent of the company, let us say. Suppose we beat him down to 10 percent and a retainer. Then, to attract really capable managers—even more crucial for a new company than an old one—one must offer them a substantial piece of the action, since their skill, experience, and dedication will make or break the enterprise. They will, after all, probably be giving up settled situations elsewhere. So let us presume that another 20 percent goes in low-priced stock or options.

And the very earliest promoters and financial backers, who take a chance before the process is proved or able managers recruited, deserve a substantial piece of the action, so let us assume they have earned 20 percent or so.

Thus, the outside investor will typically get very roughly 50 percent of the company in return for putting up all the major capital required to go into production and expand to the point of financial self-sufficiency.

Half the company for all the money! Is that attractive? Not ordinarily, considering that the company will probably fail. I mentioned that four-fifths of all new restaurants started in any given year go belly-up within twelve months, both in New York City and nationally. The record of many other businesses is worse.

It requires far less sagacity and experience and is much safer (although not socially useful) to approach investment in Buffett's spirit: You simply wait for a market collapse, or a misunderstanding of the specified stock, and buy shares of excellent companies at much less than they would be worth to a private buyer of each whole enterprise. It often happens that in a market decline you can pick up first-class assets, with strong patent positions, management in place, established markets—that is, a real going concern—for substantially less than the net cash in the bank, paying nothing for the plant, the patents, or any of the rest. In such a transaction it is hard to lose. If you succeed, you may easily do as well as most successful new ventures. Indeed, the very same original venture may be available five years after inception at far less than the outside "passive" investors paid for it. That is Graham's —and Buffett's—idea of a good deal. The bittersweet perils of venture capital he leaves to those with more of a romantic bent, courage, or specialized knowledge than himself.

Know the Values

One of the striking differences between a knowledgeable investor and, for example, an impressionistic stockbroker, is that the broker observes the direction a stock is moving, and tries to excite his customer on that basis, whereas the knowledgeable investor thinks in terms of the appraised value of the entire company whose shares he is thinking of buying. In this he acts like a successful buyer of whole companies.

Suppose, for instance, you were thinking of buying the farm next door, which happened to be owned in equal shares by four members of the same family. As mentioned earlier, what you should examine is what the entire farm is worth as compared to other similar farms, in terms of earning power and, eventually, its real estate development potential. You might conclude that you could afford to pay $200,000 for it, or $50,000 per family member. Will they sell at that price? In the same way, a masterful buyer of whole companies, using similar criteria, will consider whether he can afford to pay $200 million for a particular company. And in just this way the most successful buyers of stocks think in terms of the present value and future potential of the entire company, which they then reduce to a price per share, giving little attention to the apparent direction of the stock from day to day on the stock exchange.

For this system to work, however, you have to be able to appraise the whole company. How do you do that? As to any particular company, here are four ways:

1. Go to a friend in the industry who knows what whole companies are worth and is prepared to tell you the value of the one you're interested in.

2. Go to a company broker, investment banker, or management consultant who knows and will share the same information.

3. Go to a friend in a commercial bank who lends to this industry and thus should have a conception of the values of the companies in it.

4. Learn enough about that industry so that you know the answer yourself, the way you know the value of the farm next door.

The fourth method is the safest, unless you are a large-scale investor able to hire the appropriate talent. Few people have much incentive to tell you all they know about a company you might want to buy. If someone knows and is prepared to talk, he can probably sell his knowledge for a fee. In the end, therefore, you will want to develop this knowledge yourself.

There are, of course, a number of appraisal services available. For instance, a firm called John S. Herold, Inc., puts out *Petroleum Outlook,* which for all the major oil companies shows the appraised value of the oil and the gas in the ground. The stocks of the oil companies selling at the largest discounts from Herold's appraised values tend to act very well in the market. Of course, during periods of takeovers of entire companies, such discounts are unlikely to persist for long. Similarly, appraisals of timber, real estate and utilities, mining companies, and other "hard asset" companies are fairly easy to come by (not that Buffett himself likes these sectors). It gets tougher when you have to try to put a figure on a growth stock or, even more difficult, a high technology company. Still, there are ways. And unless you have a theory of the overall value of each company you are interested in, you cannot invest successfully.

Buffett points out that to be successful it is not necessary for an investor to know more than one thing, although he certainly has to know that. He sometimes mentions a friend of his who had gotten almost completely wiped out, and then decided to follow this principle—knowing one thing and knowing it well. The subject he chose was water companies. In Buffett's salty language. he attained such expertise that "he knew what it did to the earnings per share every time someone flushed a toilet." Having gained that degree of wisdom, Buffett's friend, not surprisingly, prospered hugely. Right here is where a large number of unsuccessful investors go wrong. They do not realize that what counts is their batting *average,* nothing else. So they attempt too many different styles. That is, they try to achieve superiority as investors in too many different industries. As a result they are masters in none.

As an alternative to concentrating on one industry, one can also concentrate on a particular investment approach—companies in bankruptcy, specialty growth companies, convertibles, and so forth. The point is that, whatever one does, one has to do it in a way that brings consistent success. Only a genius can be successful in a great number of different areas; Buffett himself does not pretend to that ability.

Reverse Engineering

One of the easiest ways to invest like Buffett is coattailing—buying what he buys, or the equivalent: often one stock can be a surrogate for another. You figure out the rationale behind the investment after the fact. Thus, when Buffett was buying newspapers, TV stations, ad agencies, or food companies, you could have asked around about why he was doing what he was doing—or read his company's annual reports. Then you could have bought cither the same stocks or others in the same industry. This principle would work, for example, for regional banks, which Buffett has always been fond of, and of course insurance companies, if you chose the right ones.

Berkshire Hathaway only publishes its holdings once a year. However, it has become so large now that its positions often exceed 4.9 percent of the stock of the target company—the level at which they must be reported to the SEC. The SEC in turn releases this information. A number of subscription services track these releases, some with quite full descriptions of the buyers and the target companies. If you are interested, you can request annual and quarterly reports, proxy material, and the voluminous 10K reports from the company itself. You can also get the principal magazine stories on it from a large library and follow up by asking your bank or broker for the best available brokerage house writeups on the company.

However, although Berkshire Hathaway would have been the perfect investment almost any time since 1970, stockbrokers have never liked the company. The customer has little reason to sell it, so the stockbroker gets no commissions. The stock scarcely trades at all. Buffett has stated that 95 percent of the shares have not changed hands in the past five years. He also deliberately keeps the number of shares fairly constant to discourage trading. Since the stock has so little activity, it does not pay brokers to study it. For that reason, less attention is paid to its holdings than they deserve.

A key point in tracking Buffett's thinking is to ignore the initial reaction of your investing friends. Most people will miss the point of the purchase; otherwise the stock would not be underpriced. Above all, don't expect the company to be "exciting" or "hot." A perfect reaction to your inquiry about a Buffett stock among your Wall Street friends would be "It seems cheap, but I can't see it doing anything for at least six months. It's dead." If you hear that, you may be on the right track.

In the first quarter of 1979 Buffett started buying General Foods, continuing his purchases all through 1979 and 1980. Loews Corporation, the Tisch brothers vehicle, in turn filed a 13D report in the spring of 1980, indicating that it owned 5 percent of General Foods. Wall Street was excited by the news, and the stock ran up several points. Loews thereupon sold some of its stock into the resulting strength. Their next 13D report indicated that they had dropped below 5 percent again. Wall Street was baffled. However, this has in fact been Loews' usual procedure when making purchases of this sort, as in their purchases of Storer, Firestone, and CBS. The surge of strength right after the 13D announcement has generally created a chance to take a quick profit. Buffett, however, went right on buying steadily, eventually accumulating the major position that he later sold to Reynolds Industries.

In this as in other instances, many astute buyers would have been able to copy Buffett if they could have overcome their own "not invented here" attitude. When the first announcement appears of a large Buffett purchase of a security, there is usually a "window" in which others can follow at much the same price. Often, however, investors assume—even investors who should know much better— that at last Buffett has lost his grip, and that this time it is not worth paying attention to what he is doing.

The same situation arose when Buffett bought into Capital Cities in connection with the ABC deal. Just before the announcement the stock was selling in the area of $172–173. By the end of the day it was still there. In other words, an alert investor could have taken a number of hours to make up his mind to follow Buffett at Buffett's own price. In the following days the stock shot up to $220, but then it sank back to $185, or almost the original price. By this time, however, it was becoming apparent that Capital Cities was getting much more money for the ABC assets it proposed to sell than it had originally expected, so in a way it was actually a better deal than when originally announced.

(Capital Cities had expected to realize $770 million from certain broadcast properties that it had to sell to comply with FCC regulations; the actual figure was $1.25 billion, or almost $500 million more.)

Nonetheless, a curious paralysis prevented most investors from taking advantage of this opportunity. What does Capital Cities, a TV station and newspaper owner, know about TV programming? many asked. The answer was that only 20 percent of the profit of the merged Capital Cities/ABC derived from programming. Even if Tom Murphy of Capital Cities could not get a good handle on the programming aspects, that is not where this deal will stand or fall. Murphy was a known master of what was needed to make the acquisition work: cutting overhead. If he merely succeeds in bringing costs in the ABC stations down to the levels of Capital Cities' existing stations, then the transaction will be a colossal success. This, indeed, is what is happening. Of course, if he can increase ABC's market share, that will be a great advantage.

Incidentally, the parallel thinking of Buffett and Larry Tisch can also be seen in the TV network area. When Buffett/Murphy took ABC out of play, only two targets remained among the major television networks. Not surprisingly, Tisch went after one of them and did in fact achieve control. The reader will perhaps recall that a beleaguered CBS encouraged Tisch to buy stock in order to fend off an unwelcome acquisitor. Like a Renaissance condottiere hired by a town to protect it against assault, Tisch, having achieved that objective, then became actual master of the domain.

It has been noted that Tukman Capital Management sometimes closely follows Buffett. Buffett watchers have sometimes used Melvin Tukman's transactions as a clue to Buffett's thinking. A recent Tukman Capital Management portfolio appears as Appendix VI, page 192.

Another Buffettlike figure is Rick Guerin, of Pacific Partners, which has had an outstanding record. The period 1965–1983, for example, beheld a compound gain of 316 percent for the S & P and *22,200 percent* for Pacific Partners. Guerin, who became a disciple of Buffett's through their mutual friend Charlie Munger, has reportedly attributed his success in part to his lack of a business school education. Guerin is chairman and the largest shareholder of PSA, which will perhaps over the long term become a personal investing vehicle similar to Berkshire Hathaway.

One interesting point that emerges from a study of Berkshire Hathaway's transactions is that Buffett, like Benjamin Graham, does a lot of risk arbitrage, especially among consumer products companies. For instance, he had a big position in Nabisco at the time of the Reynolds merger and in Burroughs convertibles in the deal with Sperry. Buffett says himself that Berkshire Hathaway sometimes enters risk arbitrage transactions "when we have more money than ideas" but only in transactions that have already been announced.[83]

Still another approach is to follow the transactions of Sequoia Fund, run by Buffett's friend Bill Ruane, to whom Buffett sent a number of his investors in 1969 when he closed up Buffett Partnership, Ltd. They remain very close. You can get its reports, showing the latest transactions, by asking for them.* See Appendix IV, p. 189.

Incidentally, never be diffident about analyzing what the great investors are buying. They do it themselves, you may be sure! After all, Buffett's interest in GEICO, which eventually led to one of his greatest coups, was first aroused when he noticed that his then mentor, Benjamin Graham, was a director of the company.

Buffett has often reiterated a curious point, which is that some people can understand and accept the value approach to investing, whereas others simply cannot accept it. One of the odder phenomena in modern investing history is that Benjamin Graham followed his simple technique year after year, and wrote it up, describing its results, in his lectures and publications. Nonetheless, year after year he had almost no imitators. Similarly, Buffett's own career was very far advanced before this second generation Grahamite became a figure of interest in the investing community. Even today, he is little known outside that community. Only in recent years, indeed, have his transactions been widely followed in the press. Most of his purchases and sales have gone virtually unremarked. And yet, had you merely copied Buffett, or for that matter bought stock in Berkshire Hathaway when the excellence of its record was already more than apparent, you could not have failed to amass a huge profit.

---

* Mutual funds send out reports to anyone who requests them, to build up their constituencies.

The Secret: Steady Compounding

There is nothing in the world like compound interest. If you put $2,000 a year into an IRA starting when you are nineteen and continuing *just for eight years,* until you are twenty-seven, when you retire at sixty-five the $16,000 will have grown to over a million dollars! This assumes you keep the money working at 10 percent per annum compounded, but in fact that's quite a conservative assumption. Buffett, of course, began building his fortune earlier than age nineteen and compounded at a higher rate. But there's no reason to try that hard.

The key thing is to *keep the process working steadily.* The occasional sensational year isn't necessary, and the bad years likely to follow from a speculative policy may throw the whole business out of gear. In value investing you try for a high consistent batting average, and don't worry about the homers.

Avoid Risk

I'm putting this principle at the end of this sequence for emphasis, not because it's last and least. On the contrary, it's the key to success. Risk taking, including venture capital, built America, while extracting money from the stock market has no social value. Still, you have to know your objective. If all you want to do is extract money from the stock market, then risk taking isn't necessary. You just follow Graham's rules and be patient. The price of a bad move in a diversified Grahamite portfolio is usually minor. The price of a bad move in a concentrated risk-taking portfolio can set you back very seriously.

To be fair, we must recognize that there are quite different and equally successful philosophies, notably investing in long-term growth or backing innovation, in which risk must be assumed. However, while they also involve a higher degree of skill than Grahamite investing, for most people they are more satisfying.

What It Takes to Be a Good Investor

Investing calls for much the same qualities as those required to become a first-class ballet dancer or concert pianist.

1. You have to want to do it enough to overcome the difficulties. I know lots of aspiring writers. Without doubt one of the biggest differences between the ones that make it and the ones that don't is simply that the successful ones have the drive to win through in spite of all the frustrations. A dedicated author writes and writes day after day, sometimes having nothing published for years at a time. For something that you desperately want to do, the difference between the professional and the amateur is often just that the professional will work terribly hard and keep at it. The "ruling passion" (to use the eighteenth century expression) of the great investor is usually greed—typically deriving from a less-than-prosperous childhood—but many great investors also have the element of the performing artist about them. They are highly conscious of each other's feats. It takes so much concentration to be in the top rank that, although great investors are almost always rich, they rarely live in a grandiose way during their most successful period, or form collections, engage in public works, or pursue arts or sports. The great investor, like the great chess player, is determined to become a master of that particular craft, sometimes without caring whether he only gets rich or immensely rich. It has been rightly said that the reward of the general is not a bigger tent but command. It is, in other words, succeeding in the process itself that fascinates the greatest investors.

2. Closely related to this is originality. Many if not most great artists are innovators. Shakespeare, for example, coined thousands of words. To succeed in investing requires a vigorously independent turn of mind, and indeed often an element of perversity, since the money is made by doing the opposite of the crowd at key points. To pull off a great investment coup it is best to be the only substantial buyer of a stock in which you are building up a position. Napoleon observed that one good general was enough for an army, and the best generals of his time rarely held councils of war. Similarly, committee investing is almost always mediocre investing.

3. However, you should not invest unless you are sure of what you are doing. Since there will be some things that you can buy with certainty, why bother with those that you cannot? Only if you are perfectly certain that you are right will you have the confidence to buck the opinion of the crowd at the critical moments; only then will you make your fortune. By the same token, you must be completely honest with yourself about what you know and do not know.

4. If possible, be flexible about buying stocks in different industries, always subject to the criterion that you know your facts for sure.

5. Only buy a stock the way you would buy a house that you intended to live in. You should understand it well enough and like it well enough so that you would be content to own it in the absence of any market. Buffett finds it useful to write down the main reasons why a stock should be attractive and then contemplate them; once he has considered a case for a time, he makes up his mind, and that is that.

6. Be thorough, cautious, and risk-averse. Remember Buffett's two key rules for successful investing:

Rule No. 1. Never lose money.

Rule No. 2. Never forget Rule No. 1.[84]

7. All this requires energy and determination. That is why the investor should have the same quality Buffett insists on in management: dedication to the job. He talks of his one-line employment form, whose only question is, "Are you a fanatic?"[85] Great investors, Buffett included, always are.

What Makes a Bad Investor

1. The unsuccessful investor is usually the opposite of the successful one. He does not have the qualifications or the mentality or the interest to do his homework, and flits from one titillating story to another like a butterfly.

2. He is excited by the emotions of the crowd, buying hot ideas near their tops and being flushed out in despair near bottoms—what Buffett calls "fashion investing."[86]

3. He doesn't know what a business is really worth, so he can't determine for sure whether he is paying a fair price for it.

4. He has a high turnover in his portfolio.

5. He thinks of a stock as a thing to bet on like a racehorse, rather than what it is—a share of a business, whose fortunes derive from the success of that business.

Conclusion

What, then, is the essence of Warren Buffett as an investor? He is a supremely clever and experienced business analyst, specializing in media and financial companies. He learns about the anatomy of a business primarily from the figures, much in the style of his master Graham. He does not try to be a futurologist. He looks for the impregnable business franchise, rather than the prospect of dramatic new developments. He is not the person you would go to for a prediction on the changes in the shape of the world in the year 2020, or the outlook for fiber optics or beta blockers. I doubt if he would venture a guess on whether some consumer fashion would last a third year. (Fudge seems to be a perennial.)

In addition, he pays close attention to the cash position of a company he buys into, and stands ready to redeploy that cash for the next purchase, and to buy back common stock. This completely business-like approach is perhaps the least understood part of his strategy.

He is, in other words, the opposite of the ordinary market plunger driven by hopes and fears, greed and dreams, excited by generalities, not analyzing the specifics. Buffett, like most successful investors, particularly of the "value" school, begins by purging himself of emotion and substituting intellect. Where he has forgotten to do that, it has usually cost him money. He was never able to run Berkshire Hathaway itself successfully, although he liked the company and its big cash dowry; the same is true for some of his other consumer operations.

Buffett knows a few things particularly well, starting with media-related companies, notably newspapers, which he has been around since infancy and which have been a marvelous field to be involved with. (As noted, some other media magnates have succeeded about as well as Buffett.) He is also at home in insurance, banks and financial businesses in general.

He can recognize and work with a dedicated manager, without feeling he should get involved in operations, as distinct from giving financial advice.

Then, he has learned what he doesn't know and what he isn't. People often try to appear what they fear they are not. Buffett doesn't have that problem. Berkshire's shareholders needn't start worrying about it until they read about Buffett's influential committees, cultural endeavors or statesmanlike utterances. The manager who concentrates fully will usually beat one who is distracted. When Wellington beat Napoleon, Wellington's attention was utterly focused on his campaign, while Napoleon, as emperor, had to cope with a host of wider problems. It's hard to do more than one thing superlatively well at a time, and Buffett, so far at least, doesn't try. He does, however, become fond of certain businesses, potentially lowering his rate of return. It may turn out, for example, that Buffett was too eager to get locked into ABC. Considerations of prestige and sentiment could conflict with a policy of waiting for "the perfect pitch."

How applicable is Buffett's method today?

In discussing some Grahamite performance records (see the table on page 52), Buffett showed that it is possible for an able investor—and note that Graham's disciples were carefully selected for their ability—to do well applying the value approach. Should other able investors reasonably also hope to succeed in the future using that technique? Yes, *unless the circumstances have changed.*

But beware: circumstances do change. Graham himself used to point out bemusedly that for decades after his publication of the essence of his method, only a handful of investors followed it. He held the funds he managed down to $20 million or so—say $200 million in today's money.

Graham sought—and achieved—the prestige of being the alchemist who finally discovered the Philosopher's Stone of a simple and consistently successful investment technique. He eschewed the uncertain benefits of making colossal amounts of money personally, of acquiring, like Croesus, more gold than he knew what to do with.

But today Buffett alone and those he influences represent many billions of dollars. Adherents of the Grahamite technique have proliferated in recent years, since it is "bankerly" and well adapted to computerized analysis. But as I write, a number of the wisest and most successful value-oriented groups have suspended taking new money, claiming that they find too few opportunities.

Indeed, at Berkshire's annual meeting in Omaha on May 20, 1986, Buffett himself said that he couldn't find good values in the market at the moment, and that he had sold most of Berkshire's equity holdings except for GEICO, the *Washington Post* and Capital Cities/ABC. He added that the prices now being paid for media properties, wonderful assets that they are, no longer made sense—what I call the "nothing exceeds like success" syndrome. He noted that the government's guarantees of their deposits had made banks and savings and loan companies less attractive by undermining prudence; also that the up-cycle in property and casualty insurance might not carry as far as usual, because of the huge amounts of capital the industry has raised.

Thus, there are two sides to the problem: the overall market is high, and within it, the Graham school has finally gotten too popular.

So Buffett and his peers, wielding their billions, can expect difficulty executing Graham's theories.

The value technique will be attractive again when its results have been dull for long enough that its discredited practitioners are thinned down to a more modest level. When the doctrine is no longer so widely followed it can once more be useful.*

What, then, should the prudent investor do now?

Buffett has given us his opinion and indeed has voted with his feet. But Grahamite investing is not the only style: There are also growth investing, high technology, liquidating situations, arbitrage and the foreign markets, among other techniques. The growth-oriented investor knows that growth stock price-earning multiples are at the bottom of their range. The high-tech adept sees wonderful opportunities unfolding in biotechnology and elsewhere. The internationalist sees the popularity of some foreign markets compared to the Dow growing as

---

* This situation arose in reverse in 1972–73. Twenty years before, in the early 1950s, the idea of growth stocks was unfamiliar. There were only a handful of growth funds. So growth stocks did very well. (The one with which I was then associated had the top performance record among all funds for the decade.) But by 1972 there were some 170 growth funds. All the volatile money was chasing growth, although for several years growth funds had done worse than income funds. Everybody was aboard the bandwagon, which, indeed, had become a mania. The end of the vogue for growth had to be near. This was the subject of my first column on investments, "End of an Era," published in the *Christian Science Monitor*. And sure enough, in 1973–74 the growth stocks collapsed. Some declined by 80 percent.

U.S. institutional investors pour money abroad, and continues to find opportunities there.

However, the market sector that is most in view today is the take-over (or leveraged buyout) candidates, usually value stocks of the type that Grahamite methods should enable one to analyze. Huge pools of money have been assembled to take advantage of any opportunities that may appear in this area. The sellers are well aware of this, so prices are high. That is why the conservative investor can't find bargains.

But shouldn't these huge pools constitute a firm support for the market, preventing it from declining?

No. This kind of money is fickle. After a few disasters the huge pools will melt away like an army of underpaid mercenaries, the over-priced market will have no support, and prices will slide down easily enough.

And when the part of the market that everybody is watching collapses, the rest usually follows along. "When the paddy wagon rolls up, they take away the good girls with the bad girls," goes the Wall Street saw. So in addition to imagination and thoroughness—as always—the successful investor today must have flexibility; or if he lacks flexibility, then patience.

APPENDIX I

Some of Berkshire Hathaway's Principal
Equity Transactions
(1964–1986)

American Express

In 1964, in the wake of the Tino de Angelis salad oil scandal, American Express collapsed on the stock market to $35 per share from a high of $62.38 a share in 1963. Buffett, believing that the company's strongest operations—credit cards and travel services—would not be hurt by the scandal and that consumers' faith in the American Express name would protect the company, bought heavily. The stock rose to $189 a share in the next five years. (This transaction was in the Buffett Partnership; Berkshire was acquired in 1965.)

American Express 112L

NYSE Symbol AXP Options on ASE & CBOE (Jan-Apr-Jul-Oct) In S&P 500

Price	Range	P-E Ratio	Dividend	Yield	S&P Ranking	Beta
May 30'86 62½	1986 70⅛–50½	15	1.36	2.2%	A	1.66

Summary

A leader in travel-related services, American Express is also active in international banking, investment services and insurance. The company has expanded its financial services network through acquisitions, including Investors Diversified Services (IDS) and Lehman Brothers Kuhn Loeb Holding Co. in 1984 and the non-U.S. banking subsidiary of Trade Development Bank Holding S.A. in 1983. AXP has reduced its interest in Fireman's Fund Corp. to 27% from 100% through two public offerings.

Current Outlook

Earnings in 1986 are estimated at $4.90 a share, up from 1985's $3.55.

Dividends should continue at $0.34 quarterly.

Earnings for 1986 are expected to benefit from continuing growth of travel-related services. Both Shearson Lehman and IDS should enjoy increased profitability stemming from strong investor demand for financial assets. Despite a smaller interest in Fireman's Fund, AXP will benefit from the turnaround in the property-casualty insurance area. Share earnings will be aided by a recently announced, second 10 million share repurchase program.

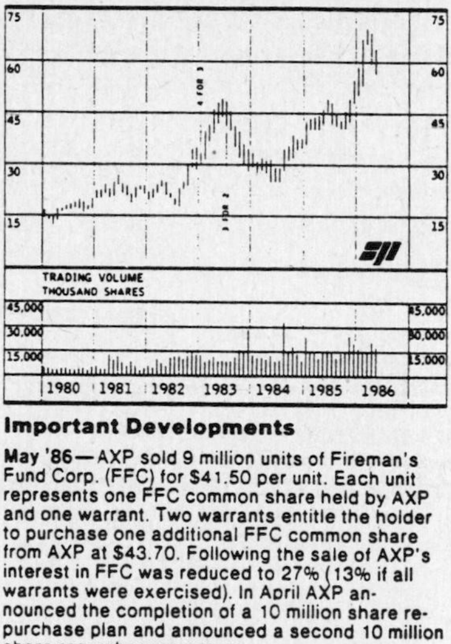
75
60
45
30
15
TRADING VOLUME
THOUSAND SHARES
45,000
30,000
15,000
1980 1981 1982 1983 1984 1985 1986

Total Revenues (Billion $)

Quarter:	1986	1985	1984	1983
Mar.	3.61	2.63	2.90	2.29
Jun.		2.90	3.15	2.46
Sep.		2.98	3.35	2.49
Dec.		3.35	3.50	2.53
		11.85	12.90	9.77

Total revenues for the three months ended March 31, 1986 rose 37%, year to year. Paced by Shearson Lehman, the Insurance and IDS segments, consolidated net income increased 112%. Share earnings were $1.40, compared with $0.67.

Common Share Earnings ($)

Quarter:	1986	1985	1984	1983
Mar.	1.40	0.67	0.54	0.80
Jun.		0.61	0.64	0.96
Sep.		1.08	0.85	0.88
Dec.		1.19	0.76	d0.11
		3.55	2.79	2.79

Important Developments

May '86—AXP sold 9 million units of Fireman's Fund Corp. (FFC) for $41.50 per unit. Each unit represents one FFC common share held by AXP and one warrant. Two warrants entitle the holder to purchase one additional FFC common share from AXP at $43.70. Following the sale of AXP's interest in FFC was reduced to 27% (13% if all warrants were exercised). In April AXP announced the completion of a 10 million share repurchase plan and announced a second 10 million share repurchase program.

Apr. '86—AXP said first quarter earnings included a $140 million gain from the sale of its interest in Warner Amex Cable, $34 million from the reversion of excess pension assets, and a $80 million charge to develop new business opportunities.

Next earnings report due in late July.

Per Share Data ($)

Yr. End Dec. 31	1985	1984	1983	1982	1981	1980	1979	1978	1977	1976
Book Value[1]	22.82	20.21	18.95	15.91	14.31	15.17	12.87	10.85	9.41	8.50
Earnings	3.55	2.79	2.53	3.02	2.79	2.63	2.41	2.15	1.83	1.35
Dividends	1.32	1.28	1.24	1.10	1.02½	1.00	0.90	0.77½	0.65	0.45
Payout Ratio	37%	46%	49%	36%	37%	38%	37%	36%	36%	33%
Prices—High	55	39	49⅝	35½	27⅛	20⅛	18⅜	21⅛	20⅞	21⅛
Low	35⅞	25	28	17¾	18¾	12⅝	13⅞	13⅞	17½	15½
P/E Ratio—	15–10	14–9	20–11	12–6	10–7	8–5	8–6	10–6	11–10	16–11

Data as orig. reptd Adj. for stk. div(s). of 50% Aug. 1983, 33⅓% Feb. 1983. 1. As reptd. by co. after 1976. d-Deficit. E-Estimated.

Standard NYSE Stock Reports
Vol. 53/No. 109/Sec. 5

June 6, 1986
Copyright © 1986 Standard & Poor's Corp. All Rights Reserved

Standard & Poor's Corp.
25 Broadway, NY, NY 10004

112L   **American Express Company**

Income Data (Million $)

Year Ended Dec. 31	Life Insur. In Force	Insur. Prems.	Premium & Other Income Commiss. & Fees	Int. & Divs.	Total Revs.	Net Bef. Taxes	Net Oper. Inc.	Net Inc.	% Return On Revs.	Assets	¹Equity
1985	46,803	1,919	6,108	3,292	11,850	1,247	810	810	6.8%	1.2%	16.8%
1984	37,436	4,371	4,814	3,291	12,895	736	610	610	4.7%	1.2%	14.4%
1983	28,715	3,243	4,037	2,227	9,770	517	515	515	5.3%	1.4%	14.5%
1982	10,223	2,932	3,235	1,759	8,093	754	581	581	7.2%	2.2%	20.4%
1981	8,726	2,730	2,648	1,688	7,211	694	518	518	7.2%	2.2%	20.3%
1980	6,351	2,589	1,522	1,264	5,504	421	376	376	6.8%	2.0%	18.8%
1979	4,790	2,451	1,130	1,006	4,667	391	345	345	7.4%	2.2%	20.1%
1978	3,372	2,342	912	759	4,085	371	308	308	7.5%	2.3%	21.3%
1977	2,492	2,080	738	579	3,446	304	252	262	7.3%	2.2%	19.6%

Balance Sheet Data (Million $)

Dec. 31	Total Assets	Cash Items	³Bonds	Investment Assets Stocks	Loans	Total	Accts. Receiv.	Cust. Deposits	Travel Cheques Outstg.	²Debt	Common Equity
1985	74,777	7,968	21,640	1,319	9,898	33,552	18,140	16,203	2,679	5,399	5,069
1984	61,848	7,490	20,305	892	7,830	29,419	14,802	13,262	2,454	3,839	4,382
1983	43,981	5,949	11,827	1,359	7,564	21,328	11,497	12,511	2,362	2,643	4,043
1982	28,311	3,194	6,986	580	4,602	12,571	9,204	6,810	2,177	1,798	3,039
1981	25,103	2,854	6,390	935	3,928	11,411	8,087	6,188	2,468	1,280	2,661
1980	19,709	2,153	6,020	1,069	3,690	10,779	4,887	5,087	2,542	1,099	2,162
1979	17,108	2,028	5,667	928	3,369	9,963	3,597	4,749	2,343	688	1,833
1978	14,670	1,735	4,979	832	3,320	9,131	2,717	4,192	2,105	479	1,548
1977	12,346	1,532	4,340	781	2,571	7,692	2,164	3,755	1,859	329	1,339

Data as orig. reptd. 1. Common. 2. Long-term; incl. curr. portion. 3. Incl. short term invest.

Business Summary

American Express is a major financial service company principally engaged in providing travel-related, investment, international banking and insurance services worldwide. Industry segment contributions in 1985 (profits in million $):

	Revs.	Profits
Travel related	36%	$461
Shearson Lehman	27%	201
Am. Express Bank	13%	164
IDS	19%	76
Insurance	5%	1

The Travel Related Services segment is comprised of the Payment Systems division, which includes travelers cheques and the American Express card, a major credit card with about 22 million cards in force; the Travel Services division, which in addition to providing vacation and leisure travel services include corporate card and business travel activities; and other activities, including publishing, direct mail merchandise services operations, and life insurance.

American Express Bank Ltd. and its affiliated Trade Development Banks, acquired in 1983, provide specialized banking services through a network of 85 offices in 39 countries.

Shearson Lehman Brothers is one of the largest

full-line investment service firms serving U.S. and foreign securities and commodities markets. IDS Financial Services provides financial products to individuals, businesses and institutions.

In August, 1985 Fireman's Fund Corp. (FFC) then wholly-owned by AXP, sold its life insurance operations to AXP for $330 million in cash. AXP has since reduced its stake in FFC to 27%.

Dividend Data

Dividends have been paid since 1870. A dividend reinvestment plan is available.

Amt. of Divd. $	Date Decl.	Ex-divd. Date	Stock of Record	Payment Date
0.34	Sep. 23	Sep. 30	Oct. 4	Nov. 8'85
0.34	Nov. 25	Dec. 27	Jan. 3	Feb. 10'86
0.34	Mar. 24	Mar. 31	Apr. 4	May 9'86
0.34	May 21	Jun. 27	Jul. 3	Aug. 8'86

Next dividend meeting: late Sep. '86.

Capitalization

Long Term Debt: $5,399,000,000.

Series A & B Money Market Pfd. Stk.: 600 shs.

Common Stk.: 224,804,296 shs. ($0.60 par).
Institutions hold approximately 63%.
Shareholders of record: 51,211.

Office—American Express Plaza, NYC 10004. Tel—(212) 323-2000. Chrmn & CEO—J. D. Robinson III. Pres—L. V. Gerstner, Jr. Secy—S. P. Norman. VP-CFO—H. L. Clark. Investor Contact—C. Streem. Dirs—A. L. Armstrong, M. R. Bohm, P. A. Cohen, D. M. Culver, C. W. Duncan, Jr., G. R. Ford, R. M. Furlaud, R. L. Genniard, L. V. Gerstner, Jr., F. R. Johnson, V. E. Jordan, Jr., F. M. Kirby, H. A. Kissinger, A. L. Lewis, Jr., A. R. McCardell, J. D. Robinson III, R. V. Roosa, M. R. Wallace, R. Warner, Jr., J. H. Williams. Transfer Agent & Registrar—Morgan Guaranty Trust Co., NYC. Organized in Buffalo in 1850; incorporated in 1965

Information has been obtained from sources believed to be reliable, but its accuracy and completeness are not guaranteed   Richard M. Levine

Affiliated Publications

Buffett acquired his original position in Affiliated Publications, publisher of the *Boston Globe,* in 1973. At year's end 1985 Buffett owned 1,555,752 shares (adjusted for a 3 for 2 split in 1986) at an average price of $2.26 per share. On April 15, 1986, Buffett sold his entire holdings in Affiliated Publications for $48.24 a share.

Affiliated Publications 7047P

ASE Symbol AFP

Price	Range	P-E Ratio	Dividend	Yield	S&P Ranking	Beta
Sep. 16'86	1986					
54½	67¾-34⅞	28	0.44	0.8%	A+	1.04

Summary

This media company is the owner of The Boston Globe, the largest newspaper in New England. It also has a 45% interest in McCaw Communications Companies, a cable TV and radio common carrier. In June 1986, the company agreed to sell its radio properties for $65.5 million in order to place greater emphasis on its newspaper and cellular telephone activities. Long-term prospects are favorable, aided by tax reform measures currently pending.

Current Outlook

Earnings for 1986 are projected at about $2.00 a share (excluding gains from the planned sale of radio stations), versus the $1.69 (including $0.21 nonrecurring gains) reported for 1985.

The $0.11 quarterly dividend is the minimum expected.

Revenues and earnings in 1986 will largely benefit from improved newspaper results, reflecting solid gains in advertising and circulation revenues. Equity losses are expected to be larger, reflecting start-up and acquisition costs. Another strong earnings advance is likely in 1987, boosted by a lower effective tax rate.

Revenues (Million $)

13 Weeks:	1986	1985	1984	1983
Mar.	94.6	86.3	77.3	64.9
Jun.		93.0	86.6	73.2
Sep.		88.6	81.7	71.5
Dec.		99.5	[3]98.2	84.3
		367.3	343.8	293.8

Revenues for the 1986 first half rose 12%, year to year. Operating earnings rose 21%. After other items, and taxes at 50.4%, versus 55.1%, income from continuing operations climbed 34%, to $0.95 a share from $0.60. Results exclude a loss of $0.01 and a gain of $0.01 in the respective periods from discontinued operations.

Common Share Earnings ($)

13 Weeks:	1986	1985	1984	1983
Mar.	0.34	0.29	0.25	0.17
Jun.	0.61	0.41	0.40	0.31
Sep.		0.39	0.35	0.32
Dec.		0.60	[3]0.50	0.44
		1.69	1.49	1.24

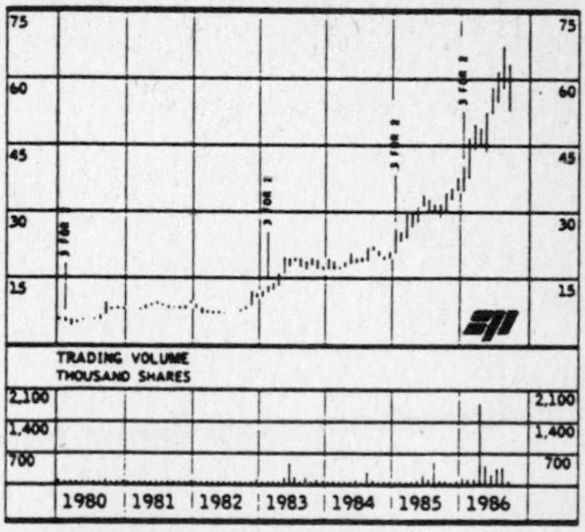
75
60
45
30
15
TRADING VOLUME
THOUSAND SHARES
2,100
1,400
700
1980
1981
1982
1983
1984
1985
1986

Important Developments

Jun. '86—Affiliated agreed to sell its nine radio stations for $65.5 million in order to emphasize its newspaper and cellular telephone activities. The sale is expected to generate a $35-$40 million pretax gain.

Dec. '85—McCaw completed acquisitions of cable systems in New York, Arizona, Oregon and Hawaii with a total of over 120,000 subscribers. Acquisition of some 136,000 radio common carrier subscribers and interests in 12 cellular radio telephone franchises for $120 million is pending, subject to regulatory approvals.

Next earnings report due in mid-October.

Per Share Data ($)

Yr. End Dec. 31	1985	1984	1983	1982	1981	1980	1979	1978	1977	[1]1976
Book Value	7.86	6.95	5.88	4.46	3.57	3.01	2.70	2.07	2.23	1.93
Earnings	[2]1.69	1.49	1.25	0.90	0.81	0.74	0.73	0.53	0.41	0.33
Dividends	0.40	0.35½	0.28½	0.24⅞	0.22½	0.19	0.15¾	0.12¾	0.11⅛	0.09½
Payout Ratio	24%	24%	23%	28%	28%	26%	22%	24%	27%	29%
Prices—High	38	22½	20	12½	10	9¾	6	4¾	3½	2⅛
Low	20⅞	17	10⅞	7	7⅞	4⅜	3⅞	3¼	2⅛	1⅜
P/E Ratio—	22-12	15-11	16-9	14-8	12-10	13-6	8-5	9-6	8-5	6-4

Data as orig. reptd. Adj. for stk. divs. of 50% Jan. 1986, of 50% Jan. 1985, 50% Feb. 1983, 50% Feb. 1980. 1. Refl. merger or acq. 2. Incl. 0.21 gain on asset sales. 3. 14 wks.

Standard ASE Stock Reports
Vol. 21/No. 76/Sec. 3

September 23, 1986
Copyright © 1986 Standard & Poor's Corp. All Rights Reserved
Standard & Poor's Corp.
25 Broadway, NY, NY 10004

7047P   Affiliated Publications, Inc.

Income Data (Million $)

Year Ended Dec. 31	Revs.	Oper. Inc.	% Oper. Inc. of Revs.	Cap. Exp.	Depr.	Int. Exp.	Net Bef. Taxes	Eff. Tax Rate	Net Inc.	% Net Inc. of Revs.
1985	367	80.0	21.8%	22.2	14.8	4.65	²66.1	53.2%	31.0	8.4%
1984	344	72.0	20.9%	43.1	11.6	2.10	²56.8	51.8%	27.4	8.0%
1983	294	57.3	19.5%	32.8	6.9	1.90	²46.5	52.2%	22.2	7.6%
1982	259	44.3	17.1%	29.4	6.0	1.71	²33.8	53.3%	15.8	6.1%
1981	236	34.9	14.8%	9.3	5.9	0.99	²29.0	51.0%	14.2	6.0%
1980	206	31.1	15.1%	5.6	5.2	0.60	26.2	50.8%	12.9	6.2%
1979	183	27.4	15.0%	8.4	4.6	1.11	25.2	50.0%	12.6	6.9%
¹1978	160	21.7	13.6%	12.3	3.2	0.30	18.9	52.5%	9.0	5.6%
1977	138	18.6	13.4%	4.8	3.2	0.23	14.7	52.5%	7.0	5.0%
¹1976	122	13.9	11.4%	6.2	2.6	0.23	11.4	52.1%	5.5	4.5%

Balance Sheet Data (Million $)

Dec. 31	Cash	Current Assets	Current Liab.	Ratio	Total Assets	Ret. on Assets	Long Term Debt	Common Equity	Total Cap.	% LT Debt of Cap.	Ret. on Equity
1985	2.3	65.7	29.7	2.2	285	12.3%	59.3	161	238	25.0%	20.4%
1984	5.9	61.4	30.0	2.0	219	10.9%	21.5	143	173	12.4%	16.7%
1983	17.7	59.3	27.4	2.2	188	12.9%	19.0	123	147	12.9%	20.1%
1982	5.4	40.8	24.0	1.7	149	11.5%	18.5	94	115	16.1%	17.8%
1981	3.4	40.5	18.3	2.2	126	12.3%	14.0	83	99	14.2%	18.3%
1980	9.7	38.2	20.4	1.9	105	12.9%	2.4	72	77	3.1%	19.0%
1979	7.3	34.0	19.2	1.8	95	14.0%	3.8	63	68	5.5%	21.9%
1978	7.9	27.1	16.3	1.7	86	11.7%	8.5	53	62	13.6%	18.2%
1977	7.9	25.8	10.3	2.5	65	11.2%	2.9	45	49	5.9%	16.5%
¹1976	4.1	20.1	9.3	2.2	59	9.6%	3.3	40	44	7.4%	14.4%

Data as orig. reptd. 1. Refl. merger or acq. 2. Incl. equity in earns. of nonconsol. subs. NA-Not Available.

Business Summary

Affiliated Publications, Inc. publishes The Boston Globe newspaper, owns eight radio stations (which it plans to sell), and has interests in cable television and radio common carrier industries. Contributions in 1985:

	Revs.	Profits
Newspapers	95%	99%
Broadcasting	5%	1%

The Boston Globe has the largest combined daily and Sunday circulation of all newspapers in the Boston primary market, and it carries more than 80% of all advertising linage placed in Boston newspapers.

Affiliated Broadcasting, wholly owned, owns three AM and five FM radio stations, including KONC-FM (formerly KHEP-FM) in Phoenix, Ariz., acquired in February 1985; KFYE-FM in Fresno, California, acquired in March 1985; KRAK (AM) and KEWT (FM) in Sacramento, Calif.; KMPS-AM and FM in Seattle, Wash.; and WOKV-AM and WAIV-FM in Jacksonville, Fla.

McCaw Communications Companies, Inc. (45% owned) is a cable television and radio common carrier operating primarily in the Northwest Southwest, Northwest and South, which owns ca-

ble systems with over 381,000 basic subscribers under management at the end of March 1986. The company plans to grow aggressively through the remainder of this decade. McCaw's radio common carriers serve some 72,500 subscribers in seven states. McCaw and joint-venture partners have been awarded cellular radio licenses in four markets.

Dividend Data

The company and its predecessor have paid dividends every year since 1882.

Amt. of Divd. $	Date Decl.	Ex-divd. Date	Stock of Record	Payment Date
0.15	Oct. 24	Nov. 7	Nov. 14	Dec. 1'85
3-for-2	Dec. 5	Jan. 27	Dec. 27	Jan. 24'86
0.11	Dec. 5	Feb. 7	Feb. 14	Mar. 1'86
0.11	Mar. 27	May 12	May 17	Jun. 1'86
0.11	Jun. 30	Aug. 11	Aug. 15	Sep. 1'86

Next dividend meeting: Oct. 18'86.

Capitalization

Long Term Debt: $59,300,524 (12/85).

Common Stock: 17,842,000 shs. ($0.01 par). About 44% is closely held. Shareholders: 3,521 of record.

Office—135 William T. Morrissey Blvd. (Box 2337), Boston, Mass. 02107. Tel—(617) 929-2889. Chrmn & CEO—W. O. Taylor. Pres & COO—J. P. Giggio. SVP-Treas & CFO—A. F. Kingsbury. VP-Investor Contact—D. Orr (617) 929-3035. Dirs—J. L. Cash Jr., R. T. H. Davidson, J. P. Giggio, R. D. Grimm, R. Heydock Jr., R. A. Lawrence, A. Simmons, R. Z. Sorenson, C. H. Taylor, Jr., W. O. Taylor. Transfer Agent & Registrar—State Street Bank and Trust Co., Boston. Incorporated in Massachusetts in 1973.

Information has been obtained from sources believed to be reliable, but its accuracy and completeness are not guaranteed.   William H. Donald

Interpublic Group of Companies

Buffett began purchasing Interpublic Group in 1973, amassing a holding of 1,422,360 shares (adjusted for a 2 for 1 split in 1984) at an average price of $3.19 per share by year's end 1982. From May 1983 through February 1985 Buffett sold over 784,980 shares at an average price of $33.62 per share.

Interpublic Group

1236S

NYSE Symbol IPG

Price	Range	P-E Ratio	Dividend	Yield	S&P Ranking	Beta
Oct. 15'86 28³/₈	1986 30¹/₂−21	16	0.60	2.1%	A−	1.01

Summary

Interpublic is the largest advertising agency system in the world. The level of billings reflects both worldwide economic conditions and success in expanding the agency network and in adding clients. Long-term growth patterns for the industry appear favorable, and Interpublic's large size provides a greater cushion to account shifts than is the case for many smaller agencies. The shares were split 2-for-1 in June, 1986.

Current Outlook

Earnings for 1986 are tentatively projected at about $1.80 a share, up from 1985's $1.68, as adjusted. A stronger profit rise is expected in 1987.

The $0.15 quarterly dividend is the minimum expected.

Gross income and earnings for 1986 will benefit from modest growth in the U.S. advertising market, contributions from new business, some strengthening in international markets, and continuing cost-control measures. Earnings will also benefit from a weaker U.S. dollar against foreign currencies. The company, along with the industry, stands to benefit significantly over the longer-term from tax reform measures.

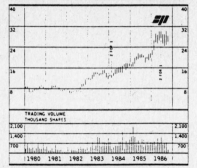

TRADING VOLUME
THOUSAND SHARES

Gross Income (Million $)

Quarter:	1986	1985	1984	1983
Mar.	167.9	148.1	146.4	131.2
Jun.	215.3	180.7	169.5	156.7
Sep.	---	156.2	145.0	137.0
Dec.	---	206.4	183.5	178.2
	---	691.5	644.4	603.0

Gross income for the 1986 first half advanced 17%, year to year. Costs rose more rapidly, and pretax earnings were flat. After taxes at 50.0%, against 57.2%, net income rose 18%, to $1.02 a share from $0.87.

Common Share Earnings ($)

Quarter:	1986	1985	1984	1983
Mar.	0.20	0.18	0.23	0.08
Jun.	0.82	0.70	0.68	0.57
Sep.	E0.20	0.16	0.15	0.12
Dec.	E0.58	0.65	0.46	0.45
	E1.80	1.68	1.52	1.22

Important Developments

Jun. '86—IPG said that it was negotiating to acquire 20 ad agencies worldwide, including at least one U.S. agency with over $100 million in billings. IPG hoped to close at least 25% of these acquisitions by year-end 1986 and another 25% in 1987. The purchases were planned to increase IPG's size in several key foreign countries and in the U.S.

Jan. '86—IPG formed a joint venture with the Lowe Howard-Spink Holding Co. (LHSHC) to create a new London-based international agency network called Lowe Marschalk Worldwide. The agency network includes The Marschalk Co., The Lowe Howard-Spink Agency and Campbell-Ewald operations in Europe, Canada and Australia.

Next earnings report due in late October.

Per Share Data ($)

Yr. End Dec. 31	1985	1984	1983	1982	1981	1980	¹1979	1978	1977	1976
Book Value	7.70	6.22	5.51	4.67	5.36	4.94	4.23	3.88	3.24	2.78
Earnings	1.68	1.52	1.22	1.07	0.83	1.10	²1.23	1.03	²0.80	²0.63
Dividends	0.54	0.50	0.45	0.41³/₈	0.40	0.40	0.36³/₄	0.31³/₈	0.25¹/₂	0.18¹/₈
Payout Ratio	32%	33%	38%	39%	49%	37%	30%	30%	31%	28%
Prices—High	21⁷/₈	18	15¹/₂	12¹/₂	9¹/₂	9¹/₂	8⁷/₈	8¹/₄	6¹/₄	4¹/₂
Low	16⁵/₈	12¹/₄	11¹/₂	6¹/₂	7¹/₈	6³/₄	6¹/₂	5¹/₂	4	2³/₈
P/E Ratio—	13–10	12–8	13–9	12–6	11–9	9–6	7–5	8–5	8–5	7–4

Data as orig. reptd. Adj. for stk. div(s) of 100% Jun. 1986, 100% Feb. 1984, 20% Aug. 1979, 50% Oct. 1977. 1. Reflects merger or acquisition. 2. Ful. dil.¹ 1.22 in 1979, 0.80 in 1977, 0.63 in 1976. E-Estimated.

1236S

The Interpublic Group of Companies, Inc.

Income Data (Million $)

Year Ended Dec. 31	Revs.	Oper. Inc.	% Oper. Inc. of Revs.	Cap. Exp.	Depr.	Int. Exp.	Net Bef. Taxes	Eff. Tax Rate	³Net Inc.	% Net Inc. of Revs.
1985	667	74.5	11.2%	³16.3	13.4	6.57	²80.0	53.5%	36.6	5.5%
1984	623	69.1	11.1%	³11.4	12.6	5.31	²73.5	54.6%	32.8	5.3%
¹1983	586	65.1	11.1%	³ 8.0	11.9	4.32	²66.1	60.8%	25.4	4.3%
⁴1982	532	53.5	10.1%	³13.2	10.3	6.26	²50.7	60.4%	⁴19.8	3.7%
1981	433	42.4	9.8%	³ 8.1	7.6	4.24	²40.3	61.3%	15.2	3.5%
1980	417	48.6	11.7%	10.1	7.3	5.46	²43.8	53.1%	19.7	4.7%
¹1979	367	49.3	13.4%	10.2	6.3	4.22	²46.5	52.2%	21.6	5.9%
1978	305	42.0	13.8%	9.5	3.6	2.01	²42.0	54.2%	18.0	5.9%
1977	244	32.4	13.3%	5.4	3.2	1.90	²31.4	53.3%	13.8	5.7%
1976	199	26.7	13.4%	4.7	2.6	1.41	²26.7	57.5%	10.7	5.4%

Balance Sheet Data (Million $)

Dec. 31	Cash	Current Assets	Current Liab.	Ratio	Total Assets	Ret. on Assets	Long Term Debt	Common Equity	Total Cap.	% LT Debt of Cap.	Ret. on Equity
1985	113	660	527	1.3	802	4.8%	8.6	208	221	3.9%	19.0%
1984	101	585	478	1.2	714	4.7%	11.8	176	191	6.2%	19.6%
1983	101	565	463	1.2	683	3.6%	14.8	157	175	8.4%	16.7%
1982	86	510	431	1.2	624	3.6%	17.3	129	149	11.6%	15.7%
1981	51	387	320	1.2	481	3.2%	11.6	122	137	8.5%	12.9%
1980	39	379	312	1.2	471	4.3%	20.2	111	134	15.1%	19.0%
1979	36	346	287	1.2	435	5.4%	25.0	96	124	20.2%	24.5%
1978	32	303	245	1.2	350	5.7%	6.3	78	87	7.3%	24.8%
1977	41	242	194	1.3	283	5.3%	6.3	67	75	8.5%	22.4%
1976	29	202	163	1.2	236	4.9%	5.8	55	63	9.2%	20.6%

Data as orig. reptd. 1. Reflects merger or acquisition. 2. Incl. equity in earns. of nonconsol. subs. 3. Net of curr. yr. retirement and disposals. 4. Reflects acctg. change

Business Summary

The Interpublic Group of Companies is the world's largest factor in the advertising field, based on 1985 billings of $4.75 billion. The advertising agency functions of the company are carried on in over 50 countries through IPG's five agency systems including McCann-Erickson Worldwide; SSC&B:Lintas Worldwide; Dailey & Associates; Campbell-Ewald Co.; and Lowe Marschalk Worldwide. The company also offers advertising agency services in 26 other countries through association arrangements with local agencies.

The principal functions of the company's advertising agencies are to plan and create advertising programs for clients and to place the advertising in various media, such as radio, television, magazines and newspapers. The usual advertising agency commission is 15% of the gross charge (billings) for advertising space or time. During 1985 IPG's five largest clients accounted for some 40% of income from commissions, fees and publications.

Operations outside the U.S. accounted for 51% of income from commissions, fees and publications, and 32% of income before taxes and unallocated expenses in 1985.

In addition to advertising agency activities, IPG is engaged in publishing, market research, sales promotion, public relations, product development and other related services.

Dividend Data

Dividends have been paid since 1971. A dividend reinvestment plan is available.

Amt. of Divd. $	Date Decl.	Ex-divd. Date	Stock of Record	Payment Date
0.27	Oct. 15	Nov. 20	Nov. 26	Dec. 16'85
0.30	Feb. 18	Feb. 21	Feb. 27	Mar. 17'86
0.30	May 20	May 23	May 30	Jun. 16'86
2-for-1	May 20	Jun. 24	May 30	Jun. 23'86
0.15	Jul. 15	Aug. 22	Aug. 28	Sep. 15'86

Next dividend meeting: Oct. 21'86.

Capitalization

Long Term Debt: $22,975,000.

Minority Interest: $5,920,000.

Common Stock: 22,255,594 shs. ($0.10 par). Institutions hold about 69%; some 12% owned by Berkshire Hathaway Inc. and related parties. Shareholders of record: 2,850.

Office—1271 Avenue of the Americas, NYC 10020. Tel—(212) 399-8000. Chrmn & CEO—P. H. Geier, Jr. Pres—J. D. McNamara. VP-Secy—E. A. Kiernan, Jr. Exec VP-Fin & Investor Contact—E. P. Beard. Dirs—E. P. Beard, P. H. Geier, Jr., R. L. James, R. D. O'Connor, L. H. Olsen, M. G. R. Sandberg, R. Shepley, J. J. Sisco, F. Stanton, W. V. Werthas, J. G. Wexler. Transfer Agent & Registrar—United States Trust Co., NYC. Incorporated in Delaware in 1930.

Information has been obtained from sources believed to be reliable, but its accuracy and completeness are not guaranteed. William H. Donald

Ogilvy & Mather International

Buffett began buying Ogilvy & Mather in 1973 and by year's end 1982 owned 782,800 shares (adjusted for a 2 for 1 split in 1984) at an average cost of $4.74 a share. In May and June 1983 companies controlled by Buffett sold 238,000 shares at an average price of $29.07 per share. Buffett later sold 147,000 shares at an average price of $33.20 per share, lowering his holdings to 397,800 shares, or 4.3 percent.

Ogilvy Group   4857

NASDAQ Symbol OGIL   (Incl. in Nat'l Market; marginable)

Price	Range	P-E Ratio	Dividend	Yield	S&P Ranking	Beta
Aug. 1'86	1986					
29	42–28⁷/₈	14	0.80	2.8%	A	1.00

Summary

This major international advertising agency has a record of growth in revenues and earnings spanning more than a decade, except for recession-affected 1982. Ogilvy established a public relations group in August, 1986, following its acquisition of Adams & Rinehart, Inc. Dividends have been raised frequently; a three-for-two stock split was effected in early 1986.

Business Summary

The Ogilvy Group, Inc. (formerly Ogilvy & Mather International) is the fourth largest advertising agency group in the world and the third largest in the U.S., based on 1985 revenues. The company specializes in developing and implementing advertising campaigns, using television, radio, newspapers, magazines and other media. Clients in 44 countries are provided with a full range of services needed for the planning, creation, preparation and execution of advertising campaigns.

For the most part, the company is paid for its services on a commission basis, receiving in most cases an amount equal to 15% of billings on media and 17.65% on production. Sometimes, particularly in the U.S., compensation is set by negotiated fixed-fee contracts and by time-related charges. Billings in 1985 totaled $2.7 billion, up from $2.4 billion in 1984. Contributions to total revenues in recent years were:

	1985	1984	1983
Commissions	63%	65%	66%
Fees	27%	27%	26%
Other income	10%	8%	8%

About 37% of 1985 revenues and half of net income came from foreign operations. The company serves nearly 2,000 clients. The 10 largest accounts in 1985 represented 27.3% of revenues, and the largest client accounted for 6.0%.

The Ogilvy Group has augmented its internal growth with the acquisition of other advertising agencies. The company established a second international agency network with the 1977 acquisition of Scali, McCabe, Sloves, Inc. and also established independent associated agencies such as Cole & Weber, Inc., Hal Riney & Partners, the

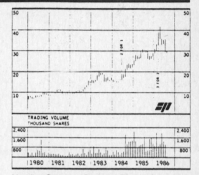

TRADING VOLUME
THOUSAND SHARES

Meridian Group and Davidson Pearce. Ogilvy also has instituted an international network of direct-response offices and, in 1983, expanded in public relations with the acquisition of Dudley-Anderson-Yutzy in New York and the purchase of a substantial equity in Actis, a leading public relations firm in Paris.

Important Developments

Aug. '86—Ogilvy acquired Adams & Rinehart, Inc., a public relations firm, and established a public relations group under the Ogilvy name. Earlier, it agreed to buy a substantial minority interest in the Washington, D.C., lobbying firm of Charles E. Walker Associates. Ogilvy plans to acquire the market research unit of Unilever N.V., which had 1985 revenues of about $50 million.

Next earnings report due in late October.

Per Share Data ($)

Yr. End Dec. 31	1985	1984	1983	1982	1981	1980	1979	1978	¹1977	¹1976
Book Value⁴	7.15	6.37	5.45	4.67	4.53	4.23	3.63	3.04	2.34	3.03
Earnings²	2.12	1.84	1.33	³1.15	1.30	1.09	1.10	1.05	³0.93	³0.67
Dividends	0.72	0.60³/₈	0.54³/₄	0.52	0.46³/₄	0.42³/₄	0.38³/₄	0.31³/₄	0.23³/₈	0.19³/₈
Payout Ratio	33%	32%	41%	45%	36%	39%	35%	30%	25%	29%
Prices—High	31¹/₈	24¹/₈	20³/₈	15⁷/₈	11³/₄	10¹/₈	8¹/₈	9¹/₂	6⁷/₈	5³/₈
Low	23¹/₈	15	14⁵/₈	9¹/₂	8¹/₂	6³/₄	6¹/₈	6¹/₄	5¹/₈	2⁷/₈
P/E Ratio—	15–11	13–8	15–11	14–8	9–6	9–6	7–6	9–6	7–6	8–4

Data as orig. reptd. Adj. for stk. divs. of 50% Mar. 1986, 100% Jun. 1984, 100% Aug. 1978. 1. Refl. merger or acq. 2. Bef. spec. item of +0.03 in 1976. 3. Ful. dil.: 1.14 in 1982, 0.9¹ in 1977, 0.66 in 1976. 4. Excl. intangibles.

4857

The Ogilvy Group, Inc.

Income Data (Million $)

Year Ended Dec. 31	Oper. Revs.	Oper. Inc.	% Oper. Inc. of Revs.	Cap. Exp.	Depr.	Int. Exp.	[2]Net Bef. Taxes	Eff. Tax Rate	[3]Net Inc.	% Net Inc. of Revs.
1985	490	55.5	11.3%	$16.6	10.9	3.55	57.7	47.5%	30.2	6.2%
1984	429	57.2	13.4%	13.8	9.2	3.15	53.9	52.1%	25.8	6.0%
1983	352	44.8	12.7%	11.8	8.6	2.59	39.3	54.7%	17.8	5.1%
1982	321	43.4	13.5%	11.0	8.1	2.44	37.8	60.7%	14.8	4.6%
1981	295	42.2	14.3%	12.7	6.7	2.99	39.1	56.3%	[4]16.5	5.6%
1980	258	37.5	14.6%	10.9	5.8	2.91	34.3	58.8%	13.7	5.3%
1979	219	35.2	16.1%	8.3	4.5	2.06	31.9	56.2%	13.5	6.1%
1978	179	30.9	17.3%	7.4	3.8	1.66	28.7	54.7%	12.6	7.1%
[1]1977	148	27.0	18.2%	7.0	2.8	1.13	26.0	57.8%	10.7	7.2%
[1]1976	110	18.7	17.0%	2.9	1.9	0.51	17.7	56.6%	7.4	6.7%

Balance Sheet Data (Million $)

Dec. 31	Cash	Current—— Assets	Current—— Liab.	Ratio	Total Assets	Ret. on Assets	Long Term Debt	Com- mon Equity	Total Cap.	% LT Debt of Cap.	Ret. on Equity
1985	78.1	541	480	1.1	650	5.1%	2.5	140	142	1.7%	23.1%
1984	43.0	462	406	1.1	550	5.2%	1.7	122	124	1.4%	22.2%
1983	43.9	356	311	1.1	438	4.1%	1.1	107	109	1.0%	17.3%
1982	51.4	328	293	1.1	408	3.8%	2.2	95	97	2.3%	16.1%
1981	28.9	301	267	1.1	374	4.7%	3.3	89	92	3.6%	19.4%
1980	43.1	257	220	1.2	319	4.4%	4.8	80	85	5.6%	18.1%
1979	27.7	252	217	1.2	305	4.9%	5.9	70	76	7.8%	20.6%
1978	22.8	187	156	1.2	234	5.7%	8.0	59	67	11.9%	22.9%
1977	14.0	154	128	1.2	195	6.3%	11.8	48	60	19.6%	24.1%
1976	15.0	117	90	1.3	137	5.9%	-0.9	39	40	2.2%	20.7%

Data as orig. reptd. 1. Refl. merger or acq. 2. Incl. equity in earns. of nonconsol. subs. 3. Bef. spec. item in 1976. 4. Refl. acctg. change. 5. Net.

Commission & Fee Income (Million $)

Quarter:	1986	1985	1984	1983
Mar.	120.9	103.9	93.1	79.7
Jun.	137.9	121.2	108.1	86.4
Sep.		115.2	99.9	79.3
Dec.		150.2	127.6	106.3
		490.5	428.6	351.6

Commission and fee income for the six months ended June 30, 1986, advanced 15%, year to year, aided by the dollar's decline against certain foreign currencies and increased business from existing clients and business from new clients. Costs and expenses rose more rapidly, and net income fell 12%, to $9,675,000 ($0.68 a share), from $11,036,000 ($0.78, as adjusted).

Common Share Earnings ($)

Quarter:	1986	1985	1984	1983
Mar.	0.23	0.25	0.23	0.17
Jun.	0.45	0.53	0.46	0.28
Sep.		0.34	0.32	0.20
Dec.		1.00	0.83	0.67
		2.12	1.84	1.33

Dividend Data

Cash has been paid each year since 1961. Dividend reinvestment and stock purchase plans are available.

Amt. of Divd. $	Date Decl.	Ex-divd. Date	Stock of Record	Payment Date
0.27	Oct. 24	Nov. 8	Nov. 15	Nov. 29'85
3-for-2	Jan. 20	Mar. 3	Feb. 14	Feb. 28'86
0.20	Jan. 20	Feb. 19	Feb. 14	Feb. 28'86
0.20	Apr. 15	May 9	May 15	May 30'86
0.20	Jun. 23	Aug. 11	Aug. 15	Aug. 29'86

Finances

The company had no commitments for large capital expenditures at the start of 1986 and expected to continue to finance routine capital spending from funds provided by operations. Ogilvy had overdraft arrangements with a number of banks amounting to $100.3 million at year-end 1985, of which $83.1 million was available.

Capitalization

Long Term Debt: $3,699,000 (3/86).

Common Stock: 13,625,643 shs. ($1 par). Institutions hold some 56%. Shareholders (of record): 2,693.

Office—2 E. 48 St., New York 10017 Tel—(212) 907-3400. Chrmn & CEO—W. E. Phillips. Secy. Treas & Investor Contact—John P. Gill. Dirs—L. Affinito, M. J. Ball, M. Baulk, J. Benson, N. C. Berry, J. Clopet, F. Correa, J. R. Cunnack, J. Elliott Jr., R. G. Engel, J. Fine, J. P. Gill, H-J. Lange, G. N. Lindsay, D. Ogilvy, G. Phillips, W. E. Phillips, M. Richardot, K. Roman, P. Warren, W. H. Weed. Transfer Agent & Registrar—Morgan Guaranty Trust Co., NYC. Incorporated in New York in 1964

Information has been obtained from sources believed to be reliable, but its accuracy and completeness are not guaranteed.   William H. Donald

Washington Post Company

Buffett purchased all of his *Washington Post* holdings in mid-1973. At year's end 1984 Buffett owned 1,868,600 shares of the *Washington Post* at an average cost of $5.69 per share. On April 12, 1985, the *Washington Post* repurchased on a pro rata basis about 142,700 shares from Buffett at $112 per share. The *Washington Post* is selling at $174 per share.

Washington Post

9517S

ASE Symbol WPO.B

Price	Range	P-E Ratio	Dividend	Yield	S&P Ranking	Beta
Sep. 16'86	1986					
132	184½–115	17	1.12	0.8%	A	1.04

Summary

This company is primarily engaged in publishing The Washington Post, the principal newspaper in the Washington, D.C., area, and Newsweek, a weekly news magazine; it also operates four television stations, and is involved in cellular radio telephones, programming for cable TV and education. The company's acquisition of 53 cable systems in January 1986 for $350 million is restricting 1986 earnings, but a strong recovery is anticipated in 1987. Longer-term prospects are favorable.

Current Outlook

Earnings for 1986 are expected to fall to about $7.70 a share from the $8.66 (including nonrecurring gains) reported for 1985. A strong advance is expected in 1987.

The $0.28 quarterly dividend is the minimum expected.

Revenues and earnings in 1986 will benefit from gains in each major operating segment and from higher equity earnings. The improvement will largely reflect higher ad rates, increased circulation and operating efficiencies. Dilution from the purchase of cable TV systems, however, will amount to about $18.5 million ($1.44 a share).

TRADING VOLUME
THOUSAND SHARES

Revenues (Million $)

13 Weeks:	1986	1985	1984	1983
Mar.	277	244	220	197
Jun.	313	284	256	224
Sep.		259	225	203
Dec.		291	284	254
		1,079	984	878

Revenues for the 1986 first half rose 12%, year to year. Profitability was impaired by a major acquisition, and net income fell 28%. Share earnings were $3.33, on fewer shares, versus $4.41.

Common Share Earnings ($)

13 Weeks:	1986	1985	1984	1983
Mar.	0.96	1.78	0.64	0.43
Jun.	2.37	2.61	1.94	1.50
Sep.		1.69	1.08	0.86
Dec.		2.53	2.47	2.02
		8.66	6.11	4.82

Important Developments

Jun. '86—The company announced plans to sell its 20% interest in the Washington-Baltimore nonwireline cellular systems, from Capital Cities Communications, at an aftertax gain of $20–$25 million.

Jan. '86—The company completed the acquisition of 53 cable systems, serving over 360,000 subscribers, from Capital Cities Communications. The purchase price of about $350 million will cause 1986 earnings dilution of about $18.5 million ($1.44 a share). Separately, the company announced that it had increased its ownership of Cowles Media Co., which publishes newspapers in five Western states, to 20%. The company began buying common shares of Cowles in March 1985.

Next earnings report due in late October.

Per Share Data ($)

Yr. End Dec. 31	1985	1984	1983	1982	[1]1981	1980	[1]1979	1978	1977	1976
Book Value	19.74	21.68	16.92	12.82	9.57	6.86	5.07	5.22	4.12	2.81
Earnings[2]	[3]8.66	6.11	4.82	3.70	2.32	2.44	2.75	3.06	2.09	1.36
Dividends	0.96	0.80	0.66	0.56	0.50	0.44	0.36	0.30	0.18	0.12½
Payout Ratio	11%	13%	14%	15%	22%	18%	12%	10%	8%	9%
Prices—High	130	85	73¼	60⅞	33	24¾	26¾	24⅜	18	12⅝
Low	77¾	60¾	54½	27⅜	19⅜	15⅞	18¾	15½	10¾	5½
P/E Ratio—	15–9	14–10	15–11	16–7	14–8	10–7	10–7	8–5	9–5	9–4

Data as ong. reptd. Adj. for stk. divs. of 100% Jan. 1979 & Dec. 1976. 1. Refl. acctg. change. 2. Bef. spec. items of −0.86 in 1979. 3. Incl. 0.93 from sale of assets.

September 23, 1986
Copyright © 1986 Standard & Poor's Corp. All Rights Reserved

Standard & Poor's Corp.
25 Broadway, NY, NY 10004

9517S

The Washington Post Company

Income Data (Million $)

Year Ended Dec. 31	Revs.	Oper. Inc.	% Oper. Inc. of Revs.	Cap. Exp.	Depr.	Int. Exp.	[3]Net Bef. Taxes	Eff. Tax Rate	[2]Net Inc.	% Net Inc. of Revs.
1985	1,079	232	21.5%	43.6	27.6	9.69	221	48.4%	114	10.6%
1984	984	190	19.3%	33.6	24.0	1.79	166	48.3%	86	8.7%
[1]1983	878	155	17.6%	21.6	22.3	2.73	135	49.2%	68	7.8%
1982	801	118	14.8%	30.6	20.0	3.11	104	49.4%	52	6.5%
1981	753	84	11.1%	41.2	18.2	5.71	62	47.6%	[4] 33	4.3%
1980	660	77	11.7%	69.0	11.3	[4]3.83	65	47.1%	34	5.2%
1979	593	90	15.1%	35.5	9.3	1.80	85	49.4%	[4] 43	7.2%
1978	520	97	18.7%	10.2	8.3	1.79	101	50.6%	50	9.6%
1977	436	78	17.8%	10.9	6.5	2.33	74	51.8%	35	8.1%
1976	376	55	14.8%	7.3	6.4	3.07	51	52.3%	24	6.5%

Balance Sheet Data (Million $)

Dec. 31	Cash	Current Assets	Current Liab.	Ratio	Total Assets	Ret. on Assets	Long Term Debt	Com- mon Equity	Total Cap.	% LT Debt of Cap.	Ret. on Equity
1985	203	359	157	2.3	885	15.5%	222	350	603	36.9%	32.7%
1984	74	219	114	1.9	646	14.2%	6	360	413	1.5%	24.7%
1983	69	191	109	1.8	571	12.7%	9	319	357	2.4%	23.6%
1982	40	171	108	1.6	501	10.9%	11	259	298	3.6%	22.2%
1981	11	135	101	1.3	458	7.4%	23	213	265	8.7%	16.3%
1980	10	126	85	1.5	429	8.8%	44	187	256	17.0%	19.7%
1979	14	112	76	1.5	358	13.2%	18	165	197	8.9%	26.6%
1978	48	119	66	1.8	329	16.6%	20	177	222	9.0%	31.7%
1977	53	114	56	2.0	279	13.7%	22	140	183	12.2%	27.8%

Data as orig. reptd. 1. Refl. merger or acq. 2. Bef. spec. items. 3. Incl. equity in nonconsol. subs. 4. Refl. acctg. change.

Business Summary

Contributions by business segment in 1985:

	Sales	Profits
Newspaper publishing	52%	56%
Magazine publishing	30%	14%
Broadcasting	14%	28%
Other	4%	2%

The Newspaper division publishes The Washington Post, which had an average circulation of 753,577 daily and 1,057,895 Sunday in the 12 months through September 1985, and The Everett Herald (Everett, Wash.), which has a daily and Sunday circulation of over 55,000. The division also includes newspaper feature syndication and other publications and a 94%-owned newsprint warehousing firm.

The Magazine division publishes Newsweek, which has a circulation rate base of 3,050,000. It also publishes three international editions of Newsweek, sells books and produces TV news features and information programming.

The Broadcast division operates four VHF network-affiliated television stations: WFSB-TV in Hartford, Conn.; WDIV in Detroit, Mich.; WPLG-TV in Miami, Fla.; and WJXT-TV in Jacksonville, Fla. Post-Newsweek productions produces and syndicates video programming. Joint-venture cable TV

programming services include Bravo, American Movie Classics, PRISM and The Sports Channel. The company owns interests in two paper companies, The International Herald Tribune, and the Los Angeles Times-Washington Post News Service. Interests are also held in cellular telephone systems in Detroit and Miami. The Stanley H. Kaplan Educational Centers were acquired in 1985.

Dividend Data

Cash has been paid each year since 1956.

Amt. of Divd. $	Date Decl.	Ex-divd. Date	Stock of Record	Payment Date
0.28	Jan. 10	Jan. 17	Jan. 24	Feb. 7'86
0.28	Mar. 17	Apr. 14	Apr. 18	May 9'86
0.28	Jul. 14	Jul. 21	Jul. 25	Aug. 8'86
0.28	Sep. 12	Oct. 10	Oct. 17	Nov. 17'86

Capitalization

Long Term Debt: $351,803,000 (6/86).

Class A Common Stock: 2,168,702 shs. ($1 par); conv. sh. for sh. into cl. B; all owned by the Graham family and related trusts.

Class B Common Stock: 10,657,756 (7/31/86) limited-voting shs. ($1 par).
Berkshire Hathaway Inc. owns about 13%.
Institutions hold about 52%.
Shareholders: 1,930 of record.

Office—1150 15th St., N.W., Washington, D.C. 20071. Tel—(202) 334-6600. Chrmn & CEO—Katharine Graham. Pres—R. D. Simmons. VP-Secy—A. R. Finberg. VP-Treas & Investor Contact—M. Cohen. Dirs—G. J. Gillespie III, D. E. Graham, K. Graham, N. deB. Katzenbach, R. S. McNamara, A. Miller, R. M. Paget, B. S. Preiskel, W. J. Ruane, R. D. Simmons, G. W. Wilson. Transfer Agents & Registrars—Morgan Guaranty Trust Co., NYC. Riggs National Bank of Washington, D.C. Incorporated in Delaware in 1947.

Information has been obtained from sources believed to be reliable, but its accuracy and completeness are not guaranteed.   William H. Donald

GEICO Corporation

Buffett became interested in this auto insurer in 1976 when it was on the brink of bankruptcy. During that year he purchased 1,294,308 shares at an average price of $3.18 per share. By December 1980, he had acquired 7,200,000 shares, or about 33 percent, at an average price of $6.55 a share. According to Buffett in the 1980 Berkshire Hathaway annual report, "GEICO represents the best of all investment worlds—the coupling of a very important and very hard to duplicate business advantage with an extraordinary management whose skills in operations are matched by skills in capital allocation." The management to whom Buffett referred was supplied by Jack Byrne, who took over as CEO of the ailing company in 1976.

Buffett compared GEICO's situation with that of American Express, in that both were one-of-a-kind companies, temporarily beset by problems that "did not destroy their underlying economics." In a share buy-back dated August 23, 1983, GEICO on a pro rata basis repurchased about 350,000 shares from Buffett at $60 a share. He later got over $135 per share.

GEICO Corp. 932F

NYSE Symbol GEC

Price	Range	P-E Ratio	Dividend	Yield	S&P Ranking	Beta
Aug. 22'86 104¼	1986 105¼-77¾	20	1.08	1.0%	B+	1.39

Summary

This holding company's principal subsidiary is Government Employees Insurance Co., whose primary business is writing preferred risk private passenger auto insurance and homeowners insurance. The company has compiled an impressive underwriting record in recent years (although an underwriting loss was sustained in 1985). Other subsidiaries offer life and health insurance, reinsurance and diversified financial services. Steady policy growth, higher rates, and cost controls should drive earnings upward in 1986 and 1987.

Current Outlook

Net operating earnings for 1986 are estimated at $6.20 a share, up from 1985's $4.21. An earnings increase to $7.20 a share is projected for 1987.

The $0.27 quarterly dividend is the minimum expected.

Premium income is expected to rise in 1986, reflecting growing new policy sales, higher rates and good persistency (renewals on existing policies). GEC is seeking to reduce costs further, and with tighter underwriting controls, underwriting is expected to return to profitability. The above scenario should lead to higher cash flow and increased investment income. Per-share comparisons will be aided by share repurchases.

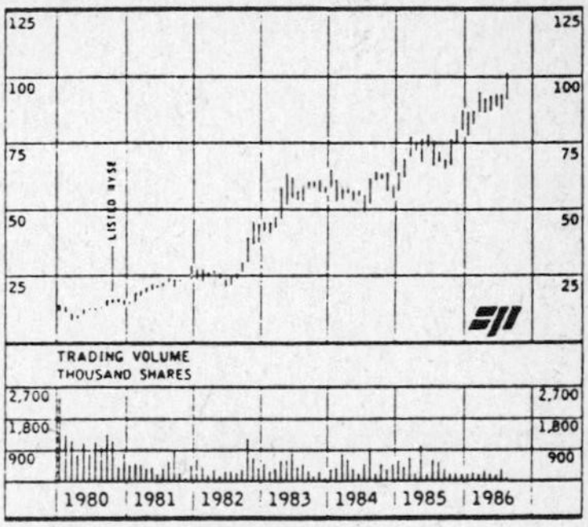
125
100
75
50
25
LISTED NYSE
TRADING VOLUME
THOUSAND SHARES
2,700
1,800
900
1980
1981
1982
1983
1984
1985
1986

Review of Operations

Total revenues for the six months ended June 30, 1986 rose 19%, year to year, primarily reflecting a 21% gain in earned premiums and a slight rise in net investment income. Losses and benefits were 17% higher, with total benefits and expenses up 16%. Pretax operating income expanded 73%. After taxes at 5.9%, versus tax credits of $5.8 million, operating income advanced 38%. Share earnings were $2.93 on 6.3% fewer shares, versus $1.99, before realized investment gains of $2.71 and $1.66.

Net Operating Share Earnings ($)

Quarter:	1986	1985	1984	1983
Mar.	1.43	1.04	1.20	0.99
Jun.	1.50	0.96	1.28	1.15
Sep.	E1.60	0.95	1.30	1.16
Dec.	E1.67	1.28	1.34	1.18
	E6.20	4.21	5.11	4.48

Important Developments

Aug. '86—GEC reported that its combined ratio for the first half of 1986 was 97.5%, versus 102.3% in the year-earlier period. Its efforts to return to underwriting profitability had slowed new business sales and decreased renewals, resulting in an annualized voluntary auto policy growth rate of 3%. GEC said that this was acceptable as its plan for 1986 called for careful risk selection of new and renewal business and adequate pricing. Separately, during the second quarter of 1986 GEC repurchased 257,000 common shares, bringing the total shares repurchased in 1986 to approximately 597,000. In November, 1985 directors had authorized a three million share repurchase program.

Next earnings report due in early November.

Per Share Data ($)

Yr. End Dec. 31	1985	1984	1983	1982	1981	1980	1979	1978	1977	1976
Book Value[4]	29.14	22.40	19.88	16.85	11.75	9.26	8.16	7.79	4.49	1.20
Oper. Earnings[3]	4.21	5.11	4.48	[2]3.80	[2]3.11	[2]2.87	[2]3.24	[2]2.99	[2]1.78	d1.51
Earnings[1,3]	9.25	6.68	5.38	2.39	4.02	2.92	3.20	2.61	1.79	d1.51
Dividends	1.00	0.88	0.72	0.56	0.48	0.43	0.36	0.20	0.03	Nil
Payout Ratio	11%	13%	13%	23%	12%	15%	11%	8%	29%	Nil
Prices—High	88	65⅝	64	45¾	29⅜	16½	13⅛	9⅝	8⅝	12
Low	57⅛	48⅞	41	21	14⅜	8⅛	6⅞	5⅝	5	2⅛
P/E Ratio—	21-14	13-10	14-9	12-6	9-5	6-3	4-2	3-2	5-3	NM

Data as orig. reptd. 1. Aft. gains/losses on security trans. 2. Ful. dil.: 3.67 in 1982, 2.98 in 1981, 2.59 in 1980, 2.14 in 1979, 1.74 in 1978, 1.10 in 1977. 3. Bef. spec. item(s) of +0.89 in 1979, +1.81 in 1978, +1.17 in 1977. 4. As reptd. by co. after 1981. NM-Not Meaningful. d-Deficit. E-Estimated.

Standard NYSE Stock Reports
Vol. 53/No. 168/Sec. 14

August 29, 1986

Copyright © 1986 Standard & Poor's Corp. All Rights Reserved

Standard & Poor's Corp.
25 Broadway, NY, NY 10004

932F

GEICO Corporation

Income Data (Million $)

Year Ended Dec. 31	Premium Income	Net Invest. Inc.	Total Revs.	[3]Property & Casualty —Underwriting Ratios—			Net Bef. Taxes	[1]Net Oper. Inc.	[1]Net Inc.	—% Return On—	
				Loss	Expense	[6]Comb.				Revs.	[2]Equity
1985	1,078	118	1,219	87.9%	15.0%	102.9%	68	78	171	6.4%	16.5%
1984	875	108	995	82.1%	15.6%	97.7%	107	100	131	10.1%	24.3%
1983	768	97	873	76.9%	16.4%	95.5%	106	95	114	10.9%	25.3%
1982	732	83	816	80.0%	15.3%	95.3%	91	77	49	9.5%	26.6%
1981	657	66	727	81.1%	15.1%	96.2%	77	64	83	8.9%	30.3%
1980	653	74	726	80.5%	15.9%	96.4%	79	60	61	8.2%	32.4%
1979	635	70	706	79.8%	16.2%	96.3%	82	60	59	8.4%	34.5%
1978	605	64	670	80.8%	15.1%	95.9%	101	62	55	9.3%	49.0%
1977	464	41	505	84.1%	15.0%	99.1%	61	38	38	7.5%	58.7%
1976	575	38	614	98.1%	12.6%	100.7%	d26	d26	d26	NM	NM

Balance Sheet Data (Million $)

Dec. 31	Cash & Equiv.	Pre-miums Due	— — —Investment Assets— — —				Invest. Yield	Deferred Policy Costs	Total Assets	[5]Debt	Common Equity
			[4]Bonds	Stocks	Loans	Total					
1985	34.8	361	1,206	478	Nil	1,684	7.7%	63.1	2,378	184	516
1984	33.5	281	836	543	Nil	1,379	8.1%	49.6	1,907	187	420
1983	33.7	251	807	499	Nil	1,306	7.9%	41.8	1,776	157	405
1982	24.9	238	796	336	Nil	1,132	8.1%	35.3	1,564	147	345
1981	21.1	217	662	244	Nil	906	7.4%	37.2	1,362	143	237
1980	29.3	202	762	268	24.3	1,057	7.2%	63.2	1,475	138	188
1979	35.5	188	782	207	22.9	1,015	7.1%	62.1	1,412	120	176
1978	38.3	187	758	181	21.9	961	8.0%	55.1	1,345	47	151
1977	28.7	226	601	22	Nil	623	6.8%	14.2	990	48	80
1976	28.0	245	562	20	Nil	582	6.6%	Nil	912	48	28

Data as orig. reptd. 1. Bef. spec. item(s) in 1979, 1978, 1977. 2. Common. 3. As reptd. by co.; GEICO and Criterion combined. 4. Incl. short term investments. 5. incl. short term debt. 6. Aft. policyholder dividends. NM-Not Meaningful. d-Deficit.

Business Summary

GEICO Corp. is an insurance and financial services company whose principal subsidiary, Government Employees Insurance Co. (GEICO), is a multiple line property and casualty insurer engaged in direct response writing of preferred risk private passenger auto insurance. GEICO also offers homeowners, fire and extended coverage, professional and comprehensive personal liability, excess business liability, and boatowners insurance. Wholly-owned Criterion Insurance Co., which emphasizes marketing to military personnel, and GEICO General Corp., write standard and nonstandard private passenger auto insurance. Other wholly-owned subsidiaries include Government Employees Financial Corp., which provides consumer credit and industrial banking services; Resolute Group, a property-casualty reinsurer; and GEICO Investment Services, a registered investment adviser and broker dealer. Life insurance operations are conducted through wholly-owned Garden State Life Ins. Co. and GEICO Annuity and Insurance Co.

GEICO is one of the nation's largest writers of private passenger auto insurance, which accounts for over 90% of its business. The company operates in the District of Columbia and all states except Massachusetts (where it is licensed to write nonautomobile lines) and New Jersey.

Dividend Data

Omitted in 1976, cash payments were resumed the following year.

Amt. of Divd. $	Date Decl.	Ex-divd. Date	Stock of Record	Payment Date
0.25	Nov. 20	Dec. 2	Dec. 6	Dec. 31'85
0.27	Feb. 26	Mar. 4	Mar. 10	Mar. 31'86
0.27	Apr. 16	Jun. 2	Jun. 6	Jun. 30'86
0.27	Aug. 20	Aug. 26	Sep. 2	Sep. 30'86

Finances

In September, 1983 GEC acquired an additional 422,631 shares of Avemco Corp. at $20 each, boosting its stake in the aviation insurer to 33⅓%. Under an agreement, GEC cannot buy any more of Avemco's shares until 1987.

Capitalization

Debt: $165,000,000.

Common Stock: 17,099,738 shs. ($1 par).
Berkshire Hathaway Inc. owns about 36%.
Institutions hold about 33%.
Shareholders of record: 4,491.

Office—GEICO Plaza, Washington, D.C. 20076. Tel—(301) 986-3000. Chrmn, Pres & CEO—W. B. Snyder. Secy—J. M. O'Connor. Treas—A. M. McKenney. Investor Contact—S. Hill. Dirs—T. E. Bolger, S. C. Butler, J. J. Byrne, J. E. Cheek, T. G. Pownall, R. G. Rosenthal, L. A. Simpson, J. J. Sisco, J. C. Steggles, W. B. Snyder, F. A. Weil, H. E. Wrapp. Transfer Agents & Registrars—Riggs National Bank, Washington, D.C.; Manufacturers Hanover Trust Co., NYC. Incorporated in District of Columbia in 1937; reorganized in Delaware in 1979.

Information has been obtained from sources believed to be reliable, but its accuracy and completeness are not guaranteed.   Richard M. Levine

American Broadcasting Co.

In 1978 Buffett purchased for Berkshire Hathaway's portfolio 246,450 shares at an average price of $24.68 per share. Apparently he sold this position in 1980. ABC had risen to $39.25 by the end of 1979. Berkshire Hathaway disclosed ownership of 740,400 ABC shares in 1984 and by year's end 1985 held 900,800 ABC shares at an average price of $60.43 a share. In January 1986 Capital Cities purchased ABC for $121 per share.

American Broadcasting 94

NYSE Symbol ABC Options on Pac (Feb-May-Aug-Nov) In S&P 500

Price	Range	P-E Ratio	Dividend	Yield	S&P Ranking
Nov. 26'85	1985				
$119\frac{3}{4}$	$120-59\frac{7}{8}$	20	[3]---	[3]---	A

Summary

Shareholders of American Broadcasting and Capital Cities Communications (CCB) on June 25, 1985 approved a proposal for the merger of the two companies, pursuant to which each ABC common share would be converted into at least $118 in cash plus at least 0.10 warrant to purchase CCB common stock. The agreement is subject to FCC approval and other conditions.

Current Outlook

Earnings for 1986 (for ABC as an independent entity) are projected to rise to about $6.50 a share from the reduced $5.80 estimated for 1985.

Dividends are at $0.40 quarterly.

Revenues for 1986 are expected to be relatively flat, reflecting continuing weakness in advertising demand in the broadcasting and publishing divisions. However, earnings should benefit from stringent cost control measures, reduced losses anticipated from motion pictures, and the attainment of profitability in video enterprises.

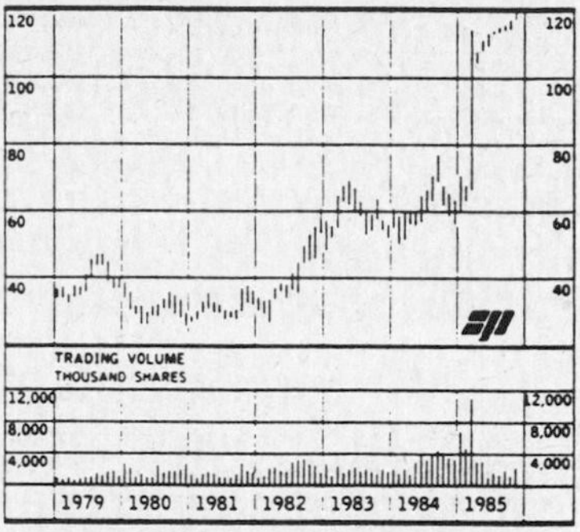

120
100
80
60
40
TRADING VOLUME
THOUSAND SHARES
12,000
8,000
4,000
1979
1980
1981
1982
1983
1984
1985

Total Revenues (Million $)

Quarter:	1985	1984	1983	1982
Mar.	798	837	663	613
Jun.	856	854	755	685
Sep.	707	1,084	660	607
Dec.	---	933	871	760
	---	3,708	2,949	2,665

Revenues for the nine months ended September 28, 1985 fell 15%, year to year. After other items, including sharply higher general and corporate expenses, net income fell 15%, to $4.20 a share from $4.91.

Common Share Earnings ($)

Quarter:	1985	1984	1983	1982
Mar.	0.67	0.81	0.48	0.84
Jun.	2.51	2.49	2.20	2.06
Sep.	1.02	1.61	1.08	1.22
Dec.	E1.60	1.80	1.69	1.42
	E5.80	6.71	5.45	5.54

Acquisition Agreement

Jun. '85—Shareholders of ABC and Capital Cities Communications (CCB) approved a merger agreement pursuant to which each share of ABC common stock would be converted into $118 cash plus 0.10 of a warrant to purchase CCB common stock. Each whole warrant would entitle the holder to purchase one share of CCB common at $250 over a two-and-one-half year period following the merger. For 90 days following the merger, the warrants may be sold to CCB at $30 each, giving the transaction a total value to ABC shareholders of at least $121 a share. If the merger were not completed by January 6, 1986 the $118 cash portion would be increased at the rate of 6% annually until June 30, 1986 (reduced for ABC dividends paid) and at increasing rates thereafter. ABC also began a program to buy back up to $300 million of its common shares. ABC will pay any net gains from the stock buybacks to remaining shareholders, and will divide the attached warrants among the remaining shareholders. The agreement is subject to FCC approval and other conditions.

Per Share Data ($)

Yr. End Dec. 31	1984	1983	1982	1981	1980	1979	1978	1977	1976	1975
Book Value[2]	38.00	39.13	35.46	31.45	28.09	24.41	20.78	16.71	13.89	11.56
Earnings[1]	6.71	5.45	5.54	5.13	5.18	5.67	4.60	4.03	2.70	0.66
Dividends	1.60	1.60	1.60	1.60	1.60	1.30	1.00	$0.73\frac{3}{8}$	$0.56\frac{3}{4}$	$0.53\frac{3}{8}$
Payout Ratio	24%	29%	29%	31%	31%	23%	22%	18%	21%	81%
Prices—High	$77\frac{1}{4}$	$69\frac{3}{4}$	$61\frac{1}{4}$	$38\frac{1}{4}$	39	$47\frac{5}{8}$	$43\frac{1}{4}$	$31\frac{1}{2}$	$26\frac{7}{8}$	$18\frac{1}{4}$
Low	$50\frac{1}{4}$	$48\frac{3}{8}$	$26\frac{3}{4}$	$26\frac{3}{4}$	$25\frac{5}{8}$	$32\frac{3}{8}$	$23\frac{1}{8}$	24	$13\frac{1}{4}$	$8\frac{3}{4}$
P/E Ratio—	12-7	13-9	11-5	7-5	8-5	8-6	9-5	8-6	10-5	28-13

Data as orig. reptd. Adj. for stk. div(s). of 50% Oct. 1978. 1. Bef. results of disc. opers. of +0.29 in 1978. 2. Excl. intangibles. 3. See Acquisition Agreement. E-Estimated.

December 5, 1985

Copyright © 1985 Standard & Poor's Corp. All Rights Reserved

Standard & Poor's Corp.
25 Broadway, NY, NY 10004

94
American Broadcasting Companies, Inc.

Income Data (Million $)

Year Ended Dec. 31	Revs.	Oper. Inc.	% Oper. Inc. of Revs.	Cap. Exp.	Depr.	Int. Exp.	Net Bef. Taxes	Eff. Tax Rate	[3]Net Inc.	% Net Inc. of Revs.
1984	3,703	429	11.6%	168	59.0	22.2	[2]369	47.2%	195	5.3%
1983	2,940	361	12.3%	127	56.9	15.5	[2]312	48.8%	160	5.4%
1982	2,641	319	12.1%	116	49.2	16.9	[2]293	45.4%	160	6.1%
1981	2,421	326	13.5%	54	43.8	18.3	[2]297	50.8%	146	6.0%
1980	2,256	319	14.1%	111	35.0	[4]18.3	[2]295	50.3%	146	6.5%
1979	2,029	337	16.6%	128	28.7	17.8	[2]319	50.1%	159	7.8%
[1]1978	1,767	311	17.6%	68	23.1	16.9	[2]271	53.0%	128	7.2%
1977	1,617	260	16.2%	46	21.1	16.1	[2]232	52.6%	110	6.8%
1976	1,342	177	13.3%	29	18.1	15.8	[2]149	51.8%	72	5.4%
1975	1,065	76	7.1%	31	17.4	12.1	[2] 36	52.1%	17	1.6%

Balance Sheet Data (Million $)

Dec. 31	Cash	Current Assets	Current Liab.	Ratio	Total Assets	Ret. on Assets	Long Term Debt	Common Equity	Total Cap.	% LT Debt of Cap.	Ret. on Equity
1984	154	1,148	595	1.9	2,335	8.9%	140	1,352	1,577	8.9%	15.3%
1983	52	1,109	477	2.3	2,091	7.9%	171	1,214	1,409	12.1%	13.8%
1982	66	945	439	2.2	1,922	9.1%	176	1,098	1,288	13.6%	15.4%
1981	194	963	367	2.6	1,588	9.7%	212	975	1,195	17.8%	15.7%
1980	147	807	291	2.8	1,411	10.8%	220	870	1,092	20.2%	17.8%
1979	213	777	277	2.8	1,274	13.3%	226	760	986	22.9%	22.8%
1978	251	761	258	3.0	1,101	12.2%	192	628	821	23.4%	22.3%
1977	181	650	235	2.8	963	12.0%	199	504	703	28.3%	24.0%
1976	166	609	230	2.6	844	9.3%	188	403	591	31.9%	19.2%
1975	81	468	146	3.2	698	2.6%	194	339	533	36.5%	5.1%

Data as orig. reptd. 1. Excludes discontinued operations. 2. incl. equity in earns. of nonconsol. subs. 3. Bef. results of disc. opers. in 1978 4. Reflects accounting change.

Business Summary

American Broadcasting Companies operates the nationwide ABC television and radio networks and owns TV and radio stations in major cities. ABC is also engaged in publishing, motion picture production and video enterprises. The leisure attractions division was sold in May, 1984. Contributions by business segment in 1984:

	Revs.	Profits
Broadcasting	89%	$427.8
Publishing	9%	34.2
Video enterprises / scenic attractions and other	2%	– 44.8

Five television stations and 12 radio stations are owned and operated in New York City (WABC-TV & AM, WPLJ-FM), Los Angeles (KABC-TV & AM, KLOS-FM), San Francisco (KGO-TV & AM), Detroit (WXYZ-TV & WRIF-FM), Chicago (WLS-TV, AM & FM), Houston (KSRR-FM), Washington, D.C. (WTQX-FM & WMAL-AM), and Dallas/Fort Worth (KTKS-FM). At the beginning of 1985 ABC's TV network had 212 affiliates and its radio network served over 1,790 affiliates.

Farm, business, database, high tech leisure and specialty magazines and books are published by several subsidiaries. Word, Inc. publishes religious books and materials, and produces and distributes records, tapes, sheet music and instructional materials.

Video enterprises produce programming for video-cassettes, video discs, and cable and subscription TV. Cable program networks include ESPN, Lifetime, ARTS & Entertainment Network, and Satellite News Channel. Theatrical feature-length films are also produced.

Dividend Data

Dividends have been paid since 1950.

Amt. of Divd. $	Date Decl.	Ex-divd. Date	Stock of Record	Payment Date
0.40	Feb. 11	Feb. 19	Feb. 25	Mar. 15'85
0.40	Apr. 8	May 13	May 17	Jun. 15'85
0.40	Aug. 12	Aug. 19	Aug. 23	Sep. 14'85
0.40	Nov. 11	Nov. 18	Nov. 22	Dec. 14'85

Capitalization

Long Term Debt: $136,989,000, incl. $23,541,000 capital lease obligations.

Common Stock: 28,389,288 shs. ($1 par). Institutions hold about 59%. Shareholders of record: 11,870.

Office—1330 Ave. of the Americas, NYC 10019. Tel—(212) 887-7777. Chrmn & CEO—L. H. Goldenson. Pres—F. S. Pierce. VP-Secy—J. B. Golden. Treas—D. J. Vondrak. Investor Contact—J. M. Fitzgerald. Dirs—R. C. Adam, F. T. Cary, J. T. Connor, E. H. Erlick, L. H. Goldenson, A. Greenspan, J. Hausman, L. Haas, G. P. Jenkins, F. S. Jones, T. M. Macioce, M. P. Mallardi, N. T. Pace, F. S. Pierce, E. H. Rule, M. J. Schwab. Transfer Agent—Morgan Guaranty Trust Co., NYC. Registrar—Bank of New York, NYC. Incorporated in New York in 1949.

Information has been obtained from sources believed to be reliable, but its accuracy and completeness are not guaranteed.　　　　　William H. Donald

SAFECO Corp.

In 1978 Buffett purchased 953,750 shares of SAFECO at $25.02 per share. The 1978 Berkshire annual report describes SAFECO's property and casualty insurance operation as better than Berkshire's own, including excellent underwriting capabilities with conservative loss reserving and sensible investing: perhaps the best-run such company in the country. Buffett continued to buy, and by the end of 1980 held 1,250,525 shares at an average price of $25.64 per share. After rising to $39.50 a share by year's end, the position was sold in 1982.

SAFECO Corp.   5141F

NASDAQ Symbol SAFC   Nat'l Market   Options on NYSE (Feb-May-Aug-Nov) In S&P 500

Price	Range	P-E Ratio	Dividend	Yield	S&P Ranking	Beta
Sep. 4'86	1986					
63¾	64–45½	15	1.70	2.7%	A–	0.90

Summary

Predominantly a property-casualty insurer, this holding company also engages in life, health, title and surety insurance. Other activities include real estate, investment management and commercial credit services. SAFECO's underwriting record continues to be among the best in the industry. In September, 1985, the company purchased 9.5% of its common shares previously held by Lincoln National Corp. A healthier property-casualty environment should lead to higher earnings in 1986 and 1987.

Current Outlook

Net operating earnings for 1986 are estimated at $5.15 a share, up from 1985's $3.29. A further gain to $6.00 is projected for 1987.

In May, 1986, the quarterly dividend was raised 6.3%, to $0.42½ per share.

Increases in premium income, from both personal and commercial property-casualty lines, are expected in 1986 and profits are likely to rise. Greater risk selectivity and a slowing of the frequency and severity of claims should improve underwriting results. These factors should lead to enhanced cash flow and higher investment income. Competition in group medical business is likely to restrain group profitability, while individual lines and financial services should register solid gains. Depite the absence of losses from real estate sold in 1985, profits from real estate operations are expected to remain under pressure. Per-share comparisons will be aided by the 1985 repurchase of 3.48 million shares.

Review of Operations

Total revenues for the six months ended June 30, 1986, rose 18%, year to year, primarily reflecting gains of 18% in premiums, 28% in net investment income and 3.5% in real estate revenues. With a significantly smaller underwriting loss from property-casualty operations ($31.4 million versus $64.6 million), pretax operating income expanded 80%. After taxes at 3.2%, versus tax credits of $8.4 million, net operating income was up 47%. Share earnings were $2.38 (on fewer shares), compared with $1.47, before nonoperating income of $1.24 and $0.56 in the respective periods.

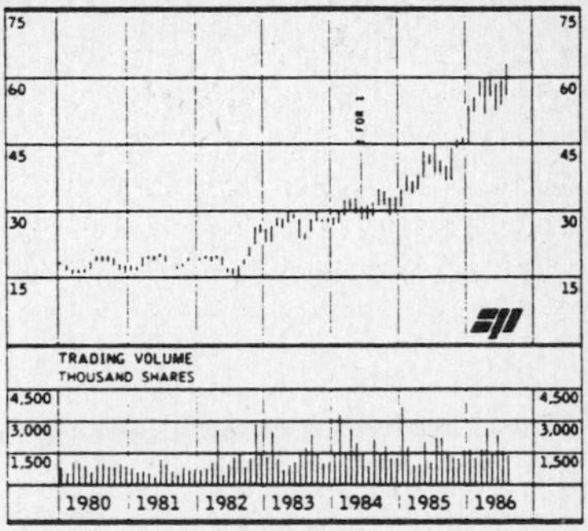

TRADING VOLUME THOUSAND SHARES

|1980 |1981 |1982 |1983 |1984 |1985 |1986

Net Operating Share Earns. ($)

Quarter:	1986	1985	1984	1983
Mar.	1.05	0.64	0.88	0.81
Jun.	1.33	0.83	0.55	0.73
Sep.	E1.37	0.90	1.15	0.99
Dec.	E1.40	0.94	0.46	1.03
	E5.15	³3.29	3.04	3.56

Important Developments

Jul. '86—The company reported that its combined ratio for the first six months of 1986 was 105.1%, compared with 112.3% in the year-earlier period. The improvement was attributed to rate increases in both personal and commercial lines and better experience in non-weather-related claims in homeowner lines.

Next earnings report due in late October.

Per Share Data ($)

Yr. End Dec. 31	1985	1984	1983	1982	1981	1980	1979	1978	1977	1976
Book Value²	32.87	28.80	27.75	24.30	22.64	21.67	19.60	16.05	13.90	11.97
Oper. Earnings	3.29	3.04	3.56	2.87	2.89	2.79	3.51	3.17	2.46	1.79
Earnings¹	4.74	3.25	3.74	2.10	2.94	2.40	3.48	3.20	2.66	1.72
Dividends²	1.55	1.40	1.20	1.10	1.00	0.90	0.75	0.57½	0.45⅞	0.36⅝
Payout Ratio	33%	43%	32%	52%	35%	32%	21%	18%	19%	21%
Prices—High	46⅞	35¼	30	27½	20⅞	20¾	19	15⅜	15⅞	16⅛
Low	30⅞	26¾	22⅞	14⅞	16½	15⅞	13⅞	10⅞	12½	11¾
P/E Ratio—	14–9	12–9	8–6	10–5	7–6	7–6	5–4	5–3	6–5	9–7

Data as ong. reptd. Adj. for stk. div. of 100% in June 1984, 50% in 1978. 1. Aft. gains/losses on security trans. and sale of real estate. 2. As reptd. by co. 3. Does not reconcile with full-year amount, owing to repurchase of shs. E-Estimated.

September 12, 1986
Copyright © 1986 Standard & Poor's Corp. All Rights Reserved

Standard & Poor's Corp.
25 Broadway, NY, NY 10004

5141F

SAFECO Corporation

Income Data (Million $)

Year Ended Dec. 31	Life Insur. In Force	Life A & H	Premium Income — Prop./ Casul.	Net Inv. Income	Total Revs.	[1]Comb. Loss-Exp. Ratio	Net Bef. Taxes	Net Oper. Inc.	[2]Net Inc.	Return On— Revs.	Equity
1985	15,925	396	1,099	296	2,165	110.0%	104	118	170	5.5%	10.9%
1984	14,602	336	943	238	1,845	109.8%	85	113	121	6.1%	10.8%
1983	13,145	265	873	202	1,643	102.6%	153	133	140	8.1%	13.7%
1982	12,279	190	833	165	1,445	101.0%	116	108	79	7.4%	12.2%
1981	11,830	156	827	142	1,386	98.2%	132	110	112	7.9%	13.1%
1980	10,834	127	798	123	1,254	96.7%	134	107	92	8.5%	13.5%
1979	10,231	111	732	108	1,146	89.8%	193	138	137	12.0%	19.7%
1978	8,648	103	664	90	1,019	88.2%	184	126	127	12.3%	21.2%

Balance Sheet Data (Million $)

Dec. 31	Cash & Equiv.	[3]Prem- iums Due	Investment Assets Bonds	Stocks	Loans	Total	Invest. Yield	Deferred Policy Costs	Total Assets	[4]Debt	Common Equity
1985	130	207	2,617	518	127	3,695	8.9%	175	4,764	759	1,106
1984	115	176	1,975	443	115	2,982	8.5%	160	3,884	552	1,069
1983	110	133	1,621	497	118	2,622	8.3%	158	3,415	419	1,036
1982	78	122	1,388	409	117	2,226	7.9%	158	2,992	381	908
1981	69	110	1,160	410	117	1,947	7.4%	156	2,706	305	855
1980	58	102	1,018	465	91	1,847	6.9%	158	2,624	349	828
1979	81	92	982	471	77	1,724	6.7%	149	2,507	334	762
1978	70	83	896	394	42	1,513	6.2%	136	2,176	286	635

Data as orig. reptd. 1. As reptd. by co. (bef. divs. to policyholders). 2. Incl. gain on sale of real estate. 3. Incl. other service fees receiv. 4. Incl. notes and mortgages payable (incl. current portion).

Business Summary

SAFECO Corp. is a holding company whose subsidiaries engage in property-casualty, life, health and title insurance throughout the U.S. and Canada. Other interests include real estate, commercial credit and investment management. Contributions by business segment in 1985 were:

	Revs.	Oper. Inc.
Property-casualty	57%	44%
Life-health insurance	25%	41%
Title insurance	7%	1%
Real estate	10%	1%
Other	1%	13%

Property-casualty insurance is the company's principal line of business. Through independent agents, most major lines of personal and commercial p-c coverage are offered in nearly all states and Canada. Gross p-c premiums written in 1985 amounted to $1.25 billion, of which personal auto accounted for 43%, homeowner 18%, other personal lines 6%, commercial lines 27%, surety 4% and other lines 2%. In recent years, SAFECO's underwriting record has compared favorably with the p-c industry's overall averages.

The life and health companies provide a broad range of life and health insurance coverages on both an individual and group basis. Products are offered through independent agents in all states except New York. Total life insurance in force at 1985 year-end amounted to $15.9 billion, of which

group life accounted for 74%. SAFECO Title Insurance Co. and its subsidiaries are qualified in 49 states, the District of Columbia, Puerto Rico and the U.S. Virgin Islands.

SAFECO Properties Inc. is the parent of three real estate subsidiaries involved in the development and management of regional shopping centers and office buildings (Winmar Co.), medical care real estate (Safecare Co.), and health-care management (Safecare Health Services). SAFECO Credit provides commercial credit and two investment management subsidiaries manage the SAFECO family of mutual funds.

Dividend Data

Cash has been paid each year since 1933.

Amt. of Divd. $	Date Decl.	Ex-divd. Date	Stock of Record	Payment Date
0.40	Nov. 6	Jan. 6	Jan. 10	Jan. 27'86
0.40	Feb. 5	Apr. 7	Apr. 11	Apr. 28'86
0.42½	May 7	Jul. 7	Jul. 11	Jul. 29'86
0.42½	Aug. 6	Oct. 6	Oct. 10	Oct. 27'86

Next dividend meeting: in early November.

Capitalization

Notes & Mtges. Payable: $761,341,000 (6/86).

Common Stock: 33,709,855 shs. ($5 par).
Institutions hold about 57%.
Shareholders: 6,199.

Office—SAFECO Plaza, Seattle, Wash. 98185. Tel—(206) 545-5000. Chrmn—R. M. Tranton. Pres & CEO—B. Maines. VP-Treas—R. W. Hubbard. VP-Secy & Investor Contact—Boh Dickey. Dirs—J. Ellis, W. P. Gerberding, D. G. Graham Jr., J. Green, III, H. W. Haynes, W. M. Jenkins, C. Knudsen, B. Maines, B. A. Nordstrom, W. G. Reed Jr., T. Rembe, H. T. Segerstrom, D. E. Skinner, R. M. Tranton, G. H. Weyerhaeuser. Transfer Agent—Seattle-First National Bank. Registrar—Morgan Guaranty Trust Co., NYC. Incorporated in Washington in 1929.

Information has been obtained from sources believed to be reliable, but its accuracy and completeness are not guaranteed. Richard M. Levine

Amerada Hess

A 112,545 share position purchased in 1979 at an average price of $25.42 per share was sold in 1980, after rising to $48.75 per share by year's end 1979.

Amerada Hess

80

NYSE Symbol AHC Options on Phila (Feb-May-Aug-Nov) In S&P 500

Price	Range	P-E Ratio	Dividend	Yield	S&P Ranking	Beta
Jun. 17'86	1986					
20 5/8	29-18 7/8	NM	[1]---	[1]---	B–	1.35

Summary

Amerada Hess, traditionally viewed as a major petroleum refiner/marketer, is also aggressively engaged in petroleum exploration/production activities both in the U.S. and abroad. Unfortunately, the refining/marketing part of the business almost consistently operates at a loss, and finding costs for petroleum reserves have tended to be among the highest for major oil companies in recent years. Because of the impact of sharply lower oil prices and AHC's use of first-in, first-out (FIFO) inventory accounting, the company reported a large 1986 first-quarter loss and omitted the dividend.

Current Outlook

AHC's prospective net loss for 1986 may not vary markedly from 1985's $3.08 a share loss (the latter after $5.12 nonrecurring charge).

The $0.27 1/2 dividend for the March, 1986 quarter was omitted by directors March 5.

Revenues for 1986 are projected down on much lower average prices for oil, natural gas, and refined products. And another loss is expected, since AHC's use of first-in, first-out (FIFO) inventory accounting exaggerates refining losses when petroleum prices are falling. Under FIFO, the older, higher-cost crude is charged against finished product being sold at current depressed prices. There could also be some charges associated with a prospective withdrawal from Libya.

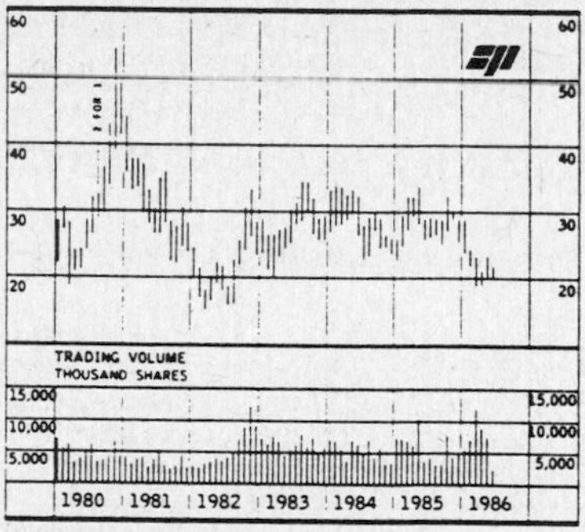

Total Revenues (Million $)

Quarter:	1986	1985	1984	1983
Mar.	1,432	2,102	2,428	1,844
Jun.	---	1,837	2,018	1,904
Sep.	---	1,802	1,951	2,353
Dec.	---	1,981	1,962	2,321
	---	7,723	8,354	8,422

Revenues for the 1986 first quarter declined 32%, year to year. A net loss of $339 million ($4.02 a share) contrasted with net income of $37 million ($0.44).

Common Share Earnings ($)

Quarter:	1986	1985	1984	1983
Mar.	d4.02	0.44	1.04	0.06
Jun.	E0.34	0.38	0.54	0.81
Sep.	E0.34	0.43	0.48	0.88
Dec.	E0.34	d4.33	d0.05	0.68
	Ed3.00	d3.08	2.01	2.43

Important Developments

Mar. 5'86—Management said that as a result of the drastic reductions in prices for crude and refined petroleum products since January 1, AHC was experiencing a substantial 1986 first-quarter loss. AHC took several actions in response. The $0.27 1/2 quarterly dividend that would have been paid on March 31, 1986 was omitted (with a view toward restoring it in full as soon as management concludes that its payment would be consistent with sound business practices). Also, capital expenditures for 1986 have been reduced to less than $300 million, from expenditures of $699 million in 1985, the work force is being cut, and refinery runs are being reduced.

Next earnings report due in late July.

Per Share Data ($)

Yr. End Dec. 31	1985	1984	1983	1982	1981	1980	1979	1978	1977	1976
Book Value	26.84	30.63	30.07	30.73	29.86	28.42	22.76	15.51	12.95	9.61
Earnings	d3.08	2.01	2.43	2.00	2.53	6.44	6.08	1.71	2.14	1.81
Dividends	1.10	1.10	1.10	1.10	1.10	1.00	0.64 3/8	0.45 7/8	0.35 3/8	0.17 1/4
Payout Ratio	NM	54%	45%	54%	43%	15%	10%	27%	12%	7%
Prices—High	34	34 1/8	34 3/4	33 1/2	44 1/2	54 3/4	24 7/8	15 7/8	17 1/2	15
Low	22 3/4	22 7/8	20 1/4	15 1/8	22 1/8	18 3/4	12 3/8	10 7/8	12 3/8	7 1/2
P/E Ratio—	NM	17-11	14-8	17-8	18-9	9-3	4-2	9-6	8-6	8-4

Data as orig. reptd. Adj. for stk. div(s). of 100% Aug. 1980, 2 1/2% in Jun. 1979, 2 1/2% in Jul. 1978, 2 1/2% Jul. 1977, 2 1/2% Jun. 1976. 1. Dirs. omitted divd. Mar. 5, 1986. NM-Not Meaningful. d-Deficit. E-Estimated.

Standard NYSE Stock Reports
Vol. 53/No. 121/Sec. 2

June 24, 1986

Copyright © 1986 Standard & Poor's Corp. All Rights Reserved

Standard & Poor's Corp.
25 Broadway, NY, NY 10004

80

Amerada Hess Corporation

Income Data (Million $)

Year Ended Dec. 31	Revs.	Oper. Inc.	% Oper. Inc. of Revs.	Cap. Exp.	Depr.	Int. Exp.	Net Bef. Taxes	Eff. Tax Rate	Net Inc.	% Net Inc. of Revs.
1985	7,653	1,294	16.9%	699	484	195	[2] 153	270.0%	d260	NM
1984	8,277	1,323	16.0%	900	445	230	[2] 760	77.6%	170	2.1%
1983	8,369	1,351	16.1%	726	[1]490	216	[2] 747	72.5%	[1] 205	2.5%
1982	8,343	1,109	13.3%	875	553	223	[2] 483	65.1%	169	2.0%
1981	9,396	1,126	12.0%	1,260	476	235	[2] 546	61.0%	213	2.3%
1980	7,869	2,102	26.7%	985	358	[1]137	[2]1,731	68.8%	540	6.9%
1979	6,770	1,725	25.5%	659	288	82	[2]1,399	63.8%	[1] 507	7.5%
1978	4,701	773	16.4%	353	254	74	[2] 484	70.6%	142	3.0%
1977	4,591	768	16.7%	400	230	55	[2] 514	65.2%	179	3.9%
1976	3,915	625	16.0%	291	180	55	[2] 425	64.1%	153	3.9%

Balance Sheet Data (Million $)

Dec. 31	Cash	Current Assets	Current Liab.	Ratio	Total Assets	Ret. on Assets	Long Term Debt	Common Equity	Total Cap.	% LT Debt of Cap.	Ret. on Equity
1985	171	2,166	1,721	1.3	6,219	NM	1,674	2,228	4,121	40.6%	NM
1984	153	2,308	1,663	1.4	6,353	2.7%	1,852	2,537	4,621	40.1%	6.7%
1983	121	2,300	1,555	1.5	6,217	3.3%	1,853	2,485	4,597	40.3%	8.1%
1982	100	2,103	1,494	1.4	6,145	2.7%	1,784	2,521	4,591	38.9%	6.7%
1981	219	2,576	1,960	1.3	6,322	3.5%	1,522	2,433	4,322	35.2%	8.9%
1980	227	2,944	2,156	1.4	5,895	9.6%	1,091	2,285	3,699	29.5%	26.0%
1979	167	2,600	2,038	1.3	4,899	11.3%	855	1,679	2,848	30.0%	35.1%
1978	197	1,592	1,255	1.3	3,435	4.2%	782	960	2,174	36.0%	14.0%
1977	122	1,325	937	1.4	2,998	6.0%	753	701	2,053	36.7%	25.5%
1976	185	1,308	922	1.4	2,777	5.9%	682	484	1,844	37.0%	30.4%

Data as orig. reptd. 1. Reflects accounting change. 2. Incl. equity in earns. of nonconsol. subs.

Business Summary

Amerada Hess is an integrated petroleum company.

Sales	1985	1984
Petroleum products	64%	65%
Crude oil	28%	27%
Natural gas	4%	5%
Other	4%	3%

Net results in 1985 (excluding the $433 million special charge related to the marine transportation business) broke down 31% U.S., 44% Europe, and 25% other foreign. Exploration and production earnings were $233 million in 1985. Excluding the special charge, refining and marketing operations had a net loss of $49 million in 1985.

Refinery runs averaged 337,000 barrels a day in 1985 and refined products sold 417,000 b/d. Operating refineries are located at St. Croix, U.S. Virgin Islands (capacity of 545,000 b/d) and Purvis, Miss. (30,000 b/d).

The company's exploration and production activities are conducted in the U.S., Canada, the Norwegian and U.K. sectors of the North Sea, Abu Dhabi, and other areas.

In 1985 net crude and natural gas liquids production averaged 171,054 barrels a day and natural gas production 481.6 million cubic feet a day. Net proved reserves at the 1985 year-end stood at 692,000,000 barrels of crude oil and liquids and 1,882 billion cubic feet of natural gas.

Dividend Data

Common dividends were omitted March 5, 1986 after having been paid since 1922. Recent payments:

Amt. of Divd. $	Date Decl.	Ex-divd. Date	Stock of Record	Payment Date
0.27½	Sep. 4	Sep. 10	Sep. 16	Sep. 30'85
0.27½	Dec. 4	Dec. 10	Dec. 16	Jan. 3'86

Capitalization

Long Term Debt: $1,850,759,000.

$3.50 Conv. Preferred Stock: 307,972 shs. ($1 par); ea. conv. into 4.345 com.

Common Stock: 83,101,220 shs. ($1 par). Leon Hess controls about 15% of common. Institutions hold about 51%. Shareholders of record: 23,416 common.

Office—1185 Ave. of the Americas, NYC 10036. Tel—(212) 997-8500. Chrmn—L. Hess. Pres—R. F. Wnght. Secy & Investor Contact—C. T. Tursi. Treas—G. A. Jamin. Dirs—E. B. Birch, J. B. Collins II, B. T. Devenn, P. A. Dysert, R. M. Heann, J. B. Hess, L. Hess, P. Kramer, C. C. F. Laidlaw, H. W. McCollum, R. B. Oresman, W. S. Ronchard, R. B. Sellars, W. I. Spencer, R. V. Van Fossan, D. T. Wilentz, R. F. Wnght. Transfer Agents—Manufacturers Hanover Trust, NYC; First Fidelity Bank, Newark, N.J. Registrar—Chase Manhattan Bank, NYC. Inc. in Delaware in 1920.

Information has been obtained from sources believed to be reliable, but its accuracy and completeness are not guaranteed. Earl L. Lester, CFA

Handy & Harman

This leading refiner and fabricator of precious metals first appeared in Berkshire Hathaway's portfolio in 1979. By the end of 1985 Berkshire Hathaway held 2,379,200 shares purchased at an average price of $11.48 a share. It later reached $35 a share.

Handy & Harman 1093K

NYSE Symbol HNH

Price	Range	P-E Ratio	Dividend	Yield	S&P Ranking	Beta
Aug. 26'86 17¾	1986 24-16¾	NM	0.66	3.7%	B	0.51

Summary

This company is a leading refiner, processor and fabricator of silver and other precious metals, and also produces a variety of specialty metal products for industrial use. A net loss was recorded for the first half of 1986, reflecting a $2.7 million nonrecurring charge for doubtful accounts and narrower margins.

Business Summary

Handy & Harman manufactures precious metals products and provides refining services, and produces automotive parts, electronic materials and other non-precious metal products. Contributions by industry segment in 1985:

	Sales	Profits
Precious metals	42%	40%
Automotive replacement	14%	12%
Automotive (OEM)	13%	14%
Electronics	8%	6%
Non-precious metals	23%	28%

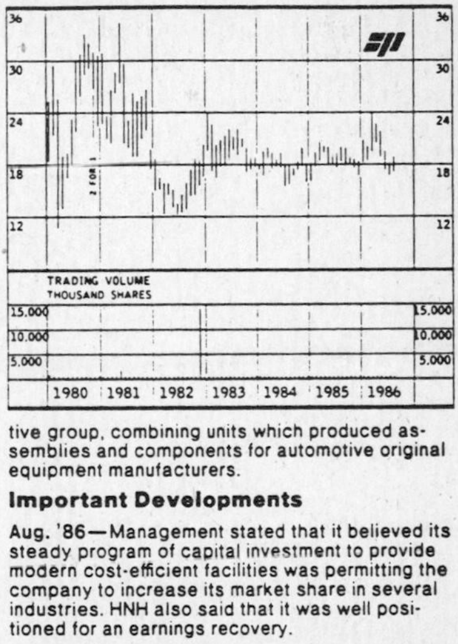

Precious metals operations include the manufacture of a variety of products, generally in mill forms, containing silver, gold and other precious metals in combination (alloys) with non-precious metals, which are sold to industrial users in the silverware and jewelry, electrical and electronic, automotive, and appliance industries. HNH also provides metal refining services for the recovery of precious metals from jewelry and industrial scrap, as well as the recovery of high grade mining concentrates and bullion. During 1984 HNH started-up a new refinery in Singapore.

Automotive replacement operations consist of the manufacture of replacement radiator cores, complete radiators and heaters, and more than 2,300 radiator models for trucks, off-the-road vehicles, and a variety of other industrial applications. The products are sold through 66 distributors or warehouses in the U.S.

Electronics business includes the manufacture of materials for the electronic high-technology industry consisting of either clad metal or plated products.

Non-precious metals operations consist of a variety of specialty metals products, using copper, steel, nickel, plastics and other raw materials.

Effective January, 1985 HNH formed an Automotive group, combining units which produced assemblies and components for automotive original equipment manufacturers.

Important Developments

Aug. '86—Management stated that it believed its steady program of capital investment to provide modern cost-efficient facilities was permitting the company to increase its market share in several industries. HNH also said that it was well positioned for an earnings recovery.

Mar. '86—HNH announced a realignment of three of its subsidiaries, Brunner Engineering and Manufacturing, O & M Manufacturing, and Industrial Heat Exchange Manufacturing, to form a division of engineering and fabrication companies with compatible products and services. The subsidiaries will retain their corporate indentities, but as a group will be known as the Industrial Heat Exchange Companies.

Next earnings report due in mid-November.

Per Share Data ($)

Yr. End Dec. 31	1985	1984	1983	1982	1981	1980	1979	[1]1978	[1]1977	1976
Book Value	8.92	9.13	9.11	8.98	9.02	7.82	6.28	5.64	4.94	4.34
Earnings	0.46	1.03	0.77	0.61	1.71	2.04	1.02	0.96	0.82	0.75
Dividends	0.66	0.61½	0.60	0.60	0.52½	0.38¾	0.31⅜	0.26⅜	0.21⅜	0.17½
Payout Ratio	143%	60%	78%	99%	31%	19%	31%	28%	26%	22%
Prices—High	20⅝	20	24	20⅜	34½	33¼	19½	9⅝	5⅞	5⅜
Low	16⅛	15½	16½	12¼	17½	10¾	7⅞	5⅝	4⅞	3⅝
P/E Ratio—	45-35	19-15	31-21	33-20	20-10	16-5	19-8	10-6	7-6	7-5

Data as orig. reptd. Adj. for stk. div(s). of 100% Dec. 1980, 100% Dec. 1978, 50% Dec. 1976. 1. Reflects merger or acquisition.

Standard NYSE Stock Reports
Vol. 53/No. 170/Sec. 10

September 3, 1986
Copyright © 1986 Standard & Poor's Corp. All Rights Reserved

Standard & Poor's Corp.
25 Broadway, NY, NY 10004

1093K

Handy & Harman

Income Data (Million $)

Year Ended Dec. 31	Revs.	Oper. Inc.	% Oper. Inc. of Revs.	Cap. Exp.	Depr.	Int. Exp.	Net Bef. Taxes	Eff. Tax Rate	Net Inc.	% Net Inc. of Revs.
1985	557	44.7	8.0%	38.0	15.2	21.6	² 8.1	22.4%	6.3	1.1%
1984	620	57.5	9.3%	35.4	12.5	22.5	²23.9	40.8%	14.2	2.3%
1983	576	47.8	8.3%	24.9	11.6	16.6	²20.3	47.8%	10.6	1.8%
1982	499	41.4	8.3%	18.5	10.0	17.2	²15.5	46.0%	³ 8.4	1.7%
1981	611	66.8	10.9%	23.1	8.3	16.2	²42.4	44.8%	23.4	3.8%
1980	761	82.0	10.8%	25.4	7.3	17.8	²54.9	49.5%	27.7	3.6%
1979	631	56.8	9.0%	17.1	6.4	26.8	²22.5	38.8%	13.8	2.2%
¹1978	468	39.7	8.5%	13.2	4.8	9.1	²26.1	50.5%	12.9	2.8%
¹1977	382	32.0	8.4%	14.3	4.1	7.1	²21.1	47.2%	11.2	2.9%
1976	348	29.6	8.5%	9.3	3.1	5.9	²20.8	49.3%	10.6	3.0%

Balance Sheet Data (Million $)

Dec. 31	Cash	——Current—— Assets	Liab.	Ratio	Total Assets	Ret. on Assets	Long Term Debt	Common Equity	Total Cap.	% LT Debt of Cap.	Ret. on Equity
1985	9.4	300	198	1.5	471	1.4%	124	132	273	45.7%	4.7%
1984	6.9	291	190	1.5	441	3.4%	105	134	252	41.7%	10.7%
1983	3.5	260	153	1.7	386	2.8%	93	130	233	39.9%	8.2%
1982	6.1	251	150	1.7	361	2.4%	76	128	210	36.0%	6.5%
1981	8.6	244	155	1.6	345	6.2%	57	129	190	29.8%	19.4%
1980	5.2	317	234	1.4	404	5.5%	55	111	170	32.2%	27.7%
1979	5.2	533	458	1.2	603	3.3%	53	89	145	36.7%	16.5%
1978	9.3	182	104	1.8	242	6.0%	57	79	138	41.1%	17.4%
1977	16.1	136	73	1.9	187	6.2%	43	69	114	37.6%	17.1%
1976	12.8	133	73	1.8	174	6.7%	38	61	100	38.0%	18.4%

Data as orig. reptd. 1. Reflects merger or acquisition. 2. Incl. equity in earns. of nonconsol. subs. 3. Reflects acctg. change. d-Deficit.

Net Sales (Million $)

Quarter:	1986	1985	1984	1983
Mar.	138.4	137.5	156.7	137.8
Jun.	142.7	150.6	163.8	144.2
Sep.		137.3	150.8	145.6
Dec.		131.3	148.1	148.3
		556.7	619.5	575.9

Sales for the six months ended June 30, 1986 fell 2.4%, year to year. Margins narrowed sharply, and following a $5.5 million ($0.20 a share, after tax) nonrecurring charge for a doubtful account, a pretax loss of $4,773,000 contrasted with a pretax profit of $10,230,000. After tax credits of $2,535,000, versus taxes at 42.0%, the net loss was $2,238,000 ($0.16 a share), versus net income of $5,930,000 ($0.43).

Common Share Earnings ($)

Quarter:	1986	1985	1984	1983
Mar.	d0.22	0.21	0.27	0.17
Jun.	0.06	0.22	0.28	0.20
Sep.		0.06	0.23	0.18
Dec.		d0.03	0.25	0.22
		0.46	1.03	0.77

Dividend Data

Dividends have been paid since 1905. A dividend reinvestment plan is available.

Amt. of Divd. $	Date Decl.	Ex-divd. Date	Stock of Record	Payment Date
0.16½	Oct. 24	Nov. 8	Nov. 15	Dec. 2'85
0.16½	Jan. 23	Feb. 10	Feb. 14	Mar. 3'86
0.16½	Apr. 24	May 9	May 15	Jun. 2'86
0.16½	Jun. 26	Aug. 11	Aug. 15	Sep. 2'86

Next dividend meeting: late Oct. '86.

Finances

At March 31, 1986, $85 million was used under credit lines totaling $164 million; $68.1 million of commercial paper was outstanding.

Capitalization

Long Term Liabilities: $122,704,000.

Common Stock: 13,831,000 shs. ($1 par). Officers and directors own about 11%. W.E. Buffett controls about 17%. Institutions hold approximately 52%. Shareholders of record: 3,508.

Office—850 Third Ave., N.Y.C. 10022. Tel—(212) 752-3400. Chrmn—M. W. Townsend. Pres & CEO—R. N. Daniel. Secy—G. P. Ekern. VP-Treas—S. B. Mudd. Controller & Investor Contact—W. H. Martinson. Dirs—P. L. Carret, R. N. Daniel, P. G. Deuchler, W. L. Grey, J. G. Hall, W. H. Newman, G. M. Nichols, M. W. Townsend, L. M. Woods, E. K. Zilkha. Transfer Agent & Registrar—Morgan Guaranty Trust Co., NYC. Incorporated in New York in 1905 as successor to business founded in 1867.

Information has been obtained from sources believed to be reliable, but its accuracy and completeness are not guaranteed.   Mark Mettke

Media General

A 282,500 share position in Media General purchased at $16.09 per share in 1979 had appreciated in price to $56.75 per share by year's end 1983. It was sold in 1984.

Media General   8508

ASE Symbol MEG.A

Price	Range	P-E Ratio	Dividend	Yield	S&P Ranking	Beta
Sep. 16'86	1986					
84	99–72	17	1.16	1.4%	A	0.73

Summary

This diversified media company is a major U.S. newspaper publisher and the world's largest manufac-
turer of recycled newsprint, owns three TV stations and three Virginia cable TV systems, and operates one of the largest media advertising placement services in the U.S. Long-term prospects remain
favorable.

Current Outlook

Earnings for 1986 are expected to rise to about
$5.05 a share from the depressed $4.61 reported for 1985.

No increase in the $0.29 quarterly dividend is ex-
pected in the near term.

Revenues and earnings for 1986 are expected to
benefit from continued improvement in newspaper
and television station results. Newsprint operations will be affected by competitive pricing.
Losses at the broadcast services unit are likely
to continue through most of the year. Higher interest expense and start-up costs for cable TV operations will also restrict gains, but higher equity
earnings will be a partial offset.

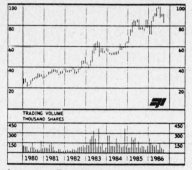

TRADING VOLUME
THOUSAND SHARES

Revenues (Million $)

Quarter:	1986	1985	1984	1983
Mar.	151.4	139.9	130.3	119.8
Jun.	161.7	147.4	141.2	128.4
Sep.		139.0	132.7	124.9
Dec.		152.3	143.4	134.6
		578.6	547.7	507.8

Revenues for the 1986 first half rose 9.0%, year
to year. Lower newsprint and auxiliary earnings
and higher interest costs were more than offset
by gains in newspaper, broadcasting and equity
earnings, and a lower tax rate (32.0%, versus
36.5%). Net income rose 9.8%, to $2.58 a share,
from $2.36.

Common Share Earnings ($)

Quarter:	1986	1985	1984	1983
Mar.	0.97	0.97	1.34	1.20
Jun.	1.61	1.39	1.54	1.44
Sep.		0.95	1.25	1.14
Dec.		1.30	1.47	1.29
		4.61	5.60	5.07

Important Developments

Aug. '86—Garden State Newspapers (40%
owned by Media General) acquired a 9,000-circu-
lation daily in California and two Texas weeklies.
Earlier, the company purchased three New Jersey dailies with combined circulation of 107,000.
Earlier, the company acquired seven dailies in
four states with 117,000 combined circulation, in
exchange for cash and the transfer of two Boston
area dailies and six Massachusetts weeklies.

Jan. '85—Mr. William B. Tanner and three associates pleaded guilty to federal charges of mail
and tax fraud following an investigation begun in
August 1983 of kickback schemes at Media General Broadcast Services, Inc. (formerly The William B. Tanner Co.). Media General, which acquired the unit in July 1982, has filed suits for
damages totaling some $275 million against Mr.
Tanner, Touche Ross & Co. and others.

Next earnings report due in mid-October.

Per Share Data ($)

Yr. End Dec. 31	1985	1984	1983	1982	1981	¹1980	1979	1978	1977	1976
Book Value	30.44	27.03	22.16	18.77	18.68	17.31	15.84	13.65	11.75	10.74
Earnings	4.61	5.60	5.07	4.60	4.41	3.91	3.42	2.40	1.82	2.22
Dividends	1.16	1.08	1.04	1.00	0.92	0.84	0.69	0.57	0.46	0.37
Payout Ratio	25%	19%	20%	21%	20%	21%	19%	23%	25%	17%
Prices—High	86¾	65⅝	65¾	50¾	39¼	34½	27¾	23⅞	20	20½
Low	63½	52	39	33⅝	29⅝	20⅞	19	13½	13½	14¼
P/E Ratio—	19–14	12–9	13–8	11–7	9–7	9–5	8–6	10–6	11–7	9–6

Data as orig. reptd. 1. Refl. merger or acq.

September 23, 1986
Copyright © 1986 Standard & Poor's Corp. All Rights Reserved

Standard & Poor's Corp.
25 Broadway, NY, NY 10004

8508

Media General, Inc.

Income Data (Million $)

Year Ended Dec. 31	Revs.	Oper. Inc.	% Oper. Inc. of Revs.	Cap. Exp.	Depr.	Int. Exp.	³Net Bef. Taxes	Eff. Tax Rate	Net Inc.	% Net Inc. of Revs.
1985	572	85.3	14.9%	90.6	30.3	13.6	50.1	34.5%	32.8	5.7%
1984	539	84.8	15.7%	89.7	22.6	10.8	64.2	38.0%	39.8	7.4%
1983	504	83.5	16.6%	58.9	18.1	8.2	63.6	43.5%	35.9	7.1%
¹1982	424	77.1	18.2%	40.1	15.6	5.8	61.8	47.4%	32.5	7.7%
1981	361	70.3	19.4%	38.3	12.9	5.1	59.4	46.9%	²31.6	8.7%
1980	328	62.5	19.1%	32.6	10.5	4.0	53.6	47.2%	28.3	8.6%
1979	278	57.7	20.7%	8.2	9.4	3.0	47.8	46.8%	25.4	9.1%
1978	244	47.4	19.4%	7.0	8.8	3.7	35.4	49.2%	18.0	7.4%
1977	217	37.6	17.3%	8.5	8.0	3.6	26.1	48.0%	13.6	6.3%
1976	199	41.6	20.9%	12.9	7.1	4.4	31.1	47.9%	16.2	8.1%

Balance Sheet Data (Million $)

Dec. 31	Cash	Current Assets	Current Liab.	Ratio	Total Assets	Ret. on Assets	Long Term Debt	Common Equity	Total Cap.	% LT Debt of Cap.	Ret. on Equity
1985	6.9	147	83.0	1.8	688	5.2%	183	305	584	31.3%	11.2%
1984	7.1	123	79.7	1.5	563	7.7%	109	278	465	23.3%	15.2%
1983	5.3	116	67.0	1.7	475	8.1%	84	245	394	21.4%	15.6%
1982	2.7	106	68.6	1.5	406	8.9%	57	216	328	17.2%	16.0%
1981	11.1	79	44.3	1.8	324	10.5%	35	191	273	12.9%	17.4%
1980	20.6	76	34.0	2.2	286	10.5%	33	176	247	13.5%	17.1%
1979	25.6	74	28.0	2.6	252	10.8%	31	154	216	14.2%	17.6%
1978	5.5	49	28.8	1.7	225	8.2%	27	140	193	13.9%	13.5%
1977	5.1	48	25.6	1.9	210	6.7%	32	126	182	17.8%	11.2%
1976	5.2	37	19.7	1.9	192	8.8%	33	116	169	19.7%	14.9%

Data as orig. reptd. 1. Refl. merger or acquisition. 2. Refl. acctg. change. 3. Incl. equity in earns. of nonconsol. subs.

Business Summary

Media General is a major newspaper publisher, recycler of newsprint, and owner of TV and cable systems. Contributions in 1985 were:

	Revs.	Profits
Newspapers	44%	73%
Newsprint	30%	32%
Broadcasting	22%	-3%
Other	5%	-2%

Daily and Sunday newspapers are published in Richmond, Va., Tampa, Fla., and Winston-Salem, N.C., with combined circulation of 554,000; 37 weekly newspapers, mostly in Southern California, have combined circulation of 600,000. Garden State Paper Co., the world's largest recycler of newsprint, accounts for 10% of all newsprint produced in the U.S. Broadcast operations include two NBC affiliates in Jacksonville and Tampa, an ABC affiliate in Charleston, and four CATV systems in Fairfax County and Fredericksburg, Va., which serve 116,000 subscribers. Media General Broadcast Services (formerly the William B. Tanner Co., acquired in July 1982) is the largest U.S. company that acquires broadcast time for resale to advertisers and their agencies. Other operations include products and services in publishing, printing and graphic arts.

Media General acquired 40% of Garden State

Newspapers Inc. (GSN) in April 1985. GSN was established in 1985 to acquire medium-sized newspapers throughout the U.S. At the end of February 1986, GSN owned eight daily newspapers with combined circulation of 221,300, plus seven weekly newspapers.

Dividend Data

Cash has been paid in each year since 1923. A dividend reinvestment plan is available.

Amt. of Divd. $	Date Decl.	Ex-divd. Date	Stock of Record	Payment Date
0.29	Sep. 20	Nov. 18	Nov. 22	Dec. 18'85
0.29	Jan. 17	Feb. 20	Feb. 26	Mar. 14'86
0.29	Mar. 21	May 23	May 30	Jun. 13'86
0.29	Jul. 29	Aug. 11	Aug. 15	Sep. 12'86

Next dividend meeting: Sep.30'86.

Capitalization

Long Term Debt: $197,711,000 (6/86).

Class A Common Stock: 6,815,741 shs. ($5 par). About 13% is closely held. Institutions hold about 67%. Shareholders: 2,500 of record.

Class B Common Stock: 280,179 shs. ($5 par). About 60% is closely held. Cl. B shs. elect 70% of directors.

Office—333 E. Grace St., Richmond, Va. 23219 (P.O. Box C-32333, Richmond 23293). Tel—(804) 649-6000. Pres, CEO & Investor Contact—J. S. Evans. Secy—A. J. Brent. VP-Treas—W. F. Robertson. Dirs—D. T. Bryan (Chrmn), A. J. Brent, J. S. Bryan III, A. K. Davis, A. S. Donnahoe, J. S. Evans, T. L. Rankin, G. T. Stewart III. Transfer Agent & Registrar—United Virginia Bank, Richmond & NYC. Incorporated in Virginia in 1969.

Information has been obtained from sources believed to be reliable, but its accuracy and completeness are not guaranteed.

W.H. Donald

Times Mirror Co.

Berkshire Hathaway's 151,104 share position in *Times Mirror*, purchased at $29.43 per share in 1980, was sold in 1981 after rising to $41.50 per share by year's end 1980.

Times Mirror

2237

NYSE Symbol TMC   In S&P 500

Price	Range	P-E Ratio	Dividend	Yield	S&P Ranking	Beta
Nov. 10'86 66¼	1986 73⅞–50⅛	12	1.50	2.3%	A	1.43

Summary

This major newspaper publisher also has important interests in book publishing, information services, cable television, broadcast television, newsprint/forest products and magazine publishing. TMC has recently sold, or plans to sell, certain of its cable TV, broadcasting, microwave and newsprint assets. In October, 1986 TMC acquired The A.S. Abell Co., publisher of the Baltimore Sun newspapers, for $600 million, and in August it sold the Dallas Times Herald for $110 million.

Current Outlook

Earnings for 1987 are tentatively projected at $3.90 a share, versus the $7.80 estimated for 1986, which includes about $4.55 of capital gains.

The $0.37½ quarterly dividend is the minimum expected.

Revenues for 1987 will be boosted by the Baltimore Sun acquisition. Each major business segment should show improved profitability, but higher debt expense and the absence of gains from accounting adjustments and significant gains from asset sales will penalize comparisons.

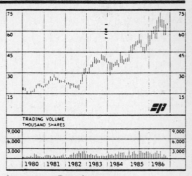

TRADING VOLUME
THOUSAND SHARES

| 1980 | 1981 | 1982 | 1983 | 1984 | 1985 | 1986 |

Total Revenues (Million $)

Quarter:	1986	1985	1984	1983
Mar.	695	695	670	567
Jun.	749	747	706	616
Sep.	698	714	681	618
Dec.	---	804	749	690
	---	2,959	2,805	2,491

Revenues for the nine months ended September 30, 1986 declined 0.7%, year to year. Largely reflecting nonrecurring gains of $192.5 million ($2.56 a share), net income rose to $308.8 million ($4.78) from $178.9 million ($2.59).

Common Share Earnings ($)

Quarter:	1986	1985	1984	1983
Mar.	0.67	0.64	0.63	0.43
Jun.	2.96	0.99	0.86	0.63
Sep.	1.15	0.96	0.68	0.66
Dec.	E3.02	0.90	1.21	1.19
	E7.80	3.49	3.38	2.90

Important Developments

Oct. '86—TMC completed the purchase of The A.S. Abell Co., publisher of the Baltimore Sun newspapers, for $600 million. Abell also owned two TV stations, which TMC sold for $200 million. The Sun newspapers had a combined daily average circulation of 397.584 and average Sunday circulation of 465.339 for the six months ended June 30, 1986. The newspapers had revenues of $172.5 million in 1985. In August TMC sold the Dallas Times Herald for $110 million. Earlier, the company sold three TV stations in Pennsylvania and New York for $79 million; sold its 50% interest in a Las Vegas cable system; and sold its microwave business and 80% of its newsprint business.

Next earnings report due in late January.

Per Share Data ($)

Yr. End Dec. 31	1985	1984	1983	1982	1981	1980	1979	1978	¹1977	1976
Book Value	8.31	12.40	10.69	9.40	8.23	6.83	7.33	8.14	7.23	6.44
Earnings	3.49	3.38	2.90	2.05	2.20	2.04	2.16	2.07	1.39	1.03
Dividends	1.36	1.20	1.00	1.00	0.86	0.72	0.60	0.50	0.37½	0.28⅞
Payout Ratio	37%	35%	34%	49%	39%	35%	28%	24%	27%	28%
Prices—High	59	45⅝	44	34¾	29¾	22⅞	18⅞	17⅝	13	11⅞
Low	38	28¼	29½	17⅞	19⅞	14½	14	11⅛	10	9⅛
P/E Ratio—	17–11	13–8	15–10	17–9	13–9	11–7	9–6	9–5	9–7	12–9

Data as ong. reptd. Adj. for stk. div(s). of 100% Feb. 1984. 1. Reflects merger or acquisition. E-Estimated.

Standard NYSE Stock Reports
Vol. 53/No. 222/Sec. 24

November 17, 1986
Copyright © 1986 Standard & Poor's Corp. All Rights Reserved

Standard & Poor's Corp.
25 Broadway, NY, NY 10004

2237

The Times Mirror Company

Income Data (Million $)

Year Ended Dec. 31	Revs.	Oper. Inc.	% Oper. Inc. of Revs.	Cap. Exp.	Depr.	Int. Exp.	Net Bef. Taxes	Eff. Tax Rate	Net Inc.	% Net Inc. of Revs.
1985	2,947	620	21.0%	252	154	62.7	[3]461	48.6%	237	8.0%
1984	2,771	540	19.5%	263	152	57.2	[3]398	41.5%	233	8.4%
1983	2,479	468	18.9%	248	108	56.7	[3]360	44.6%	200	8.1%
1982	2,200	345	15.7%	230	79	60.5	[3]250	43.9%	[2]140	6.4%
1981	2,131	361	16.9%	217	80	55.3	[3]257	41.5%	150	7.1%
1980	1,857	314	16.9%	242	71	[3]35.5	[3]230	39.4%	139	7.5%
1979	1,639	315	19.2%	268	55	14.5	254	42.3%	146	8.9%
1978	1,411	268	19.0%	92	41	3.0	266	46.5%	142	10.1%
[1]1977	1,130	209	18.5%	73	41	2.4	179	46.3%	96	8.5%
1976	965	158	16.4%	61	38	2.3	129	46.1%	70	7.2%

Balance Sheet Data (Million $)

Dec. 31	Cash	Current Assets	Current Liab.	Ratio	Total Assets	Ret. on Assets	Long Term Debt	Common Equity	Total Cap.	% LT Debt of Cap.	Ret. on Equity
1985	27	645	638	1.0	2,701	9.3%	721	974	1,903	37.9%	21.9%
1984	33	628	515	1.2	2,555	9.4%	446	1,272	1,889	23.6%	19.4%
1983	35	590	476	1.2	2,385	8.8%	513	1,120	1,781	28.8%	18.9%
1982	24	572	363	1.6	2,136	6.9%	541	988	1,642	33.0%	14.7%
1981	34	556	329	1.7	1,917	8.2%	478	915	1,479	32.3%	17.3%
1980	30	514	304	1.7	1,735	9.0%	447	823	1,330	33.6%	17.9%
1979	27	444	276	1.6	1,350	12.4%	223	732	995	22.4%	21.6%
1978	103	487	239	2.0	1,002	15.6%	41	626	699	5.8%	24.6%
1977	146	427	180	2.4	843	12.1%	36	547	616	5.9%	18.6%
1976	127	360	156	2.3	730	10.1%	38	471	538	7.1%	15.6%

Data as orig. reptd. 1. Reflects merger or acquisition. 2. Reflects accounting change. 3. Incl. equity in earns. of nonconsol. subs.

Business Summary

Contributions to revenues and operating earnings (million $) by business segment in 1985:

	Revs.	Profits
Newspaper publishing	51%	$279.3
Newsprint/forest products	13%	32.2
Other publishing	16%	85.9
Cable television	9%	47.3
Broadcast television	4%	64.3
Other	7%	22.4

TMC publishes five metropolitan newspapers — The Los Angeles Times, Newsday, The Denver Post, The Hartford (Conn.) Courant, and the Call-Chronicle Newspapers of Allentown Pa. — and two community newspapers in Connecticut.

TMC owns 272,000 acres of timberlands in Washington and Oregon, which it intends to dispose of over time. In February, 1986 the company sold 80% of Publishers Paper Co., a newsprint, particleboard and lumber company.

The company publishes a variety of books, including paperbacks and medical, art and law books. TMC also publishes magazines, flight information, road maps, telephone directories and recording charts.

Four network-affiliated TV stations are operated in Dallas, Austin, St. Louis, and Birmingham, Ala. Cable television systems (including affiliates) serve some 883,000 basic and 687,000 pay subscribers in 15 states. Xerox Learning Systems was purchased in July, 1985.

Dividend Data

Dividends have been paid since 1892.

Amt. of Divd. $	Date Decl.	Ex-divd. Date	Stock of Record	Payment Date
0.37½	Dec. 4	Feb. 14	Feb. 21	Mar. 10'86
0.37½	Mar. 5	May 23	May 30	Jun. 10'86
0.37½	Jun. 4	Aug. 25	Aug. 29	Sep. 10'86
0.37½	Aug. 28	Nov. 21	Nov. 28	Dec. 10'86

Next dividend meeting: Dec. 3'86.

Capitalization

Long Term Debt: $603,585,000.

Common Stock: 64,491,472 shs. (no par). About 35% owned by the Chandler family. Institutions hold about 40%. Shareholders of record: 5,490.

Office — Times Mirror Square, Los Angeles, Calif. 90053. Tel — (213) 972-3700. Chrmn — O. Chandler. Pres & CEO — R. F. Erburu. Secy — J. W. Wallace. Treas — J. M. Fields. Investor Contact — M. L. Schwanbeck. Dirs — G. G. Babcock, P. S. Bing, B. Chandler, O. Chandler, R. F. Erburu, F. D. Frost, W. B. Gerken, R. W. Heyns, E. S. Jacobs, A. E. Osborne, Jr., H. M. Williams, P. L. Williams, W. B. Williamson. Transfer Agent — First Interstate Bank of California, Los Angeles. Registrars — First Interstate Bank of California, Los Angeles; Bank of America, Los Angeles. Incorporated in California in 1884; reincorporated in Delaware in 1986.

Information has been obtained from sources believed to be reliable, but its accuracy and completeness are not guaranteed. William H. Donald

General Foods

In a 13D filing dated February 9, 1981, Buffett reported the purchase of 2,584,459 common shares, or 5.2 percent of General Foods, at an average price of $31.43 per share. By August 1983 he had increased his holdings to 4,573,400 shares, or 8.8 percent at an average price of $35.52 a share. In light of Philip Morris' purchase of General Foods in September 1985 at $120 per share, Buffett realized a return on his investment of 238 percent.

General Foods   972

NYSE Symbol GF   Options on CBOE (Feb-May-Aug-Nov)   In S&P 500

Price	Range	P-E Ratio	Dividend	Yield	S&P Ranking
Sep. 30'85	1985				
118³⁄₈	118³⁄₈-53¹⁄₂	18	⁸---	⁶---	A

Summary

In September, 1985 GF agreed to be acquired by Philip Morris Cos., the nation's largest cigarette producer with important positions in the beer and soft drink industries, through a cash tender offer at $120 a share, or $5.75 billion. The resulting company would have annual sales of some $23 billion, with cigarettes representing 43% and foods and beverages about 55%. The merger was expected to be effected by the end of October, 1985.

Current Outlook

For the company as a separate entity, earnings for the fiscal year ended March 31, 1986 are projected at $6.95 a share, versus 1984-5's $6.96, which included a $0.76 net nonrecurring gain, but excluded a $0.35 special charge.

The $0.62¹⁄₂ quarterly dividend should be maintained.

Earnings of the packaged foods operations are expected to post modest gains in fiscal 1985-6, aided by small unit volume and price increases, as well as favorable ingredient costs. Other segments should also contribute to the anticipated gain in earnings from operations.

TRADING VOLUME
THOUSAND SHARES

|1979 | 1980 | 1981 | 1982 | 1983 | 1984 | 1985 |

Net Sales (Million $)

Quarter:	1985-6	1984-5	1983-4	1982-3
Jun.	2,268	2,256	2,135	2,060
Sep.	---	2,259	2,137	1,994
Dec.	---	2,160	2,088	1,990
Mar.	---	2,347	2,239	2,213
	---	9,022	8,600	8,256

Sales for the 13 weeks ended June 29, 1985 edged up 0.5%, year to year. In the absence of the year-earlier $98.3 million gain from the sale of Gaines Pet Foods (partially offset by a $21.0 million restructuring charge), pretax income fell 33%. After taxes, net income declined 30%, to $1.65 a share (on 8.2% fewer shares) from $2.17, which included a $0.76 net nonrecurring gain.

Common Share Earnings ($)

Quarter:	1985-6	1984-5	1983-4	1982-3
Jun.	1.65	2.17	1.15	1.24
Sep.	E1.33	1.20	1.41	1.34
Dec.	E1.20	1.06	1.28	1.00
Mar.	E2.77	2.53	2.26	2.15
	E6.95	6.96	6.10	5.73

Acquisition Agreement

Sep. '85—GF agreed to be acquired by Philip Morris Cos. (MO), the nation's largest cigarette producer with important interests in the beer and soft drink industries, for $120 a share in cash, or about $5.75 billion. On September 30 MO commenced a tender offer for GF's 47.9 million common shares outstanding; the offer was to expire October 28, unless extended. Under the agreement, MO has an option to purchase 8.5 million GF shares at $120 each, and five GF representatives would be added to MO's board of directors. The resulting company, with sales of some $23 billion, would be the largest consumer products company in the U.S., with cigarettes representing some 43% of sales and foods and beverages comprising 55%. The transaction would be the largest non-oil takeover in history.

Next earnings report due in late October.

Per Share Data ($)

Yr. End Mar. 31 [1]	1984	1983	²1982	²1981	1980	1979	1978	1977	1976	1975
Book Value	34.62	33.47	30.30	30.86	32.11	29.15	25.98	23.00	21.18	18.95
Earnings³	6.96	6.10	ᵃ5.73	4.47	5.14	⁴5.12	⁴4.65	⁴3.40	⁴3.56	⁴3.02
Dividends	2.50	2.40	2.30	2.20	2.20	1.95	1.72	1.64	1.53¹⁄₂	1.42¹⁄₂
Payout Ratio	36%	39%	41%	49%	43%	38%	37%	48%	43%	47%
Prices⁵—High	59⁷⁄₈	53¹⁄₂	47³⁄₄	35	34¹⁄₄	37	35¹⁄₄	36¹⁄₂	34³⁄₄	29⁵⁄₈
Low	45¹⁄₄	36⁵⁄₈	29	27³⁄₄	23¹⁄₂	28¹⁄₄	26¹⁄₂	29	26¹⁄₈	18⁵⁄₈
P/E Ratio—	9-6	9-6	8-5	8-6	7-5	7-6	8-6	11-9	10-7	10-6

Data as ong. reptd. 1. Of fol. cal. yr. 2. Reflects merger or acquisition. 3. Bef. spec. item(s) of −0.35 in 1984; bef results of disc. opers. of −0.42 in 1981. 4. Ful. dil.: 5.02 in 1979, 4.56 in 1978, 3.33 in 1977, 3.49 in 1976, 2.97 in 1975. 5. Cal. yr. 6 See Acquisition Agreement. E-Estimated.

972

General Foods Corporation

Income Data (Million $)

Year Ended Mar. 31[1]	Revs.	Oper. Inc.	% Oper. Inc. of Revs.	Cap. Exp.	Depr.	Int. Exp.	Net Bef. Taxes	Eff. Tax Rate	[4]Net Inc.	% Net Inc. of Revs.
[3]1984	9,022	791	8.8%	303	165	157	[3]621	45.0%	342	3.8%
[2]1983	8,600	788	9.2%	267	156	149	[3]573	44.7%	317	3.7%
[2]1982	8,256	721	8.7%	266	133	139	[3]535	46.0%	289	3.5%
[5]1981	8,351	694	8.3%	283	131	152	[3]418	47.1%	221	2.6%
1980	6,601	565	8.6%	187	89	50	[3]473	46.0%	255	3.9%
1979	5,960	534	9.0%	262	78	39	[3]470	45.6%	256	4.3%
1978	5,472	524	9.6%	121	77	31	[3]452	48.6%	232	4.2%
1977	5,376	425	7.9%	126	70	38	[3]331	48.7%	170	3.2%
1976	4,910	448	9.1%	112	70	27	[3]368	51.8%	177	3.6%
1975	3,978	384	9.6%	96	57	24	[3]319	52.8%	150	3.8%

Balance Sheet Data (Million $)

Mar. 31[1]	Cash	Current Assets	Current Liab.	Ratio	Total Assets	Ret. on Assets	Long Term Debt	Common Equity	Total Cap.	% LT Debt of Cap.	Ret. on Equity
1984	288	2,378	1,403	1.7	4,554	8.0%	725	1,940	2,933	24.7%	18.0%
1983	277	2,346	1,245	1.9	4,432	7.2%	750	2,040	3,007	24.9%	16.2%
1982	285	2,315	1,342	1.7	4,310	6.9%	736	1,872	2,804	26.3%	16.1%
1981	163	2,254	1,215	1.9	3,861	6.3%	731	1,626	2,499	29.2%	13.6%
1980	309	2,019	929	2.2	3,130	8.4%	391	1,610	2,121	18.4%	16.6%
1979	178	1,951	1,047	1.9	2,978	9.2%	255	1,480	1,845	13.8%	18.3%
1978	291	1,736	845	2.1	2,565	9.3%	251	1,321	1,681	14.9%	18.6%
1977	132	1,618	860	1.9	2,433	7.1%	260	1,174	1,535	16.9%	15.0%
1976	129	1,569	850	1.8	2,345	8.1%	253	1,085	1,448	17.4%	17.1%
1975	216	1,252	654	1.9	2,013	7.7%	235	983	1,312	17.9%	15.9%

Data as orig. reptd. 1. Of fol. cal. yr. 2. Reflects merger or acquisition. 3. Incl. equity in earns. of nonconsol. subs. 4. Bef. results of disc. opers. in 1981, 1974. 5. Excl. disc. opers. and refl. merger or acqn.

Business Summary

General Foods is a leading producer of packaged foods. In fiscal 1984-5 sales and profit contributions by industry segment were:

	Sales	Profits
Packaged foods	42%	60%
Coffee	28%	18%
Processed meat	18%	15%
Food service	12%	7%

International operations accounted for 19% of 1984-5 sales, and 16% of operating income.

Packaged foods include a variety of beverage mixes (including Kool-Aid and Crystal Light), Post ready-to-eat cereals, Log Cabin syrup, Birds Eye vegetables, desserts (Jell-O, Cool Whip, D-Zerta), main meal dishes (Shake'n Bake, Stove Top stuffing mix, Minute Rice), baked goods (Entenmann's, Oro-weat) and specialty cheese.

GF is the largest processor of coffee in the U.S., with such brands as Maxwell House, Yuban, Sanka, Maxim, and Brim.

Oscar Mayer & Co. (acquired 1981) is the leading U.S. producer of branded meat products.

The Food Service division provides a wide-range of food products to restaurants, hotels, hospitals, offices and other institutional customers.

The company's Gaines pet food business was sold in June, 1984.

Dividend Data

Dividends have been paid since 1922. A dividend reinvestment plan is available.

Amt. of Divd. $	Date Decl.	Ex-divd. Date	Stock of Record	Payment Date
0.62½	Nov. 7	Nov. 13	Nov. 19	Dec. 5'84
0.62½	Feb. 6	Feb. 11	Feb. 19	Mar. 5'85
0.62½	May 1	May 14	May 20	Jun. 5'85
0.62½	Jul. 17	Aug. 8	Aug. 14	Sep. 5'85

Next dividend meeting: early Nov. '85.

Capitalization

Long Term Debt: $719,415,000.

Common Stock: 47,900,000 shs. ($1 par). Institutions hold about 60%. Shareholders of record: 64,373.

Offices—250 North St., White Plains, N.Y. 10625. Tel—(914) 335-2500. Chrmn & CEO—J. L. Ferguson. Pres—P. L. Smith. Secy—A. M. Shaver. VP-Treas—D. M. Brush. Investor Contact—L. S. Goodman. Dirs—W. M. Agee, A. L. Armstrong, L. M. Branscomb, C. L. Brown, H. L. Clark, R. F. Dee, J. L. Ferguson, A. Greenspan, J. H. Holland, D. J. Keller, E. J. McCormack, P. G. Peterson, H. R. Roberts, P. L. Smith, M. I. Sovern, W. P. Tavoulareas. Transfer Agents & Registrars—Manufacturers Hanover Trust Co., NYC and San Francisco. Harris Trust & Savings Bank, Chicago. Incorporated in Delaware in 1922.

Information has been obtained from sources believed to be reliable, but its accuracy and completeness are not guaranteed. George C. Piendes

Pinkerton's

First purchased for Berkshire Hathaway's portfolio in 1980 (after Blue Chip had accumulated 37 percent from 1976 through 1980 for $23,364,000) at an average price of $32.81 per share, Pinkerton's was bought in December 1982 by American Brands for $160 million or $77.50 a share (which is why there is no Standard & Poor's report on it as a separate company). Pinkerton's met Buffett's usual investment criteria, as it was relatively inflation-immune, had predictable cash flow and its business operations involved little capital expense.

RCA Corp.

In June 1983 Buffett filed a 13D statement indicating that he and Berkshire Hathaway controlled 564,904 shares of RCA's $3.65 Series D Cumulative Preference stock, purchased at an average price of $25.37 per share. Buffett continued his purchases into September 1984, raising his total ownership to 867,904 shares or 8.15 percent, purchased at an average of $27.20 a share for the entire holding. In March 1985 Buffett lowered his stake in RCA to 4.86 percent with the sale of 350,000 shares at an average price of $34.32 per share.

RCA Corp.

1891

NYSE Symbol RCA   Options on CBOE (Mar-Jun-Sep-Dec)   In S&P 500

Price	Range	P-E Ratio	Dividend	Yield	S&P Ranking	Beta
Jun. 2'86	1986					
66	66¹/₈–59¾	24	⁴---	⁴---	B+	0.97

Summary

In December, 1985 RCA Corp. entered into a definitive agreement to be acquired by General Electric. Under terms of the agreement, which now requires only certain regulatory approvals, General Electric will pay $66.50 in cash for each RCA common share. RCA has granted General Electric an option to purchase 28.3 million common shares. The exercise price of the option is to be increased to $59.75 from $53.125 under a proposed settlement of litigation. The transactions should be completed shortly.

Current Outlook

Earnings for 1986 (for the company as a separate entity) could reach $4.30 a share, up from the $2.57 earned on continuing operations in 1985.

The $0.26 quarterly dividend should continue.

Moderate sales growth is anticipated for 1986, led by continuing strong comparisons from the entertainment segment. Margins should benefit from the operating leverage of the entertainment segment, volume gains, and recent cost reductions. A higher tax rate should be only partially offsetting.

Sales (Billion $)

Quarter:	1986	1985	1984	1983
Mar.	2.29	2.07	2.36	2.03
Jun.		2.15	2.48	2.20
Sep.		2.18	2.47	2.27
Dec.		2.57	2.79	2.48
		8.97	10.11	8.98

Revenues for the three months ended March 31, 1986 rose 11%, year to year. Margins widened, and pretax income was up 23%. After taxes at 40.9%, versus 37.7%, net income advanced 17%, to $0.77 a share from $0.56, which was before earnings of $0.02 from discontinued operations.

Common Share Earnings ($)

Quarter:	1986	1985	1984	1983
Mar.	0.77	0.56	d0.72	0.18
Jun.		1.30	1.10	0.60
Sep.		d0.27	0.74	0.57
Dec.		1.00	1.03	0.75
		2.57	2.15	2.10

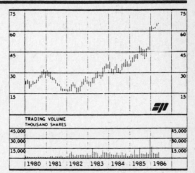

TRADING VOLUME
THOUSAND SHARES

|1980 |1981 |1982 |1983 |1984 |1985 |1986 |

Acquisition Agreement

Feb. '86 — Shareholders of RCA approved a merger between RCA and General Electric. The merger, which does not require the approval of GE shareholders, is expected to be completed after approvals are received from various regulatory agencies. Under terms of the agreement, GE will pay $6.28 billion in cash to acquire RCA ($66.50 per RCA common share). Earlier GE and RCA reached a proposed settlement with certain plaintiffs increasing to $59.75 from $53.125 the exercise price of an option granted to GE to purchase 28.3 million RCA common shares. The proposed settlement, which requires court approval, somewhat restricted GE's right to exercise the option.

Next earnings report due in mid-July.

Per Share Data ($)

Yr. End Dec. 31	1985	1984	¹1983	1982	1981	1980	1979	1978	1977	1976
Book Value	26.99	22.57	21.27	20.15	19.06	21.23	21.71	19.59	17.34	15.30
Earnings³	2.57	2.15	²2.10	²2.03	d0.19	²3.35	²3.72	²3.65	²3.23	²2.30
Dividends	1.04	1.00½	0.90	0.90	1.80	1.80	1.60	1.40	1.20	1.00
Payout Ratio	43%	47%	43%	44%	NM	54%	43%	38%	37%	43%
Prices—High	63½	40	37⅛	28⅛	32¼	33	28¼	33⅞	32½	30⅛
Low	34¾	28⅝	19¾	15¾	16¾	18½	21⅛	22⅝	24⅜	18⅞
P/E Ratio—	25–14	19–13	18–9	14–8	NM	10–6	8–6	9–6	10–8	13–8

Data as orig. reptd. 1. Reflects acctg. change. 2. Ful. dil.: 2.06 in 1983, 2.00 in 1982, 3.19 in 1980, 3.57 in 1979, 3.50 in 1978, 3.11 in 1977, 2.24 in 1976. 3. Bef. results of disc opers. of +1.47 in 1985, +0.23 and spec. item of +0.92 in 1984. 4. See Acquisition Agreement. NM-Not Meaningful. d-Deficit.

June 9, 1986
Copyright © 1986 Standard & Poor's Corp. All Rights Reserved

Standard & Poor's Corp.
25 Broadway, NY, NY 10004

1891

RCA Corporation

Income Data (Million $)

Year Ended Dec. 31	Revs.	Oper. Inc.	% Oper. Inc. of Revs.	Cap. Exp.	Depr.	Int. Exp.	Net Bef. Taxes	Eff. Tax Rate	⁴Net Inc.	% Net Inc. of Revs.
¹1985	8,972	689	7.7%	571	259	149	³370	34.0%	244	2.7%
¹1984	10,112	1,231	12.2%	1,831	614	263	³378	34.8%	246	2.4%
²1983	8,977	944	10.5%	1,701	541	294	³373	35.4%	241	2.7%
1982	8,237	954	11.6%	1,627	578	359	³321	30.7%	223	2.7%
1981	8,005	983	12.3%	1,739	497	401	³ 98	45.1%	² 54	0.7%
1980	8,011	972	12.1%	986	494	279	³507	37.8%	315	3.9%
1979	7,455	976	13.1%	865	438	²163	³472	39.8%	284	3.8%
1978	6,601	942	14.3%	700	364	113	³515	45.9%	278	4.2%
1977	5,881	848	14.4%	869	332	97	³470	47.5%	247	4.2%
1976	5,329	689	12.9%	780	300	94	³343	48.3%	177	3.3%

Balance Sheet Data (Million $)

Dec. 31	Cash	—Current— Assets	Liab.	Ratio	Total Assets	Ret. on Assets	Long Term Debt	Common Equity	Total Cap.	% LT Debt of Cap.	Ret. on Equity
1985	240	3,230	2,088	1.5	6,705	3.1%	838	2,435	3,998	21.0%	9.8%
1984	175	4,207	3,105	1.4	8,221	3.1%	1,597	1,852	4,721	33.8%	9.8%
1983	98	3,557	2,919	1.2	7,656	3.1%	1,731	1,739	4,271	40.5%	10.1%
1982	76	3,390	2,893	1.2	7,743	2.7%	1,885	1,642	4,328	43.6%	9.6%
1981	175	3,619	3,063	1.2	7,857	0.7%	1,856	1,438	4,096	45.3%	NM
1980	175	3,403	2,277	1.5	7,148	4.8%	1,771	1,597	4,183	42.3%	15.6%
1979	206	3,230	2,136	1.5	5,990	5.2%	1,474	1,625	3,234	45.6%	18.0%
1978	241	2,758	1,612	1.7	4,873	6.0%	1,118	1,464	2,717	41.1%	19.8%
1977	264	2,376	1,400	1.7	4,352	6.0%	1,076	1,295	2,507	42.9%	19.8%
1976	178	2,038	1,261	1.6	3,838	4.7%	944	1,142	2,222	42.5%	15.7%

Data as orig. reptd. 1. Excl. disc. opers. 2. Reflects acctg. change. 3. Incl. equity in earns. of nonconsol. subs. 4. Bef. results of disc. opers. in 1985, 1984, and spec. item(s) in 1984. NM-Not Meaningful.

Business Summary

RCA is a broadly diversified company. Business segment contributions in 1985 (profits in million $):

	Sales	Profits
Consumer products and services	41%	$146.8
Commercial products and services	26%	−93.8
Government systems and services	33%	124.9

Foreign businesses accounted for 8.3% of sales and 17% of pretax income in 1985.

Consumer electronics products consist of TV sets and video cassette recorders. Commercial electronics include color TV picture tubes, semiconductors and broadcasting equipment.

The Global Communications unit is an international communications common carrier.

NBC furnishes network TV and radio services and owns TV and radio stations. Electronic equipment is made for the U. S. Government.

Dividend Data

Amt. of Divd. $	Date Decl.	Ex-divd. Date	Stock of Record	Payment Date
0.26	Jun. 5	Jun. 11	Jun. 17	Aug. 1 '85
0.26	Sep. 4	Sep. 10	Sep. 16	Nov. 1 '85
0.26	Dec. 4	Dec. 10	Dec. 16	Feb. 1 '86
†0.10	Dec. 24	Dec. 24	Dec. 31	Jan. 10 '86
0.26	Mar. 5	Mar. 11	Mar. 17	May 1 '86

†Represents redemption of rights.

Next dividend meeting: early Jun. '86.

Capitalization

Long Term Debt: $709,400,000.

$3.50 Cum. Pfd. Stk.: 132,835 shs. (no par).

$3.65 Cum. Pref. Stk.: 3,306,836 shs. (no par).

Common Stock: 94,281,906 shs. (no par).
Institutions hold some 47%.
Shareholders of record: 156,747.

Office—30 Rockefeller Plaza, NYC 10020. Tel—(212) 621-6000. Chrmn—T. F. Bradshaw. Pres & CEO—R. R. Frederick. Secy—W. P. Alexander. VP-Treas—B. J. Heidtke. Investor Contact—J. H. Reynolds. Dirs—J. Brademas, T. F. Bradshaw, R. Cizik, R. R. Frederick, I. O. Funderburg, D. C. Jones, T. O. Paine, P. G. Peterson, J. R. Petty, C. C. Selby, D. B. Smiley, W. F. Smith, G. Tinker. Transfer Agent—Company's Office, NYC. Registrar—First Jersey National Bank, Jersey City, N.J. Incorporated in Delaware in 1919.

Information has been obtained from sources believed to be reliable, but its accuracy and completeness are not guaranteed.

Paul H. Valentine

Time, Inc.

First purchased in 1982 at an average price of $29.56 per share. At the end of 1985 Berkshire Hathaway's portfolio held 847,788 shares, purchased at an average price of $24.04 per share. Time, Inc. was sold in 1986 at about three times Berkshire's cost.

Time Inc.   2236

NYSE Symbol TL   Options on Phila (Mar-Jun-Sep-Dec)   In S&P 500

Price	Range	P-E Ratio	Dividend	Yield	S&P Ranking	Beta
Nov. 4'86	1986					
7 15/8	9 13/8–57 1/2	11	1.00	1.4%	B+	1.50

Summary

This company, the nation's leading magazine publisher, circulates such well-known magazines as Time, Sports Illustrated, Fortune, and People. It is also a major book publisher, operates the second largest group of cable TV systems in the U.S., and owns the largest pay cable TV programming service, Home Box Office. In June, 1986 TL acquired a 13.3% interest in Group W Cable for $229 million. In October TL agreed to purchase educational publisher Scott, Foresman & Co. for $520 million.

Current Outlook

Earnings for 1987 are projected at $4.10 a share, versus the $6.55 estimated for 1986, which includes significant capital gains.

No increase in the $0.25 quarterly dividend is anticipated over the near term.

Revenues and earnings for 1987 should benefit largely from cable system operations, books and magazines, in spite of a difficult operating environment for the magazine industry. Higher programming costs and weak demand for pay cable services, costs of launching several new magazines and business ventures, plus dilution from recent and pending acquisitions, will limit the prospective earnings improvement.

Revenues (Million $)

Quarter:	1986	1985	1984	1983
Mar.	874	747	694	605
Jun.	945	864	772	691
Sep.	914	847	751	658
Dec.	---	945	851	763
	---	3,404	3,067	2,717

Revenues for the nine months ended September 30, 1986 rose 11%, year to year. Boosted by a $318 million pretax capital gain, net income climbed to $5.72 a share from $2.34.

Common Share Earnings ($)

Quarter:	1986	1985	1984	1983
Mar.	0.78	0.70	0.67	0.35
Jun.	0.98	0.94	0.92	0.84
Sep.	3.98	0.70	0.72	0.36
Dec.	E0.81	0.81	1.06	0.70
	E6.55	3.15	3.37	2.25

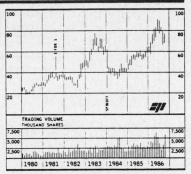

TRADING VOLUME
THOUSAND SHARES

Important Developments

Oct. '86—TL agreed to acquire Scott, Foresman & Co. from SFN Companies for $520 million. During the third quarter TL sold 20% of its cable TV subsidiary in a public offering and sold its 10% interest in Temple-Inland Inc. TL also purchased 1.1 million shares of its common stock as part of a long-range program to buy back up to 10 million shares. In June TL and a group of five others purchased Group W Cable for about $1.73 billion. TL received 13.3% of the Group W shares at a cost of $228.9 million, and formed a partnership with a unit of Houston Industries, which purchased 12.9% of Group W, to operate their holdings, serving some 500,000 basic subscribers as a joint venture.

Next earnings report due in mid-January.

Per Share Data ($)

Yr. End Dec. 31	1985	1984	1983	1982	1981	1980	1979	¹1978	¹1977	1976
Book Value	9.56	13.62	10.85	20.11	16.91	15.92	13.82	11.43	11.69	10.75
Earnings²	3.15	3.37	2.25	2.50	3.02	2.51	2.58	2.74	2.22	1.66
Dividends	1.00	0.82	1.00	1.00	0.95	0.88³/₈	0.81	0.72¹/₂	0.63¹/₈	0.53⁷/₈
Payout Ratio	32%	24%	43%	41%	29%	32%	28%	28%	28%	33%
Prices—High	65¼	62¾	78³/₈	52³/₈	41³/₈	31⁵/₈	24³/₄	25¹/₂	19⁷/₈	19⁷/₈
Low	42¹/₂	33¾	44¹/₂	25¹/₂	26³/₈	19	17⁷/₈	16⁷/₈	15¾	14³/₈
P/E Ratio—	21–13	19–10	35–20	21–10	14–9	13–8	10–7	9–6	9–7	12–9

Data as orig. reptd.; Temple-Inland Inc. spun off in Jan. 1984. Adj. for stk. div(s). of 100% Oct. 1981, 100% Oct. 1978. 1. Reflects merger or acquisition. 2. Bef. results of disc. opers. of +0.40 in 1983, −0.05 in 1982, −0.59 in 1981, and spec. item(s) of +0.16 in 1978. E-Estimated.

2236

Income Data (Million $)

Year Ended Dec. 31	Revs.	Oper. Inc.	% Oper. Inc. of Revs.	Cap. Exp.	Depr.	Int. Exp.	Net Bef. Taxes	Eff. Tax Rate	³Net Inc.	% Net Inc. of Revs.
¹1985	3,404	526	15.5%	224	139	51.0	⁴387	48.4%	200	5.9%
1984	3,067	504	16.4%	311	111	49.0	⁴421	48.6%	216	7.1%
²1983	2,717	365	13.4%	305	90	42.5	⁴280	48.8%	143	5.3%
1982	3,564	432	12.1%	319	136	58.2	⁴243	35.7%	156	4.4%
²1981	3,296	428	13.0%	353	110	51.2	⁴297	37.9%	185	5.6%
1980	2,882	303	10.5%	259	89	52.1	⁴223	36.6%	141	4.9%
1979	2,504	307	12.3%	203	70	36.2	⁴231	37.7%	144	5.7%
¹1978	1,698	241	14.2%	112	41	12.5	⁴214	44.4%	118	7.0%
¹1977	1,250	186	14.9%	50	34	10.4	⁴162	44.1%	91	7.2%
1976	1,038	135	13.0%	47	30	10.8	⁴109	38.7%	67	6.5%

Balance Sheet Data (Million $)

Dec. 31	Cash	Current Assets	Current Liab.	Ratio	Total Assets	Ret. on Assets	Long Term Debt	Common Equity	Total Cap.	% LT Debt of Cap.	Ret. on Equity
1985	172	1,042	769	1.4	3,072	6.9%	465	1,211	1,923	24.2%	17.5%
1984	480	1,119	691	1.6	2,615	8.8%	383	1,032	1,596	24.0%	22.1%
1983	330	974	542	1.8	2,273	5.4%	399	881	1,443	27.7%	12.0%
1982	39	871	547	1.6	2,896	5.2%	462	1,363	2,104	21.9%	10.7%
1981	57	952	506	1.9	2,755	7.0%	489	1,079	2,018	24.2%	15.8%
1980	34	865	431	2.0	2,371	6.2%	476	931	1,719	27.7%	14.8%
1979	75	794	396	2.0	2,104	7.4%	420	809	1,527	27.5%	17.4%
1978	84	650	379	1.7	1,801	8.0%	271	710	1,262	21.5%	18.2%
1977	164	528	195	2.7	1,053	9.4%	128	519	733	17.4%	18.6%
1976	126	407	122	3.3	866	8.2%	138	450	637	21.7%	15.7%

Data as orig. reptd. 1. Reflects merger or acquisition. 2. Excludes discontinued operations. 3. Bef. results of disc. opers. in 1983, 1982, 1981, and spec. item(s) in 1978 4. Incl. equity in earns. of nonconsol. subs.

Business Summary

Business segment contributions in 1985:

	Revs.	Profits
Magazine publishing	44%	36%
Video	40%	46%
Books & information services	16%	18%

Magazines include Time, Sports Illustrated, Life, People, Asiaweek, Fortune, Money and Discover. With the March, 1985 acquisition of Southern Progress Corp., the division also publishes Southern Living, Progressive Farmer, and Creative Ideas. The unit is test-marketing several new magazines. The book group includes Time-Life Books, Little, Brown & Co., Book-of-the-Month Club, and Oxmoor House.

Video operations consist of 80%-owned American Television and Communications Corp. (ATC) and Home Box Office, Inc. (HBO). ATC is the second largest multiple system cable TV operator, with 2.7 million basic and 2.5 million premium subscriptions as of year-end 1985. HBO programs and markets two satellite-transmitted pay TV networks, the HBO service, which had about 14.6 million subscribers at year-end 1985, and the Cin-

emax service, with about 3.7 million. Other activities include a market information service, SAMI, which provides over 600 food manufacturers with marketing information on the movement of supermarket items.

Dividend Data

Dividends paid since 1930. A dividend reinvestment plan is available. A "poison pill" stock purchase right was issued in 1986.

Amt. of Divd. $	Date Decl.	Ex-divd. Date	Stock of Record	Payment Date
0.25	Feb. 20	Feb. 25	Mar. 3	Mar. 13'86
0.25	Apr. 17	May 21	May 28	Jun. 11'86
0.25	Jul. 17	Aug. 21	Aug. 27	Sep. 11'86
0.25	Oct. 16	Nov. 20	Nov. 26	Dec. 11'86

Next dividend meeting: mid-Feb. '87.

Capitalization

Long Term Debt: $961,000,000.

Common Stock: 62,890,959 shs. ($1 par). About 12% owned or controlled by O & D's. Institutions hold about 53%. Shareholders of record: 17,273.

Office—Time & Life Bldg., Rockefeller Center, NYC 10020. Tel—(212) 586-1212. Chrmn & CEO—J. R. Munro. Pres—N. J. Nicholas Jr. VP-Secy—W. M. Guttman. VP-Treas—U. L. Uebelhoer. VP-Investor Contact—J. W. Fowlkes (212) 841-4543. Dirs—L. Banks, J. F. Bere, R. P. Davidson, M. D. Dingman, E. S. Finkelstein, H. C. Goodrich, C. J. Grum, H. A. Grunwald, A. Heard, M. S. Horner, D. T. Kearns, G. M. Levin, H. Luce III, J. R. Munro, N. J. Nicholas, Jr., J. R. Opel, D. S. Perkins, K. F. Sutton, A. Temple, C. R. Wharton, Jr. Transfer Agent & Registrar—Morgan Guaranty Trust Co., NYC. Incorporated in New York in 1922; reincorporated in Delaware in 1983.

Information has been obtained from sources believed to be reliable, but its accuracy and completeness are not guaranteed.   William H. Donald

R. J. Reynolds

In a 13D filing dated July 6, 1983, Buffett reported ownership of 5,599,721 common shares of R. J. Reynolds, purchased at an average price of $45.98 per share. Between August 1983 and January 1984 Buffett lowered his stake in R. J. Reynolds to 4.95 percent with the sale of 577,200 shares at an average price of $62.46 per share.

RJR Nabisco

1891F

NYSE Symbol RJR Options on CBOE (Feb-May-Aug-Nov) In S&P 500

Price	Range	P-E Ratio	Dividend	Yield	S&P Ranking	Beta
Oct. 30'86	1986					
53¼	55¼-31	14	1.60	3.0%	A+	0.85

Summary

Following the 1985 acquisition of Nabisco Brands, RJR Nabisco (formerly R. J. Reynolds Industries) is one of the world's largest consumer products companies. Besides its important roles in the tobacco and beverage industries, RJR now holds leading positions in numerous segments of the packaged food market. In October, 1986 RJR sold Kentucky Fried Chicken for some $840 million, and said it would redeem the final 5.4 million shares of its Series C preferred in December.

Current Outlook

Earnings for 1987 are forecast at $5.00 a share, up from the $4.05 estimated for 1986.

The quarterly dividend was raised 8.1%, to $0.40 from $0.37, with the October, 1986 declaration.

Earnings for 1987 are expected to advance at a strong pace, led by tobacco operations. While domestic cigarette volume may decline slightly, higher selling prices and productivity gains should fuel profits. Increased unit volume and favorable foreign currency exchange rates should aid tobacco earnings from abroad. Nontobacco operations, mainly Nabisco Brands, should post a moderate profit improvement on higher volumes and prices. Lower interest and preferred dividend costs and a lesser tax rate should benefit earnings; a resumption of share repurchases would boost per-share results.

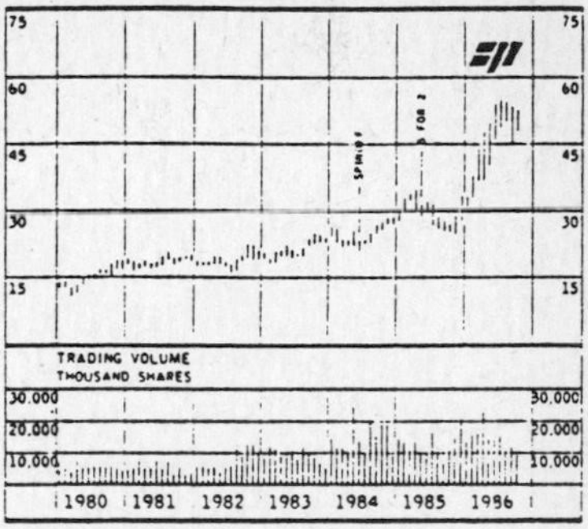

[4]Sales & Oper. Revs. (Billion $)

Quarter:	1986	1985	1984	1983
Mar.	4.62	2.90	2.86	3.05
Jun.	[7]4.63	3.40	3.36	3.62
Sep.	4.74	4.76	3.22	3.24
Dec.		5.53	3.53	3.62
		16.60	12.97	13.53

Sales from continuing operations for the nine months ended September 30, 1986 advanced 37%, year to year, reflecting respective revenue increases of 10% and 71% for tobacco and nontobacco operations. Substantially higher interest charges held the gain in pretax income to 9.5%. After taxes at 44.4%, versus 46.5%, and lower minority interest, net income from continuing operations rose 17%. After preferred dividends, share earnings were $2.64 before $0.02 loss from discontinued operations, versus $2.35 (income of $0.08).

[3]Common Share Earnings ($)

Quarter:	1986	1985	1984	[1]1983
Mar.	0.66	0.66	0.48	0.46
Jun.	[7]0.95	0.86	0.67	0.74
Sep.	1.03	0.91	0.76	0.80
Dec.		1.17	0.89	0.74
		3.60	2.80	2.74

Important Developments

Oct. '86—RJR sold Kentucky Fried Chicken to PepsiCo for some $840 million (book value). Separately, the company said it would redeem the 5.4 million outstanding shares of its Series C cumulative preferred stock on December 1, 1986; the per-share redemption price would be $135.23 plus $1.08 in accrued and unpaid dividends.

Next earnings report due in mid-February.

Per Share Data ($)

Yr. End Dec. 31	[2]1985	1984	[2]1983	[2]1982	[2]1981	1980	[5]1979	1978	[1]1977	[2]1976
Book Value	d0.50	13.26	18.44	16.93	15.05	13.24	10.76	10.14	9.11	8.18
Earnings[6]	3.60	2.80	2.74	3.13	2.83	2.49	2.09	1.80	1.74	1.50
Dividends	1.41	1.30	1.22	1.14	1.00	0.87	0.78	0.71½	0.66¾	0.62⅝
Payout Ratio	39%	43%	45%	36%	35%	35%	38%	40%	39%	42%
Prices—High	35	29	25½	22⅞	21¼	19	14½	13	14⅛	13⅝
Low	24¾	21⅛	18⅛	16	16⅜	10⅞	10⅞	10½	11⅝	11
P/E Ratio—	10-7	10-8	9-7	7-5	7-6	8-4	7-5	7-6	8-7	9-7

Data as orig. reptd. Adj. for stk. div(s). of 150% Jun. 1985, 100% Dec. 1979. 1. Reflects accounting change. 2. Reflects merger or acquisition. 3. Ful. dil. 4. Incl. excise taxes. 5. Reflects merger or acquisition and accounting change. 6. Bef. results of disc. opers. of +1.31 in 1984, +0.16 in 1983. 7. Reflects 9 mos. reclassification for 6 mos.

November 6, 1986

Copyright © 1986 Standard & Poor's Corp. All Rights Reserved

Standard & Poor's Corp.
25 Broadway, NY, NY 10004

1891F

RJR Nabisco, Inc.

Income Data (Million $)

Year Ended Dec. 31	Revs.	Oper. Inc.	% Oper. Inc. of Revs.	Cap. Exp.	Depr.	Int. Exp.	Net Bef. Taxes	Eff. Tax Rate	[3]Net Inc.	% Net Inc. of Revs.
[2]1985	13,533	2,612	19.3%	1,194	449	424	1,854	46.0%	1,001	7.4%
[3]1984	9,915	1,891	19.1%	813	272	216	1,552	45.7%	843	8.5%
[4]1983	10,371	2,061	19.9%	925	474	212	1,473	43.3%	835	8.1%
[2]1982	10,906	2,084	19.1%	926	490	217	1,610	46.0%	870	8.0%
[2]1981	9,766	1,897	19.4%	964	393	181	1,401	45.2%	768	7.9%
1980	8,449	1,633	19.3%	898	363	[1]163	1,139	41.2%	670	7.9%
[3]1979	7,133	1,399	19.6%	986	312	126	1,017	45.8%	551	7.7%
1978	4,952	1,133	22.9%	383	226	71	854	48.3%	442	8.9%
[1]1977	4,816	1,023	21.2%	285	209	84	790	46.4%	424	8.8%
[2]1976	4,291	943	22.0%	834	164	69	691	48.8%	354	8.2%

Balance Sheet Data (Million $)

Dec. 31	Cash	---Current--- Assets	Liab.	Ratio	Total Assets	Ret. on Assets	Long Term Debt	Com-mon Equity	Total Cap.	% LT Debt of Cap.	ReL on Equity
1985	589	5,878	4,130	1.4	16,930	7.7%	4,857	4,796	11,955	40.6%	19.9%
1984	1,323	5,114	2,250	2.3	9,272	9.2%	1,257	4,481	6,757	18.6%	17.0%
1983	367	4,266	1,801	2.4	9,874	8.2%	1,421	5,223	7,757	18.3%	15.4%
1982	282	4,624	2,303	2.0	10,355	9.1%	1,666	4,766	7,705	21.6%	18.5%
1981	61	3,987	1,971	2.0	8,096	9.9%	1,039	3,927	5,904	17.6%	20.0%
1980	188	3,642	1,810	2.0	7,355	9.6%	1,046	3,445	5,332	19.6%	19.6%
1979	165	3,201	1,485	2.2	6,422	9.8%	989	2,998	4,754	20.8%	18.1%
1978	114	2,141	803	2.7	4,616	9.8%	740	2,630	3,706	20.0%	17.4%
1977	94	2,021	841	2.4	4,334	9.6%	761	2,360	3,404	22.3%	18.5%
1976	105	2,009	978	2.1	4,277	9.3%	646	2,068	2,953	21.9%	17.4%

Data as orig. reptd. 1. Reflects acctg. change. 2. Reflects merger or acquisition. 3. Reflects merger or acquisition and acctg. change. 4. Excl. disc. opers. and reflects merger or acquisition. 5. Bef. results of disc. opers. in 1984, 1983 6. Excl. disc. opers.

Business Summary

RJR Nabisco (formerly R. J. Reynolds Industries) is a major factor in the tobacco, food and beverage industries worldwide. Segment contributions in 1985:

	Revs.	Profits
Tobacco	49%	66%
Food and Beverages	51%	34%

R. J. Reynolds Tobacco is the second-largest domestic cigarette producer with a 32% share of the U.S. market. Brands include Winston, Salem, and Camel. It is a defendant in numerous product-liability suits related to cigarettes, although initial rulings have been favorable. R. J. Reynolds Tobacco International sells products in more than 160 markets worldwide; cigarettes are both exported and manufactured in 30 foreign countries and territories.

Nabisco Brands (acquired in July, 1985; annual sales of some $6 billion) is a worldwide producer and marketer of packaged foods with leading shares of the cookie, cracker, confectionery and other markets. Effective January, 1986 Del

Monte, a major producer of canned fruits and vegetables, was combined with Nabisco Brands. Heublein is the world's second-largest marketer of distilled spirits and has an important position in wine.

Dividend Data

Dividends have been paid since 1900. A dividend reinvestment plan is available.

Amt. of Divd. $	Date Decl.	Ex-divd. Date	Stock of Record	Payment Date
0.37	Jan. 16	Feb. 4	Feb. 10	Mar. 5'86
0.37	Apr. 23	May 5	May 9	Jun. 5'86
0.37	Jul. 17	Aug. 4	Aug. 8	Sep. 5'86
0.40	Oct. 16	Nov. 4	Nov. 10	Dec. 5'86

Next dividend meeting: mid-Jan. '87.

Capitalization

Long Term Debt: $5,433,000,000.

Red. Cum. Preferred Stock: $968,000,000.

Common Stock: 250,290,882 shs. (no par). Institutions hold about 42%. Shareholders of record: 155,138.

Office—Reynolds Blvd., Winston-Salem, N.C. 27102. Tel—(919) 773-2000. Chrmn & CEO—J. T. Wilson. Pres—F. R. Johnson. VP-Secy—J. N. Crittenden. VP-Treas—H. M. Bains. VP-Investor Contact—H. R. Lambert. Dirs—W. S. Anderson, A. L. Butler, Jr., J. L. Clendenin, G. H. Gillespie, R. H. Grierson, J. W. Hanley, E. A. Horngan, Jr., C. E. Hugel, F. R. Johnson, V. E. Jordan, Jr., J. M. Kreps, G. H. Long, J. D. Macomber, J. G. Medlin, Jr., A. G. C. Sage II, R. M. Schaeberle, J. P. Sticht, S. D. Watson, J. O. Welch, Jr., J. T. Wilson. Transfer Agents & Registrars—Manufacturers Hanover Trust Co., NYC; First Jersey National Bank, Jersey City, N.J. Incorporated in New York in 1899; reincorporated in Delaware in 1970.

Information has been obtained from sources believed to be reliable, but its accuracy and completeness are not guaranteed. George C. Pierides

The Scott & Fetzer Company

In a 13D filing dated November 8, 1985, Berkshire Hathaway announced it had agreed to acquire Scott & Fetzer for $60 per share. Under the merger agreement Berkshire Hathaway received an option to purchase 1.3 million shares directly from the company at $55 per share, plus up to 889,533 $1.80 convertible preferred, also for $55 per share. The merger price was subsequently increased to $60.77 per share, and on January 6, 1986, the Scott & Fetzer Company became an indirectly, wholly owned subsidiary of Berkshire Hathaway.

Scott & Fetzer

1987S

NYSE Symbol SFZ

Price	Range	P-E Ratio	Dividend	Yield	S&P Ranking
Oct. 29'85	1985				
58¼	61½-53½	12	[4]---	[4]3.1	A–

Summary

In October, 1985 Scott & Fetzer agreed to be acquired by Berkshire Hathaway, Inc. for $60 a share in a leveraged buyout. As part of the agreement, Berkshire Hathaway was granted an option to purchase 1.3 million new SFZ common shares and 889,533 new convertible preferred shares at $55 each. Subject to shareholder approval, the transaction was expected to be completed in January, 1986.

Business Summary

Scott & Fetzer is a diversified marketing-oriented manufacturing company. Business segment contributions in fiscal 1984:

	Sales	Profits
Education, information & training	38%	29%
Household products & services	43%	47%
Commercial industrial	19%	24%

Foreign operations accounted for about 6% of sales in fiscal 1984.

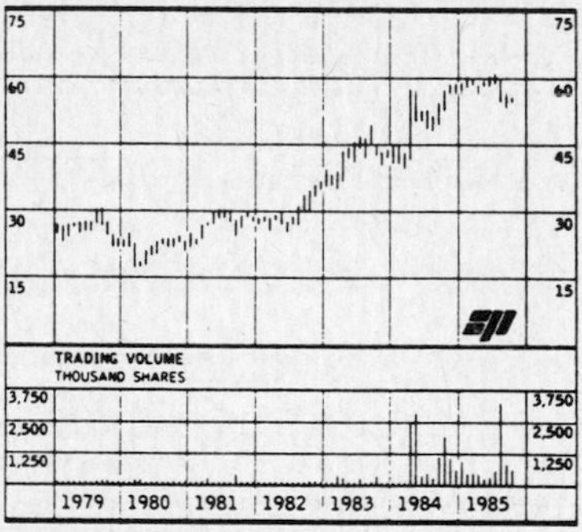

Education, information, & training products include the World Book subsidiary which publishes The World Book Encyclopedia, other reference works, and educational and instructional material primarily under the World Book and Childcraft names, as well as the development of various business and educational microcomputer software systems.

Household products & services include a wide variety of vacuum cleaners and other floor maintenance equipment and supplies for residential, industrial, and institutional use. Floor maintenance equipment for consumer use is sold primarily under the Kirby name. Certain other floor maintenance equipment is sold under both private labels of customers and under certain company trade names.

Consumer industrial products include connectors and fittings for compressed gas applications; a line of medical regulators and flowmeters; injected molded plastic items; utility service truck bodies and related equipment; explosion-proof electrical fittings; junction boxes, instrument housings, and control stations for electrical distribution systems; and precision equipment for measuring liquids.

Acquisition Agreement

Oct. '85—SFZ agreed to be acquired in a leveraged buyout by Berkshire Hathaway, Inc. for $60 a share cash. As part of the agreement, Berkshire Hathaway was granted an option to buy 1.3 million new SFZ common shares and 889,533 new convertible preferred shares, both at $55 a share. Subject to shareholder approval, the transaction was expected to be completed in January, 1986. In accepting this offer, SFZ rejected a $60-a-share bid by Equity Group Holdings. Earlier, SFZ rejected a $62-a-share bid by Kelso & Co.

Next earnings report due in late January.

Per Share Data ($)

Yr. End Nov. 30	1984	1983	1982	1981	1980	1979	[1]1978	1977	1976	1975
Book Value	36.76	32.08	29.00	26.75	24.68	23.41	20.45	18.21	16.06	14.21
Earnings[2]	5.67	4.20	4.04	4.01	3.12	4.62	4.10	3.63	3.01	2.26
Dividends	1.80	1.80	1.80	1.80	1.80	1.70	1.50	1.30	1.17	1.02
Payout Ratio	31%	42%	44%	42%	58%	37%	37%	35%	39%	45%
Prices[3]—High	59⅛	49⅞	37¼	30¾	25⅜	30⅞	36⅛	29	29⅜	22
Low	39⅞	35¼	25½	22	17¼	22	22	22¾	18	9⅛
P/E Ratio—	10-7	12-8	9-6	8-5	8-6	7-5	9-5	8-6	10-6	10-4

Data as orig. reptd. 1. Reflects merger or acquisition. 2. Bef. results of disc. opers. of +0.34 in 1984, +0.60 in 1983, +0.01 in 1978, –0.07 in 1977. 3. Cal. yr. 4. See Acquisition Agreement.

Standard NYSE Stock Reports
Vol. 52/No. 213/Sec. 17

November 5, 1985
Copyright © 1985 Standard & Poor's Corp. All Rights Reserved
Standard & Poor's Corp.
25 Broadway, NY, NY 10004

1987S   The Scott & Fetzer Company

Income Data (Million $)

Year Ended Nov. 30	²Revs.	Oper. Inc.	% Oper. Inc. of Revs.	Cap. Exp.	Depr.	Int. Exp.	Net Bef. Taxes	Eff. Tax Rate	⁴Net Inc.	% Net Inc. of Revs.
¹1984	695	80.0	11.5%	20.3	10.2	7.84	⁵71.0	45.9%	38.4	5.5%
¹1983	630	67.8	10.8%	19.4	10.2	8.73	⁵51.5	45.2%	28.2	4.5%
1982	600	62.6	10.4%	11.9	10.5	9.64	⁶48.1	43.7%	27.1	4.5%
1981	656	64.2	9.8%	11.5	1C.1	9.13	⁶56.9	48.9%	29.1	4.4%
1980	632	53.6	8.5%	14.7	9.0	9.86	⁶37.3	38.2%	23.1	3.6%
1979	697	78.4	11.2%	26.4	7.9	9.22	⁶63.1	45.9%	34.1	4.9%
³1978	478	70.1	14.7%	12.9	7.1	5.32	⁶60.8	50.4%	30.2	6.3%
¹1977	351	64.5	18.4%	8.8	5.4	3.96	56.1	52.2%	⁵26.8	7.6%
1976	343	51.0	14.9%	4.6	5.1	3.18	45.9	50.1%	22.9	6.7%
1975	284	39.5	13.9%	6.1	4.8	2.85	32.8	48.0%	17.1	6.0%

Balance Sheet Data (Million $)

Nov. 30	Cash	Assets	Current Liab.	Ratio	Total Assets	Ret. on Assets	Long Term Debt	Common Equity	Total Cap.	% LT Debt of Cap.	Ret. on Equity
1984	121	323	174	1.9	468	8.4%	33.3	244	289	11.5%	16.7%
1983	125	303	147	2.1	445	6.6%	68.2	215	293	23.3%	13.8%
1982	86	253	123	2.1	404	6.8%	74.8	194	275	26.4%	14.5%
1981	102	273	133	2.1	406	7.6%	76.9	184	268	28.7%	16.4%
1980	92	263	117	2.2	394	5.8%	79.6	185	272	29.3%	12.8%
1979	63	271	128	2.1	395	9.3%	82.3	175	263	31.3%	20.8%
1978	55	230	131	1.8	338	10.7%	46.0	153	203	22.6%	21.0%
1977	60	171	46	3.7	225	12.6%	41.8	133	179	23.4%	21.2%
1976	47	161	45	3.6	207	11.7%	34.4	124	163	21.1%	19.6%
1975	38	137	36	3.8	184	9.8%	34.8	110	148	23.5%	16.3%

Data as orig. reptd. 1. Excludes discontinued operations. 2. Incl. other income aft. 1977. 3. Excludes discontinued operations and reflects merger or acquisition. 4. Bef. results of disc. opers. in 1984; 1983, 1978, 1977. 5. Reflects accounting change. 6. Includes equity in earnings of nonconsol. subs

Revenues Sales (Million $)

Quarter:	1984-5	1983-4	1982-3	1981-2
Feb.	177.5	160.2	139.8	142.8
May	195.2	199.7	177.7	172.0
Aug.	159.3	173.6	149.6	143.5
Nov.		162.0	162.5	141.7
	695.4	629.6	600.0	

Sales for the nine months ended August 31, 1985 declined 0.3%, year to year, reflecting sluggish economic conditions. Higher profits for the education/information/training and the commercial/industrial segments were offset by lower earnings for the household products/services segment. Net income was virtually unchanged, but based on more shares outstanding, earnings per share declined to $4.42 from $4.46 (before income from discontinued operations of $0.34).

Common Share Earnings ($)

Quarter:	1984-5	1983-4	1982-3	1981-2
Feb.	1.07	0.95	0.69	0.79
May	2.08	2.09	1.41	1.32
Aug.	1.27	1.42	1.03	1.02
Nov.		1.21	1.07	0.91
	5.67	4.20	4.04	

Dividend Data

Dividends, which had been paid since 1942, were suspended in early 1985 in connection with a leveraged buyout agreement that was subsequently terminated. In September, 1985 dividends were resumed as follows:

Amt. of Divd. $	Date Decl.	Ex-divd. Date	Stock of Record	Payment Date
0.45	Aug. 20	Aug. 26	Aug. 30	Sep. 6'85
0.45 Ext.	Aug. 20	Aug. 26	Aug. 30	Sep. 6'85

Finances

In announcing the acquisition agreement with Berkshire Hathaway, SFZ said that it may complete its previously announced plan to buy back up to $150 million of its common stock for as much as $60 a share.

In September, 1985 directors authorized the repurchase of 1,400,000 SFZ common shares in the open market or through negotiated transactions.

Capitalization

Long Term Debt: $37,083,000.

Common Stock: 6,642,544 shs. (no par). Institutions hold approximately 45%. Shareholders of record: 4,816.

Office—28800 Clements Rd. Westlake. Ohio 44145. Tel—(216) 892 3000. Chrmn & Pres—R. E. Schey. VP-Secy—R. C. Weber. VP-Treas—W. T. Stephans VP-Fin & Investor Contact—K. J. Semelsberger. Dirs—R. W. Bjork, S. H. Fuller, J. A. Hughes, L. C. Jones, K. K. Kier, R. E. Schey, K. J. Semelsberger, K. W. Smith, M. A. White. Transfer Agent & Registrar—AmeriTrust Co., Cleveland Incorporated in Ohio in 1917

Information has been obtained from sources believed to be reliable, but its accuracy and completeness are not guaranteed.   N.J. DeVita

Capital Cities Communications

As disclosed in a January 9, 1986, 13D filing Buffett bought 3 million unissued shares of Capital Cities Communications at $172.50 a share in order to assist Capital Cities in the purchase of American Broadcasting Companies. Capital Cities is now selling at $278 per share.

Warren Buffett and Capital Cities/ABC

Buffett agreed to invest $517 million to help finance the acquisition of ABC by Capital Cities Communications *(CCB, NYSE, 222 ½)*. Buffett's Berkshire Hathaway Inc. will provide nearly 15 percent of the $3.5 billion that Capital Cities paid for ABC. Upon the expected completion of the merger in early 1986, Berkshire will own 18 percent of the new Capital Cities/ABC at a cost of $172.50 per share.

The CCB investment is the largest one ever made by Buffett. Although he generally holds very large positions in a small number of stocks, he historically has built up his investment position over a long period of time.

In a September 30, 1985, 13F filing at the SEC by Berkshire Hathaway, the largest portfolio holdings were GEICO Corp. at $459 million and General Foods at $478 million, two positions that had been accumulated over a long period of time and in the interim had registered enormous capital gains.

Business Background: Capital Cities/ABC

Capital Cities Communications (CCB) is a group broadcaster whose other diversified media operations include nearly forty trade and professional publications and eighteen daily and weekly newspapers. Over the last decade, CCB has experienced compound annual earnings growth of nearly 22 percent and cash flow has grown from $1.71 to $14.53 per share.

CCB has been superbly managed by Tom Murphy, who has been described by Buffett as a rare "managerial superstar" able to reinvest adeptly large amounts of free cash flow in high cash-generating businesses.

ABC, in contrast to CCB, has not been able to reinvest cash flow from its broadcasting operations successfully. In 1984, broadcasting accounted for 89 percent of revenues and over 103 percent of operating earnings.

Capital Cities/ABC 442

NYSE Symbol CCB Options on CBOE (Feb-May-Aug-Nov) In S&P 500

Price	Range	P-E Ratio	Dividend	Yield	S&P Ranking	Beta
Nov. 12'86	1986					
$271\frac{3}{4}$	276-$208\frac{1}{4}$	29	0.20	0.1%	A	0.92

Summary

Capital Cities/ABC was formed by the January, 1986 merger of American Broadcasting Companies into Capital Cities Communications in a transaction valued at about $3.5 billion. The combined company operates one of the three national TV networks and seven radio networks, owns TV and radio stations in major U.S. markets, is a major publisher of magazines and newspapers, and provides cable TV programming. Earnings are being impacted by soft national advertising demand.

Current Outlook

Earnings for 1987 are projected at $11.40 a share, versus the $8.75 estimated for 1986, which excludes a special credit from the sale of real estate.

The $0.05 quarterly dividend should continue over the near term.

Revenues and earnings in 1987 will continue to be impacted by softness in national advertising demand, which is affecting the ABC television network and the magazine publishing division. Substantial network programming costs and a heavy debt burden will also continue to restrict profitability, but the absence of certain nonrecurring charges and continuing cost-cutting measures should be more than offsetting.

Net Revenues (Million $)

Quarter:	1986	1985	1984	1983
Mar.	912	234	207	170
Jun.	1,066	267	244	194
Sep.	959	248	230	184
Dec.	---	272	260	214
	---	1,021	940	762

Revenues for the 1986 first nine months were $2.94 billion, versus $749 million, reflecting the ABC acquisition. Hurt by sharply higher costs and expenses, net income was down 0.8%. Share earnings declined to $6.28 (before a special credit of $16.43) on more shares from $7.83.

Common Share Earnings ($)

Quarter:	1986	1985	1984	1983
Mar.	0.12	2.13	2.07	1.58
Jun.	4.15	3.15	3.03	2.41
Sep.	2.01	2.55	2.36	1.95
Dec.	E2.47	3.04	2.94	2.59
	E8.75	10.87	10.40	8.53

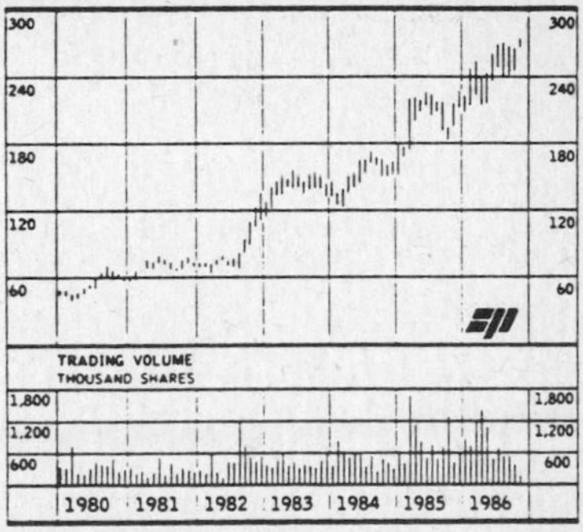

Important Developments

Oct. '86—ABC's New York headquarters building was sold for $174.2 million. Separately, in the 1986 third quarter the company took an $0.85 a share charge to earnings to reflect the cost of settling certain litigation.

Jan. '86—Capital Cities/ABC was formed through the merger of American Broadcasting Companies into Capital Cities Communications in a transaction valued at about $3.5 billion. In order to comply with FCC restrictions, CCB and ABC sold TV, radio and cable properties for a total of about $1.0 billion. To help finance the purchase, CCB sold 3 million common shares (19% of shares outstanding) to Berkshire Hathaway, Inc. for $517.5 million.

Next earnings report due in late January.

Per Share Data ($)

Yr. End Dec. 31	[1]1985	[1]1984	[1]1983	[1]1982	[1]1981	[1]1980	1979	[1]1978	[1]1977	[1]1976
Book Value[3]	**31.37**	19.97	19.39	13.77	6.75	7.13	4.37	1.04	d0.22	2.82
Earnings[2]	**10.87**	10.40	8.53	7.25	6.12	5.38	4.68	3.80	2.91	2.30
Dividends	**0.20**	0.20	0.20	0.20	0.20	0.20	0.20	$0.17\frac{1}{2}$	0.10	0.10
Payout Ratio	**2%**	2%	2%	3%	3%	4%	4%	4%	3%	4%
Prices—High	**229**	$174\frac{1}{2}$	$157\frac{1}{2}$	$136\frac{3}{4}$	$80\frac{1}{2}$	72	$49\frac{7}{8}$	$47\frac{3}{4}$	$30\frac{1}{2}$	$28\frac{1}{8}$
Low	**$152\frac{1}{4}$**	$123\frac{1}{2}$	$114\frac{3}{4}$	$64\frac{3}{8}$	$56\frac{1}{2}$	40	$36\frac{3}{4}$	$27\frac{1}{8}$	$22\frac{1}{8}$	$21\frac{1}{8}$
P/E Ratio—	**21-14**	17-12	18-13	19-9	13-9	13-7	11-8	13-7	10-8	12-9

Data as orig. reptd. Adj. for stk. div(s). of 100% Jul. 1978. 1. Reflects merger or acquisition. 2. Bef. spec. item(s) of +0.58 in 1984, +0.18 in 1980, +0.22 in 1977. 3. Excl. intangibles. E-Estimated.

November 19, 1986

Copyright © 1986 Standard & Poor's Corp. All Rights Reserved

Standard & Poor's Corp.
25 Broadway, NY, NY 10004

442

Capital Cities/ABC, Inc.

Income Data (Million $)

Year Ended Dec. 31	Revs.	Oper. Inc.	% Oper. Inc. of Revs.	Cap. Exp.	Depr.	Int. Exp.	Net Bef. Taxes	Eff. Tax Rate	²Net Inc.	% Net Inc. of Revs.
¹1985	1,021	335	32.8%	9	57.7	27.3	277	48.6%	142	13.9%
¹1984	940	319	34.0%	65	51.7	28.4	269	49.7%	135	14.4%
¹1983	762	261	34.2%	52	40.3	16.0	225	48.9%	115	15.0%
¹1982	664	224	33.7%	60	33.8	9.6	185	48.0%	96	14.5%
¹1981	574	182	31.8%	100	23.1	12.2	155	48.1%	81	14.0%
¹1980	472	152	32.3%	31	14.9	³ 5.9	138	48.9%	71	15.0%
1979	415	139	33.4%	18	13.1	6.8	125	48.9%	64	15.4%
¹1978	367	127	34.5%	20	12.5	8.6	111	51.2%	54	14.7%
¹1977	306	108	35.2%	44	10.9	9.5	90	52.1%	43	14.1%
¹1976	212	· 80	37.5%	4	6.6	4.0	73	51.0%	36	16.8%

Balance Sheet Data (Million $)

Dec. 31	Cash	Current Assets	Current Liab.	Ratio	Total Assets	Ret. on Assets	Long Term Debt	Common Equity	Total Cap.	% LT Debt of Cap.	Ret. on Equity
1985	769	1,006	175	5.7	1,885	9.2%	708	889	1,639	43.2%	17.4%
1984	236	402	161	2.5	1,208	12.1%	215	734	990	21.7%	20.1%
1983	272	403	137	2.9	1,053	12.6%	207	625	870	23.8%	19.7%
1982	41	151	134	1.1	776	13.0%	31	544	602	5.1%	19.4%
1981	10	118	113	1.0	698	13.2%	87	444	556	15.7%	19.9%
1980	40	129	92	1.4	520	14.3%	39	361	409	9.4%	21.5%
1979	43	123	87	1.4	473	14.1%	56	300	367	15.4%	23.1%
1978	32	104	85	1.2	445	12.6%	76	260	346	22.0%	22.3%
1977	37	87	78	1.1	435	11.5%	101	237	348	29.2%	19.8%
1976	57	96	58	1.7	329	11.3%	45	209	262	17.3%	18.2%

Data as org. reptd. 1. Reflects merger or acquisition. 2. Bef. spec. item(s) in 1984, 1980, 1977. 3. Reflects accounting change.

Business Summary

Capital Cities/ABC, Inc. was formed in January, 1986 with the merger of American Broadcasting Companies into a subsidiary of Capital Cities Communications. Following the merger, and the sales of certain assets, the company's business is largely comprised of broadcasting, programming and publishing.

The broadcast division includes the ABC television network with 214 affiliates, seven radio networks with 1,914 affiliates, eight owned TV stations and 12 radio stations: WPVI-TV, Philadelphia; KTRK-TV, Houston; WTVD (TV), Durham; KFSN-TV, Fresno; WABC-TV, New York; KABC-TV, Los Angeles; WLS-TV, Chicago; KGO-TV, San Francisco; WMAL (AM) and WRQX (FM), Washington, D.C.; WJR (AM) and WHYT (FM), Detroit; WPRO-AM & FM, Providence; WBAP (AM) and KSCS (FM), Fort Worth; WPLO (AM), Atlanta; WKHX (FM), Marietta; and KQRS-AM&FM, Minneapolis. Seven additional radio stations must be sold before June 1987.

The publishing division publishes nine daily newspapers in seven markets, weekly papers in four states and shopping guides in four states. Fairchild Publications publishes over two dozen trade newpapers and magazines and specialty publications, including Women's Wear Daily, W, M, Daily News Record, Institutional Investor, and others. The division also includes ABC Publishing, whose 10 operating units publish more than 100 magazines and book titles monthly and release over 25 record albums annually. The units include the Chilton Co., Hitchcock Publishing, COMPUTE! Publications, Inc., Farm Progress Companies, Miller Publishing, ABC Leisure Magazine, Los Angeles magazine, NILS Publishing, National Price Service, and Work, Inc. The company also provides programming for cable television.

Dividend Data

Dividends were initiated in 1976.

Amt. of Divd. $	Date Decl.	Ex-divd. Date	Stock of Record	Payment Date
0.05	Dec. 17	Dec. 24	Dec. 31	Jan. 28'86
0.05	Mar. 21	Mar. 24	Mar. 31	Apr. 21'86
0.05	Jun. 12	Jun. 24	Jun. 30	Jul. 21'86
0.05	Sep. 17	Sep. 30	Oct. 6	Oct. 27'86

Capitalization

Long Term Debt: $2,068,894,000.

Common Stock: 16,117,357 shs. ($1 par). Institutions hold about 75%, incl. 19% owned by Berkshire Hathaway Inc.
Shareholders of record: 5,020.

Office—24 E. 51st., New York I 0022. Tel—(212) 887-7008. Chrmn & CEO—T. S. Murphy. Pres—D. B. Burke. Secy—G. Dickler. Treas—R. W. Gelles. VP & Investor Contact—J. M. Fitzgerald. Dirs—R. P. Bauman, W. E. Buffet, D. B. Burke, F. T. Cary, G. Dickler, J. P. Dougherty, J. B. Fairchild, L. H. Goldenson, A. Greenspan, A. Hess, G. P. Jenkins, T. M. Maciocce, J. H. Muller, Jr., T. S. Murphy, F. S. Pierce, J. B. Poole, J. B. Sias, W. I. Spencer, M. C. Woodward, Jr. Transfer Agent & Registrar—Chemical Bank, NYC. Incorporated in New York in 1946.

Information has been obtained from sources believed to be reliable, but its accuracy and completeness are not guaranteed. William H. Donald

Asset redeployment is underway at ABC to refocus the company on its core broadcasting business. Several top management resignations have been asked for in 1985 in preparation for the merger with CCB.

Currently, earnings at ABC are being severely affected by the soft economic climate and rating declines. Since early 1984, ABC has fallen from first to third place among the three networks in ratings, losing considerable market share to resurgent NBC. Third quarter 1985 earnings fell 37 percent to $1.02 per share compared to $1.61 in the previous year's quarter.

Industry Environment: Network Broadcasters

The networks are characterized by the following:

- *High cash flow.* Network broadcasting companies generate considerably more cash than they need to reinvest in the business, generally termed free or excess cash flow.
- *Quasi-monopoly market positions.* ABC, CBS, and NBC dominate the network business and have considerable pricing flexibility during good times.
- *Low capital needs.* After a broadcaster has invested in basic equipment, large additional capital expenditures are not required.
- *Business franchise.* Television advertising is the most efficient way for most consumer product companies to sell their products. No other medium has such a large audience reach or has such widespread popularity. The fact that *TV Guide* is the largest circulation publication in the country indicates the power of the broadcast over the print media.
- *Stable customer base.* The majority of television advertisers are consumer product companies who must advertise during both good and bad times in order to maintain market share.
- *High earnings leverage.* Television advertising is basically a commodity business with a fixed supply of product, i.e., perishable time, and high fixed costs for programming to fill the time. Prices charged by the broadcasters rise sharply when demand rises during strong economic periods and conversely fall as economic activity slows. Thus, profits can fluctuate widely.
- *Good long-term growth outlook.* Advertising overall has been growing faster than the economy for a decade. Compared to inflation adjusted GNP growth estimated at 2.4 percent by the Commerce Department, for 1986, total advertising was projected to grow 8.0 percent, again well above the expected growth in the economy.
- *Ratings importance.* The level of program ratings (the size and demographic characteristics of the audience reached) are crucial. High ratings mean high profitability because the broadcaster charges according to the size and attractiveness of the audience reached. For example, a new snack product marketer would want to reach a large market of the group most likely to buy his products: teenagers and young adults.
- *Regulatory change.* Broadcasting station ownership rules have been greatly

expanded to allow ownership of twelve television stations, as long as market coverage is less than 25 percent of the United States population. Previously, only seven stations could be owned. Overall, regulatory pressures have been relaxed due to the more compliant policies adopted by the Reagan Administration and followed by the FCC.

Investment Rationale: Network Broadcasters

Recent improvements in the industry's long-term fundamentals due to regulatory changes will result in accelerated earnings growth for broadcasting networks.

Expansion of station ownership will allow the networks to redeploy assets into broadcasting where high rates of return have been earned historically. In 1984, CBS's operating return on assets equaled 33.3 percent for the Broadcast Group, 15.8 percent for the Records Group, and 16.9 percent for the Publishing Group. Both CBS and ABC have earned returns on equity as high as 22 percent during periods of strong advertising demand and high ratings.

Greater pricing flexibility may result from the creation of larger broadcasting entities and GE's ownership of NBC. If GE makes extensive management changes at NBC, creativity and ratings could suffer, benefiting ABC's and CBS's market positions.

Considerable cost reduction and asset redeployment are already underway at the historically inefficiently run, heavily staffed network broadcasters, in response to industry consolidation and the threat of unfriendly takeover.

More efficient asset utilization can be attained with the easing of regulatory rules that previously restricted the purchase and sale of broadcast stations.

- Investors will look beyond the current earnings slowdown and restructuring costs and focus on the intrinsic value of network properties and the potential for high levels of cash flow and earnings in the late 1980s.

  The earnings leverage at networks and their affiliated stations is immense. Consider what happened to operating margins in the late 1970s when ABC was recovering from its depressed number three ranked position, eventually eclipsing the then perennial number one CBS.

  During the 1976 to 1979 period, total corporate operating margins at ABC advanced from 13.5 percent to 17.6 percent. At CBS, where rating declines were causing market share losses, operating margins declined from 15.2 percent to 10.9 percent.

- The networks may command expanding multiple premiums in a strong advertising climate. The scarcity value of public broadcasting properties has increased greatly as many companies have already merged or gone private.

- Networks are potential takeover candidates because of their high levels of cash flow, the increased salability of broadcast stations, and the enhanced values of broadcast stations, which probably have not been fully reflected in market prices.

Investment Rationale: Capital Cities Communications

The potential for operating improvement at ABC under CCB's superior management is considerable. CCB had operating margins of 34.0 percent in 1984 versus 11.4 percent for ABC, 15.0 percent for CBS's broadcasting operations and 10.7 percent for CBS overall. The merged entity CCB/ABC will combine the best of both companies, as ABC and CCB will have sold many of their less profitable operations before the merger.

The investment outlook for CCB/ABC centers on how fast the approximately $2.1 billion in debt can be paid down with excess cash flow or through sale of properties. In 1984, premerger cash flow of the two companies totaled $447 million. However, after interest and other merger related expenses, cash flow on a pro forma basis fell to $270 million.

One industry expert believes that the merged CCB/ABC can attain large operating efficiencies quickly, estimating free cash flow (after capital expenditures and dividends) at $247 million in 1986, $356 million in 1987, and $461 million in 1988. According to these estimates, the debt to capitalization rate would be reduced to 20 percent by 1988. Under the assumption that the market would capitalize CCB/ABC's free cash flow at twelve times, the 1986 per share valuation of $185 would grow to $346 in 1988.

If operating efficiencies can be attained as quickly as projected above, earnings per share growth would accelerate by 35.6 percent in 1987 and 31.6 percent in 1988. Earnings per share would equal $14.01 in 1986, $19.00 in 1987, and $25.00 in 1988. Thus, the stock at current prices is selling at 16.3 times estimated 1986 earnings per share, 12.1 times estimated 1987 earnings, and 9.2 times estimated 1988 earnings.

(Courtesy *Street Smart Investing,* No. 164, December 26, 1985)

Fireman's Fund (Underwriting Participation)

On September 1, 1986, a Berkshire Hathaway insurance subsidiary became a 7 percent participant in the underwriting business of Fireman's Fund (FFC) except for FFC reinsurance written for unaffiliated companies, an illustration of Buffett's coolness to the reinsurance (long-tail) business. The participation runs for four years and provides that FFC remit premiums to Berkshire's subsidiary and in exchange recover losses and expenses attributable to Berkshire's 7 percent. As part of the deal, Buffett also became an adviser to FFC on investment strategy. FFC's volume of business in 1985 was about $3 billion, and its unearned premium reserve was $1.324 billion, of which 7 percent share, or $92.7 million, was transferred to Berkshire.

Fireman's Fund and John J. Byrne

A CEO greatly admired by Warren Buffett is . . . Jack Byrne, who guided the extraordinary turnaround at GEICO.

In 1985 Byrne was hired to head Fireman's Fund (*FFC, NYSE, 34 ¾*). He soon had Buffett's agreement to advise FFC on its investment portfolio strategy. When Byrne selected Robert W. Bruce from value manager Cumberland Associates to run FFC's $6 billion investment portfolio, a third outstanding investment brain was added at Fireman.

This trio of top performers indicates unusual investment opportunity at FFC. Consider the following factors:

- A turnaround in corporate results already underway with the potential of earnings surprises on the upside.
- Large price increases being implemented in commercial property and casualty insurance, the bulk of Fireman's business.
- Improving industry fundamentals that form the basis for a prolonged cyclical upturn.

By way of review, Fireman's Fund was offered to the public in October 1985 at $25.75 per share by American Express. The public offering was viewed as the best way to cut the losses being incurred at American Express from FFC's operations and to maximize proceeds from the sale of the company. . . .

Fireman's Fund

887

NYSE Symbol FFC

Price	Range	P-E Ratio	Dividend	Yield	S&P Ranking	Beta
Aug. 29'86 39⅝	1986 44½–30⅝	NM	0.30	0.8%	NR	NA

Summary

Fireman's Fund writes a full line of property and casualty insurance throughout the U.S.; on the basis of direct premiums written, it was the seventh largest property-casualty insurer in 1985. FFC's operating results and the p-c industry's in general have deteriorated in recent years, due to intense price competition and adverse claims experience. However, higher premiums and improved underwriting are expected for the foreseeable future. In June, 1986 FFC acquired a large mortgage banking firm.

Current Outlook

Operating earnings for 1986 are estimated at $2.70 a share, versus a loss incurred in 1985. A further earnings gain to $4.00 a share is projected for 1987.

Dividends should continue at $0.07½ quarterly.

Premium income should rise in 1986, reflecting the continuation of a seller's market for property-casualty insurance (particularly commercial lines), and earnings are expected. Underwriting performance should improve as FFC tightens its risk selectivity (though this selectivity may restrict policy growth). Earnings should benefit also from the acquisition of a mortgage banking firm. Aided by increased cash flow, higher investment income should further boost earnings.

Review of Operations

Total revenues for the six months ended June 30, 1986 rose 5.6%, year to year, primarily reflecting a 6.5% increase in earned premiums. Aided by a 15% decline in the provision for losses ($187 million was added to loss reserves in the second quarter of 1985), total expenses were down 11%. Pretax operating earnings totaled $75 million, in contrast to a year-earlier pretax deficit of $224 million. After taxes at 6.7%, versus tax credits of $137 million, net operating income was $70 million, compared with an $87 million net operating loss. Share earnings for the 1986 period were $1.06, before realized investment gains of $0.23.

Net Operating Earns. Per Share ($)

Quarter:	1986	1985	'1984
Mar.	0.45	---	---
Jun.	0.61	---	²0.21
Sep.	E0.74	---	---
Dec.	E0.90	0.35	²d0.07
	E2.70	---	0.14

TRADING VOLUME
THOUSAND SHARES

Recent Developments

Jul. '86—FFC said its growth and profitability in 1986's first half reflected two years of tighter underwriting, more disciplined management and better pricing. The company said it continued to benefit from higher rates on new and renewal businesses, primarily in commercial and specialty insurance. FFC said that its overall quality of its business was much improved; and noted a 14% decline in the number of in-force policies. FFC's combined ratio for the first half of 1986 improved to 109.8% from 132.5% a year earlier.

Jun. '86—FFC acquired Manufacturers Hanover Mortgage Corp. (renamed Fireman's Fund Mortgage Corp.) for $252 million in cash. The mortgage banking firm is the third largest in the U.S., servicing a portfolio of more than 367,000 loans totaling nearly $15 billion.

Per Share Data ($)
Yr. End Dec. 31

	1985	1984
Book Value	20.31	NA
Earnings	NA	¹0.14
Dividends	0.07½	Nil
Payout Ratio	NA	Nil
Prices—High	33⅞	NA
Low	25¾	NA
P/E Ratio—	NA	NA

Data as orig. reptd.; prior to 1985 data as reptd. in Preliminary Prospectus dated Sep. 11, 1985. 1. Pro forma. 2. Six mos. NA-Not Available. NM-Not Meaningful. d-Deficit. E-Estimated.

Standard NYSE Stock Reports
Vol. 53/No. 173/Sec. 6

September 8, 1986
Copyright © 1986 Standard & Poor's Corp. All Rights Reserved

Standard & Poor's Corp.
25 Broadway, NY, NY 10004

887   Fireman's Fund Corporation

Income Data (Million $)

Year Ended Dec. 31	Premium Income	Net Invest. Inc.	Total Revs.	Property & Casualty —Underwriting Ratios—			Net Bef. Taxes	Net Oper. Inc.	Net Inc.	—% Return On—	
				³Loss	³Expense	³Comb.				Revs.	Equity
1985	2,855	476	3,350	91.9%	31.6%	123.5%	d197	d45	d44	NM	NM
1984	2,834	397	3,287	88.9%	32.2%	121.1%	d192	¹ 9	¹ 9	0.3%	0.6%
1983	2,708	420	3,209	89.4%	36.6%	126.0%	d260	12	12	0.4%	0.9%
1982	2,587	328	2,970	70.7%	33.8%	104.5%	199	229	229	7.7%	17.0%
1981	2,431	299	2,770	NA	NA	103.2%	232	220	220	7.9%	17.1%
1980	2,395	265	2,689	NA	NA	103.3%	196	198	198	7.4%	NA

Balance Sheet Data (Million $)

Dec. 31	Cash & Equiv.	Accts. Receiv.	²Bonds	Stocks	Loans	Total	Invest. Yield	Deferred Policy Costs	Total Assets	Debt	Common Equity
1985	28	977	5,439	298	Nil	5,737	9.4%	268	7,986	250	1,344
1984	25	949	4,241	98	Nil	4,339	9.2%	270	6,862	Nil	1,485
1983	27	882	3,950	335	Nil	4,285	10.2%	289	6,394	Nil	1,304

Data as orig. reptd.; prior to 1985 data as reptd in Preliminary Prospectus dated Sep. 11, 1985. 1. Pro Forma. 2. Incl. short-term invest. 3. As reptd. by Co. NA-Not Available. NM-Not Meaningful. d-Deficit.

Business Summary

Fireman's Fund Corp., which was wholly-owned by American Express Co. from 1968 through October 23, 1985, is a holding company engaged through subsidiaries in providing a full line of property and casualty insurance throughout the U.S. On the basis of direct premiums written in 1984, the company ranked as the nation's seventh largest property and casualty insurer and fourth largest commercial insurer. Contributions to pretax income (loss) in recent years were as follows (million $):

	1985	1984
Commercial lines	−$590	−$558
Personal lines	−82	−40
Investment income	476	369
Other	−1	37

Net premiums written in 1985 totaled $2.9 billion, of which commercial insurance accounted for 75%. Personal lines, which consisted primarily of homeowners and automobile policies, accounted for 25%. In 1985 24% of direct premiums written originated in California.

Fireman's Fund and National Indemnity Insurance Corp., a wholly-owned subsidiary of Berkshire Hathaway Inc., have entered into a four year quota-share reinsurance agreement commencing September 1, 1985. The net effect of the reinsurance treaty is that National Indemnity is participating with FFC on an equal basis to the extent of 7% of FFC's earned premiums and costs, and, in effect, is investing a portion of its statutory surplus in support of FFC's insurance underwriting operations.

At December 31, 1985 FFC's investment portfolio aggregated $5.7 billion and included $2.0 billion of U.S. Government securities with aggregate maturities of 4.1 years and cash and cash equiva-

lents of $1.8 billion. In August, 1985 Fireman's Fund sold its life insurance operations to American Express Travel Related Services for $330 million in cash.

Dividend Data

Directors have established a policy of declaring quarterly dividends on FFC's common stock. Payments have been initiated as follows:

Amt. of Divd. $	Date Decl.	Ex-divd. Date	Stock of Record	Payment Date
0.07½	Nov. 6	Nov. 14	Nov. 20	Dec. 11'85
0.07½	Feb. 19	Feb. 21	Feb. 27	Mar. 20'86
0.07½	May 14	May 22	May 29	Jun. 19'86
0.07½	Aug. 13	Aug. 21	Aug. 27	Sep. 17'86

Finances

On October 23, 1985 underwriters headed by Shearson Lehman Brothers Inc. and Salomon Brothers Inc. sold 35.2 million common shares of Fireman's Fund Corp. at $25.75 each. Of the total, 8 million shares were sold for Firemen's Fund and 27.2 million shares for American Express Co. The sale reduced AXP's interest in FFC to 41% from 100%. This stake was further reduced to 27% in May, 1986 through AXP's sale of nine million units, each consisting of one share of FFC and one warrant to purchase FFC common stock from AXP (two warrants entitle the holder to purchase one FFC common share from AXP at $43.70 per share). The offering price was $41.50 per unit. In addition FFC acquired from AXP, for $25 million, warrants to purchase five million FFC common shares at $46 each now held by AXP.

Capitalization

Long Term Debt: $245,000,000

Common Stock: 66,219,585 shs. ($1 par).
American Express Co. holds approximately 27%.

Office—777 San Marin Drive, Novato, Calif. 94998 Tel—(415) 899-2000 Chrmn & CEO—J. J. Byrne Pres—W. M. McCormick. VP-Secy—F. W. Benedict. VP-Treas—R. M. Marto. Investor Contact—D. Kalis. Dirs—K. J. Arrow, S. T. Black, R. W. Bruce III, D. B. Burke, J. J. Byrne, H. C. Clark, H. L. Clark, Jr., W. D. Davis, A. Delaney, A. W. Eames Jr., G. L. Gillespie, L. W. Glucksman, G. L. Hough, W. M. McCormick, W. F. Miller, J. D. Robinson III, A. M. Wilson. Transfer Agent & Registrar—Morgan Guaranty Trust Co., NYC. Incorporated in Delaware in 1980.

Information has been obtained from sources believed to be reliable, but its accuracy and completeness are not guaranteed.   Richard M. Levine

When John Byrne took over as Chairman of GEICO in 1976, it was on the verge of bankruptcy. GEICO had plummeted from a high of $61.30 per share in 1972 to a low of close to $2 by 1976.

At GEICO Byrne instituted an extensive cost-cutting program that enabled the company to operate profitably in its niche as a low cost provider. As an illustration of Byrne's accomplishments, GEICO's expense ratio had declined to 15 percent by 1982 from 18 percent in 1979 while for the property and casualty industry overall the ratio rose to 28 percent.

Robert W. Bruce III established his reputation as a money manager at top performing Cumberland Associates. Cumberland has specialized in risk avoidance by broad diversification in small, out-of-favor stocks.

Cumberland ranked 13th among a group of 135 money managers for the four years ended in June 1986. The firm earned an annual return of 35.4 percent, compared to 28.5 percent for the S&P 500 during that period. Since the firm's inception in 1970 with $15 million under management, funds have grown to $566 million.

Fireman's Fund Corporation: Business

Fireman's Fund is the nation's 11th largest property and casualty (p&c) insurer and the 7th largest in the commercial area. Headquartered in Novato, California, FFC was founded in 1863 in San Francisco.

Commercial p&c insurance is the backbone of Fireman's business. A nationwide network of 48 offices services the 8,900 independent agents and brokers who sell the company's products.

Investment Case for Fireman's Fund

The considerable investment talent recently assembled at Fireman's have a high stake in the future of the company.

- Buffett's investment in FFC is through Berkshire Hathaway's reinsurance subsidiary which receives 7 percent of FFC's net premiums over the next four years. Thus Buffett's investment will grow in proportion to FFC's growth.
- Byrne's financial incentives dwarf those of other managerial superstars. His total package gives him the right to purchase 2.5 million shares for $67 million at an average cost of $26.80 per share.
- Bruce and his staff have been given a substantial profit sharing incentive on the investment results of $800 million of Fireman's assets set up in a separate account.

The involvement of Buffett, Byrne and Bruce suggests that Fireman's should be considered a core holding like Capital Cities/ABC and CBS. . . . Earnings leverage is large, and the marked turnaround in earnings already evident should result in a upward valuation of the stock. FFC is particularly well situated, as 80 percent of net premiums are derived from commercial

FIREMAN'S FUND CORPORATION

(Based on current price and 12-month data as of June 30, 1986.)

Price 9/16/86	52 week range	Earnings p/share 1986E	1987E	P/E ratio 1986	1987	*Cash flow p/sh	Price/csh flow	Bk value p/sh	Price/bv	Debt/capt.
34¾	45–26	$2.75	$4.20	12.6	8.3	$11.34	3.06	$21.81	1.59	14.5%

* From operations.

Financial Summary (dollars in millions, except per share amounts)

	Six months ended June 30 1986	1985	% Change	1985	1984	1983	1982	1981
REVENUES:								
Earned premiums	$1,497	$1,406	6.5%	$2,855	$2,834	$2,708	$2,587	$2,431
Net investment income	233	232	0.6	476	394	386	311	302
Other revenue	9	9	1.3	19	31	71	36	26
Total	$1,740	$1,647	5.7	3,350	3,259	3,165	2,934	2,759
Operating earnings (loss)	$70	$ (88)	NMF	(189)	(180)	(298)	(144)	(169)
Net income (loss)	85	(87)	NMF	(40)	2	9	208	190
Per common share:								
Operating earnings	$1.06	—	—	(189)	(180)	(298)	(144)	(169)
Net income	$1.29	—	—	(40)	2	9	208	190
PROPERTY-LIABILITY								
Net premiums written	$1,654	$1,535	7.7%	$2,912	$2,834	$2,781	$2,637	$2,476
Combined Underwriting ratio	109.8%	132.5%	22.7 pts.	123.5%	121.1%	126.0%	104.5%	103.2%
Loss and loss adjustment expense ratio	77.6%	97.6%	20.0%	89.5%	86.4%	86.5%	68.3%	67.4%
Underwriting expense ratio	31.7%	32.5%	0.8%	31.6%	32.2%	36.6%	33.8%	33.5%

Earnings per share calculated for 1986 periods only; Fireman's Fund became a publicly traded company on October 23, 1985. Six months 1986 excludes the results of life insurance operations sold August 31, 1985.

lines where dramatic price increases are being effected. . . . Commercial premium increases at FFC averaged 34 percent in 1985. Earnings per share are estimated to reach $4.50 in 1987. At FFC's current price of 34 ¾, the stock would be selling at nearly a 45 percent P/E discount to the market at current levels. Note that p&c companies typically sell at about a 20 percent discount to the market on peak earnings. Four consecutive quarters of improving profits through June 1986 have been experienced. The turnaround is solidly based on initiatives taken in 1983 when American Express put William McCormick, a highly respected American Express turnaround veteran, at FFC to correct several years of operating losses and inadequate reserve provisions. See the table above for FFC's financial history.

Important steps implemented by McCormick at FFC include:

- Operating cost reductions. Expenses were cut to 31.6 percent of premiums by year's end 1985, from 36.6 percent two years earlier.
- Loss reserve increases. $600 million in charges have bolstered loss reserves to an adequate level.
- Better quality underwriting and aggressive pricing. The underwriting ratio improved to 109.8 percent in the first half of 1986 versus 132.5 percent in the 1985 period. . . .

Fireman's is committed to top performance on its investment side as well as on its insurance side. With the help of Buffett and Bruce, Byrne will pursue active portfolio management focusing on value-oriented investments in contrast to the usually passively managed insurance portfolio. . . .

The loss-ridden years of 1982 to 1985 have wrung out the excesses in the industry. Record operating losses sustained in 1984 and 1985 due to price competition and excessive claims have caused a big shortage of capacity. An early return of pricing competition appears unlikely, based on:

- Capital shortage in the industry.
- Scarce and expensive reinsurance.
- Still inadequate return on capital.
- Considerably lower investment yields.

Also, earnings visibility is being improved by more predictable liability claims. Curbs are being put on excessive court awards in a number of states due to public outcry over the high cost and scarcity of insurance.

Risks include the sharp increases occurring in commercial p&c rates are prompting businesses to self-insure. Also, an always present risk with p&c companies is the possibility of higher than predicted claims and losses that exceed reserves. . . .

(Courtesy *Street Smart Investing,* No. 181, September 18, 1986)

APPENDIX II

Berkshire Hathaway's Principal Year's End Holdings
(1976–1986)

Table 1—1976 (over $3 million)

No. of Shares	Company	Cost
141,987	California Water Service Company	$ 3,608,711
1,986,953	Government Employees Insurance Company Convertible Preferred	19,416,635
1,294,308	Government Employees Insurance Company Common Stock	4,115,670
395,100	Interpublic Group of Companies	4,530,615
582,900	Kaiser Industries, Inc.	8,270,871
188,900	Munsingwear, Inc.	3,398,404
83,400	National Presto Industries, Inc.	1,689,896
170,800	Ogilvy & Mather International	2,762,433
934,300	The Washington Post Company Class B	10,627,604
	Total	$58,420,839
	All Other Holdings	16,974,375
	Total Equities	$75,395,214

Table 2—1977 (over $5 million)

No. of Shares	Company	Cost	Market
		(000's omitted)	
220,000	Capital Cities Communications, Inc.	$ 10,909	$ 13,228
1,986,953	Government Employees Insurance Company Convertible Preferred	19,417	33,033
1,294,308	Government Employees Insurance Company Common Stock	4,116	10,516
592,650	The Interpublic Group of Companies, Inc.	4,531	17,187
324,580	Kaiser Aluminum & Chemical Corporation	11,218	9,981
1,305,800	Kaiser Industries, Inc.	778	6,039
226,900	Knight-Ridder Newspapers, Inc.	7,534	8,736
170,800	Ogilvy & Mather International, Inc.	2,762	6,960
934,300	The Washington Post Company Class B	10,628	33,401
	Total	$ 71,893	$139,081
	All Other Holdings	34,996	41,992
	Total Equities	$106,889	$181,073

Table 3—1978 (over $8 million)

No. of Shares	Company	Cost	Market
		(000's omitted)	
246,450	American Broadcasting Companies, Inc.	$ 6,082	$ 8,626
1,294,308	Government Employees Insurance Company Common Stock	4,116	9,060
1,986,953	Government Employees Insurance Company Convertible Preferred	19,417	28,314
592,650	Interpublic Group of Companies, Inc.	4,531	19,039
1,066,934	Kaiser Aluminum & Chemical Corporation	18,085	18,671
453,800	Knight-Ridder Newspapers, Inc.	7,534	10,267
953,750	SAFECO Corporation	23,867	26,467
934,300	The Washington Post Company	10,628	43,445
	Total	$ 94,260	$163,889
	All Other Holdings	39,506	57,040
	Total Equities	$133,766	$220,929

168APPENDIXES

Table 4—1979 (over $5 million)

No. of Shares	Company	Cost	Market
		(000's omitted)	
289,700	Affiliated Publications, Inc.	$ 2,821	$ 8,800
112,545	Amerada Hess	2,861	5,487
246,450	American Broadcasting Companies, Inc.	6,082	9,673
5,730,114	GEICO Corp. (Common Stock)	28,288	68,045
328,700	General Foods, Inc.	11,437	11,053
1,007,500	Handy & Harman	21,825	38,537
711,180	Interpublic Group of Companies, Inc.	4,531	23,736
1,211,834	Kaiser Aluminum & Chemical Corp.	20,629	23,328
282,500	Media General, Inc.	4,545	7,345
391,400	Ogilvy & Mather International	3,709	7,828
953,750	SAFECO Corporation	23,867	35,527
1,868,000	The Washington Post Company	10,628	39,241
771,900	F. W. Woolworth Company	15,515	19,394
	Total	$156,738	$297,994
	All Other Holdings	28,675	38,686
	Total Equities	$185,413	$336,680

Table 5—1980 (over $5 million)

No. of Shares	Company	Cost	Market
		(000's omitted)	
434,550 (a)	Affiliated Publications, Inc.	$ 2,821	$ 12,222
464,317 (a)	Aluminum Company of America	25,577	27,685
475,217 (b)	Cleveland-Cliffs Iron Company	12,942	15,894
1,983,812 (b)	General Foods, Inc.	62,507	59,889
7,200,000 (a)	GEICO Corporation	47,138	105,300
2,015,000 (a)	Handy & Harman	21,825	58,435
711,180 (a)	Interpublic Group of Companies, Inc.	4,531	22,135
1,211,834 (a)	Kaiser Aluminum & Chemical Corp.	20,629	27,569
282,500 (a)	Media General	4,545	8,334
247,039 (b)	National Detroit Corporation	5,930	6,299
881,500 (a)	National Student Marketing	5,128	5,895
391,400 (a)	Ogilvy & Mather Int'l. Inc.	3,709	9,981
370,088 (a)	Pinkerton's, Inc.	12,144	16,489
245,700 (b)	R. J. Reynolds Industries	8,702	11,228
1,250,525 (b)	SAFECO Corporation	32,062	45,177
151,104 (b)	The Times Mirror Company	4,447	6,271
1,868,600 (a)	The Washington Post Company	10,628	42,277
667,124 (b)	F. W. Woolworth Company	13,583	16,511
		$298,848	$497,591
	All Other Common Stockholdings	26,313	32,096
	Total Common Stocks	$325,161	$529,687

(a) All owned by Berkshire or its insurance subsidiaries.

(b) Blue Chip and/or Wesco own shares of these companies. All numbers represent Berkshire's net interest in the larger gross holdings of the group.

Table 6—1981 (over $11 million)

No. of Shares	Company	Cost	Market
		(000's omitted)	
451,650 (a)	Affiliated Publications, Inc.	$ 3,297	$ 14,114
703,634 (a)	Aluminum Company of America	19,359	18,031
420,441 (a)	Arcata Corporation (including common equivalents)	14,076	15,136
475,217 (b)	Cleveland-Cliffs Iron Company	12,942	14,362
441,522 (a)	GATX Corporation	17,147	13,466
2,101,244 (b)	General Foods, Inc.	66,277	66,714
7,200,000 (a)	GEICO Corporation	47,138	199,800
2,015,000 (a)	Handy & Harman	21,825	36,270
711,180 (a)	Interpublic Group of Companies, Inc.	4,531	23,202
282,500 (a)	Media General	4,545	11,088
391,400 (a)	Ogilvy & Mather International Inc.	3,709	12,329
370,088 (b)	Pinkerton's, Inc.	12,144	19,675
1,764,824 (b)	R. J. Reynolds Industries, Inc.	76,668	83,127
785,225 (b)	SAFECO Corporation	21,329	31,016
1,868,600 (a)	The Washington Post Company	10,628	58,160
		$335,615	$616,490
	All Other Common Stockholdings	16,131	22,739
	Total Common Stocks	$351,746	$639,229

(a) All owned by Berkshire or its insurance subsidiaries.

(b) Blue Chip and/or Wesco own shares of these companies. All numbers represent Berkshire's net interest in the larger gross holdings of the group.

Table 7—1982 (over $12 million)

No. of Shares or Share Equiv.	Company	Cost	Market
		(000's omitted)	
460,650 (a)	Affiliated Publications, Inc.	$ 3,516	$ 16,929
908,800 (c)	Crum & Forster	47,144	48,962
2,101,244 (b)	General Foods, Inc.	66,277	83,680
7,200,000 (a)	GEICO Corporation	47,138	309,600
2,379,200 (a)	Handy & Harman	27,318	46,692
711,180 (a)	Interpublic Group of Companies, Inc.	4,531	34,314
282,500 (a)	Media General	4,545	12,289
391,400 (a)	Ogilvy & Mather Int'l. Inc.	3,709	17,319
3,107,675 (b)	R. J. Reynolds Industries	142,343	158,715
1,531,391 (a)	Time, Inc.	45,273	79,824
1,868,600 (a)	The Washington Post Company	10,628	103,240
		$402,422	$911,564
	All Other Common Stockholdings	21,611	34,058
	Total Common Stocks	$424,033	$945,622

(a) All owned by Berkshire or its insurance subsidiaries.

(b) Blue Chip and/or Wesco own shares of these companies. All numbers represent Berkshire's net interest in the larger gross holdings of the group.

(c) Temporary holding as cash substitute.

Table 8—1983 (over $11 million)

No. of Shares	Company	Cost	Market
		(000's omitted)	
690,975	Affiliated Publications, Inc.	$ 3,516	$ 26,603
4,451,544	General Foods Corporation[a]	163,786	228,698
6,850,000	GEICO Corporation	47,138	398,156
2,379,200	Handy & Harman	27,318	42,231
636,310	Interpublic Group of Companies, Inc.	4,056	33,088
197,200	Media General	3,191	11,191
250,400	Ogilvy & Mather International	2,580	12,833
5,618,661	R. J. Reynolds Industries, Inc.[a]	268,918	314,334
901,788	Time, Inc.	27,732	56,860
1,868,600	The Washington Post Company	10,628	136,875
		$558,863	$1,287,869
	All Other Common Stockholdings	7,485	18,044
	Total Common Stocks	$566,348	$1,305,913

[a] Wesco owns shares in these companies.

Table 9—1984 (over $27 million)

No. of Shares	Company	Cost	Market
		(000's omitted)	
690,975	Affiliated Publications, Inc.	$ 3,516	$ 32,908
740,400	American Broadcasting Companies, Inc.	44,416	46,738
3,895,710	Exxon Corporation	173,401	175,307
4,047,191	General Foods Corporation	149,870	226,137
6,850,000	GEICO Corporation	45,713	397,300
2,379,200	Handy & Harman	27,318	38,662
818,872	Interpublic Group of Companies, Inc.	2,570	28,149
555,949	Northwest Industries	26,581	27,242
2,553,488	Time, Inc.	89,327	109,162
1,868,600	The Washington Post Company	10,628	149,955
		$573,340	$1,231,560
	All Other Common Stockholdings	11,634	37,326
	Total Common Stocks	$584,974	$1,268,886

Table 10—1985 (over $43 million)

No. of Shares	Company	Cost	Market
		(000's omitted)	
1,036,461	Affiliated Publications, Inc.	$ 3,516	$ 55,710
900,800	American Broadcasting Companies, Inc.	54,435	108,997
2,350,922	Beatrice Companies, Inc.	106,811	108,142
6,850,000	GEICO Corporation	45,713	595,950
2,379,200	Handy & Harman	27,318	43,718
847,788	Time, Inc.	20,385	52,669
1,727,765	The Washington Post Company	9,731	205,172
		267,909	1,170,358
	All Other Common Stockholdings	7,201	27,963
	Total Common Stocks	$275,110	$1,198,321

174 APPENDIXES

Table 11—1986 (through September 30, 1986)

Common Stocks	No. of Shares	Market
	(000's omitted)	
Burroughs Corp.	1,850,244	92,512
	42,319	2,116
	821,518	41,076
Capital Cities/ABC Inc.	1,850,000	461,806
	950,000	237,144
	150,000	37,444
	50,000	12,481
City Natl Corp	28,784	590
GEICO Corp	4,409,012	422,163
	2,153,535	206,201
	134,431	12,872
	153,022	14,652
Handy & Harman	1,586,000	29,341
	544,800	10,079
	88,400	1,635
	160,000	2,960
National Svc Inds Inc	209,865	6,742
	52,000	1,671
	337,130	10,830
FirsTier Inc.	114,076	3,109
	18,000	490
	9,472	258
	17,600	480
Reynolds RJ Inds Inc.	14,894	1,854
	10,291	1,281
Washington Post Co	1,042,615	147,530
	648,165	91,715
	36,985	5,233
Wesco Finl Corp	5,703,087	227,411

APPENDIX III

Buffett's Epistles: Extracts from Berkshire Hathaway's Annual Reports

In the investment community, the annual reports of Berkshire Hathaway are regarded as models for such productions, and alas are sometimes considered almost the only good annual reports put out by an American corporation. Most corporate reports are designed to sell the corporation's image, both to its shareholders and to its customers, almost like a brochure for a resort hotel: huge, luscious pictures of the product line and scenes in the factory, usually embellished by irrelevant shots of pretty girls. The figures are there, but not always presented in the frankest way. The president's message sounds like an army recruiter's spiel. You know it's not the whole story. As Philip Fisher observes, if a divisional vice president of a corporation reported to his chief executive officer in the language of a corporate annual report, he would be fired. And yet, the owners of the company—the shareholders—tolerate this pap when the chief executive officer writes to them.*

Anyway, Buffett's reports are usually more cheerful reading than those of other companies, basically because Berkshire Hathaway has done well; nevertheless, they offer no pretty girls or other adornment. His messages to the shareholders are simple, chatty, and straightforward. He goes to great lengths to explain accounting concepts, to make clear what is really happening beneath the level of the figures that are being presented, and to explain the nature of the various businesses in which Berkshire Hathaway has an interest, so that the shareholder knows what to expect in future years, so far as this can be predicted.

Buffett also differs from most American CEOs in giving elaborate credit to the day-to-day operators of the businesses Berkshire controls. Rightly, since it is remarkable when the manager of a business that has sold out to a larger one goes on working as hard for the new owner as he did for himself. Such praise costs nothing and gratifies all concerned. Extracts from some of Buffett's reports follow.

---

* The annual reports of English companies have a special charm. They often avoid the technicolor hype of our reports, which the shareholders would consider vulgar, as though there were cheerleaders at a cricket match. Instead, the chairman delivers himself of several pages of pontification on the state of the economy and the world, and discusses the errors of the government in coping with them, just as though he were head of a Royal Commission, which indeed he probably has been, will be, or would like to be.

The Banking Business

Our banking subsidiary, The Illinois National Bank & Trust Company, continued to lead its industry as measured by earnings as a percentage of deposits. In 1971, Illinois National earned well over 2 percent after tax on average deposits while (1) not using borrowed funds except for very occasional reserve balancing transactions; (2) maintaining a liquidity position far above average; (3) recording loan losses far below average; and (4) utilizing a mix of over 50% time deposits with all consumer savings accounts receiving maximum permitted interest rates throughout the year. This reflects a superb management job by Gene Abegg and Bob Kline.

Interest rates received on loans and investments were down substantially throughout the banking industry during 1971. In the last few years, Illinois National's mix of deposits has moved considerably more than the industry average away from demand money to much more expensive time money. For example, interest paid on deposits has gone from under $1.7 million in 1969 to over $2.7 million in 1971. Nevertheless, the unusual profitability of the Bank has been maintained. Marketing efforts were intensified during the year, with excellent results.

With interest rates even lower now than in 1971, the banking industry is going to have trouble achieving gains in earnings during 1972. Our deposit gains at Illinois National continue to come in the time money area, which produces only very marginal incremental income at present. It will take very close cost control to enable Illinois National to maintain its 1971 level of earnings during 1972.

1971

Our banking subsidiary, The Illinois National Bank and Trust Co. of Rockford, maintained its position of industry leadership in profitability. After-tax earnings of 2.2% on average deposits in 1972 are the more remarkable when evaluated against such moderating factors as: (1) a mix of 60% time deposits heavily weighted toward consumer savings instruments, all paying the maximum rates permitted by law: (2) an unvarying strong liquid position and avoidance of money-market borrowings: (3) a loan policy which has produced a net charge-off ratio in the last two years of about 5% of that of the average commercial bank. This record is a direct tribute to the leadership of Gene Abegg and Bob Kline who run a bank where the owners and the depositors can both eat well and sleep well.

During 1972, interest paid to depositors was double the amount paid in 1969. We have aggressively sought consumer time deposits, but have not pushed for large "money market" certificates of deposit although, during the past several years, they have generally been a less costly source of time funds.

During the past year, loans to our customers expanded approximately 38%. This is considerably more than indicated by the enclosed balance sheet which includes $10.9 million in short-term commercial paper in the 1971 loan total, but which has no such paper included at the end of 1972.

Our position as "Rockford's leading bank" was enhanced during 1972. Present rate structure, a decrease in investable funds due to new Federal Reserve collection procedures, and a probable increase in already substantial nonfederal taxes make it unlikely that Illinois National will be able to increase its earnings during 1973.

1972

The Illinois National Bank & Trust Co. of Rockford again had a record year in 1973. Average deposits were approximately $130 million, of which approximately 60% were time deposits. Interest rates were increased substantially in the important consumer savings area when regulatory maximums were raised at mid-year.

Despite this mix heavily weighted toward interest bearing deposits, our operating earnings after taxes including a new Illinois state income tax were again over 2.1% of average deposits.

We continue to be the largest bank in Rockford. We continue to maintain unusual liquidity. We continue to meet the increasing loan demands of our customers. And we continue to maintain our unusual profitability. This is a direct tribute to the abilities of Gene Abegg, Chairman, who has been running the Bank since it opened its doors in 1931, and Bob Kline, our President.

1973

There is little new to say about Illinois National Bank and Trust. With Eugene Abegg running the operation, the exceptional has become the commonplace. Year after year he continues to run one of the most profitable banks in the United States, while paying maximum interest rates to depositors, operating with unusual levels of liquidity, and maintaining a superior level of loan quality.

Two factors specifically should be noted in looking at the separate income statement of the bank. The effect of filing a consolidated tax return is reflected in their figures, with the tax loss of the insurance operations used to offset the tax liability created by banking operations. Also, a property tax formerly paid by the bank now is assessed to the parent company and is reflected in corporate selling and administrative expense. Because of accruals, this had a double effect at both the bank and corporate level in 1974.

Under present money conditions, we expect bank earnings to be down somewhat in 1975 although we believe they still are likely to compare favorably with those of practically any banking institution in the country.

It is difficult to find adjectives to describe the performance of Eugene Abegg, Chief Executive of Illinois National Bank and Trust of Rockford, Illinois, our banking subsidiary.

In a year when many banking operations experienced major troubles, Illinois National continued its outstanding record. Against average loans of about $65 million, net loan losses were $24,000, or .04%. Unusually high liquidity is maintained with obligations of the U.S. Government and its agencies, all due within one year, at yearend amounting to about 75% of demand deposits. Maximum rates of interest are paid on all consumer savings instruments which make up more than half of the deposit base. Yet despite the maintenance of premier liquidity and the avoidance of "stretching" for high yield loans, the Illinois National continues as about the most profitable bank of its size, or larger, in the country.

1974

In 1975 the thirty largest banks in the United States earned an average of .5% on total assets. The Illinois National earned about four times that much. These same thirty largest banks carried down 7% of operating revenues to net income. Without counting any tax benefits from consolidation, Illinois National carried down 27%.

Gene Abegg opened the doors of the Illinois National Bank in 1931 with paid-in capital of $250,000. In 1932, its first full year of operation, it earned $8,782. No additional capital has been paid in.

Under the present interest rate structure, it is expected that earnings of the Bank will be off somewhat during 1976 but still will remain at a highly satisfactory level.

Eugene Abegg, Chief Executive of Illinois National Bank and Trust Company of Rockford, Illinois, our banking subsidiary, continues to lead the parade among bankers—just as he has ever since he opened the bank in 1931.

1975

Recently, National City Corp. of Cleveland, truly an outstandingly well-managed bank, ran an ad stating "the ratio of earnings to average assets was 1.34% in 1976 which we believe to be the best percentage for any major banking company." Among the really large banks this was the best earnings achievement but, at the Illinois National Bank, earnings were close to 50% better than those of National City, or approximately 2% of average assets.

This outstanding earnings record again was achieved while:

1. paying maximum rates of interest on all consumer savings instruments (time deposits now make up well over two-thirds of the deposit base at the Illinois National Bank),

2. maintaining an outstanding liquidity position (Federal funds sold plus U.S. Government and Agency issues of under six months' duration presently are approximately equal to demand deposits), and

3. avoiding high-yield but second-class loans (net loan losses in 1976 came to about $12,000, or .02% of outstanding loans, a very tiny fraction of the ratio prevailing in 1976 in the banking industry).

Cost control is an important factor in the bank's success. Employment is still at about the level existing at the time of purchase in 1969 despite growth in consumer time deposits from $30 million to $90 million and considerable expansion in other activities such as trust, travel and data processing.

1976

The Insurance Business

An unusual combination of factors reduced auto accident frequency, sharply higher effective rates in large volume lines, and the absence of major catastrophes produced an extraordinarily good year for the property and casualty insurance industry. We shared in these benefits, although they are not without their negative connotations.

Our traditional business and still our largest segment is in the specialized policy or non standard insured. When standard markets become tight because of unprofitable industry underwriting, we experience substantial volume increases as producers look to us. This was the condition several years ago, and largely accounts for the surge of direct volume experienced in 1970 and 1971. Now that underwriting has turned very profitable on an industry-wide basis, more companies are seeking the insureds they were rejecting a short while back and rates are being cut in some areas. We continue to have underwriting profitability as our primary goal and this may well mean a substantial decrease in National Indemnity's direct volume during 1972. Jack Ringwalt and Phil Liesche continue to guide this operation in a manner matched by very few in the business.

We entered the reinsurance business late in 1969 at a time when rates had risen substantially and capacity was tight. The reinsurance industry was exceptionally profitable in 1971, and we are now seeing rate-cutting, as well as the formation of well-capitalized aggressive new competitors. These lower rates are frequently accompanied by greater exposure. Against this background we expect to see our business curtailed somewhat in 1972. We set no volume goals in our insurance business generally—and certainly not in reinsurance—as virtually any volume can be achieved if profitability standards are ignored. When catastrophes occur and underwriting experience sours, we plan to have the resources available to handle the increasing volume which we will then expect to be available at proper prices.

We inaugurated our "home-state" insurance operation in 1970 by the formation of Cornhusker Casualty Company. To date, this has worked well from both a marketing and an underwriting standpoint. We have therefore further developed this approach by the formation of Lakeland Fire & Casualty Company in Minnesota during 1971, and Texas United Insurance in 1972. Each of these companies will devote its entire efforts to a single state seeking to bring to the agents and insureds of its area a combination of large company capability and small company accessibility and sensitivity. John Ringwalt has been in overall charge of this operation since inception. Combining hard work with imagination and intelligence, he has transformed an idea into a well organized business. The "home-state" companies are still very small, accounting for a little over $1.5 million in premium volume during 1971. It looks as though this volume will more than double in 1972 and we will develop a more creditable base upon which to evaluate underwriting performance.

A highlight of 1971 was the acquisition of Home & Automobile Insurance Company, located in Chicago. This company was built by Victor Raab from a small initial investment into a major auto insurer in Cook County, writing about $7.5 million in premium volume during 1971. Vic is cut from the same cloth as Jack Ringwalt and Gene Abegg, with a talent for operating profitably accompanied by enthusiasm for his business. These three men have built their companies from scratch and, after selling their ownership position for cash, retain every bit of the proprietary interest and pride that they have always had.

While Vic has multiplied the original equity of Home & Auto many times since its founding, his ideas and talents have always been circumscribed by his capital base. We have added capital funds to the company, which will enable it to establish branch operations extending its highly-concentrated and on-the-spot marketing and claims approach to other densely populated areas.

All in all, it is questionable whether volume added by Home & Auto, plus the "home-state" business in 1972, will offset possible declines in direct and reinsurance business of National Indemnity Company. However, our large volume gains in 1970 and 1971 brought in additional funds for investment at a time of high interest rates, which will be of continuing benefit in future years. Thus, despite the unimpressive prospects regarding premium volume, the outlook for investment income and overall earnings from insurance in 1972 is reasonably good.

1971

In the last few years we consistently have commented on the unusual profitability in insurance underwriting. This seemed certain eventually to attract unintelligent competition with consequent inadequate rates. It also has been apparent that many insurance organizations, major as well as minor, have been guilty of significant underreserving of losses, which inevitably produces faulty information as to the true cost of the product being sold. In 1974, these factors, along with a high rate of inflation, combined to produce a rapid erosion in underwriting results.

The costs of the product we deliver (auto repair, medical payments, compensation benefits, etc.) are increasing at a rate we estimate to be in the area of 1% per month. Of course, this increase doesn't proceed in an even flow but, inexorably, inflation grinds very heavily at the repair services—to humans and to property—that we provide. However, rates virtually have been unchanged in the property and casualty field for the last few years. With costs moving forward rapidly and prices remaining unchanged, it was not hard to predict what would happen to profit margins.

Best's, the authoritative voice of the insurance industry, estimate that in 1974 all auto insurance premiums in the United States increased only about 2%. Such a growth in the pool of dollars available to pay insured losses and expenses was woefully inadequate. Obviously, medical costs applicable to people injured during the year, jury awards for pain and suffering, and body shop charges for repairing damaged cars increased at a dramatically greater rate during the year. Since premiums represent the sales dollar and the latter items represent the cost of goods sold, profit margins turned sharply negative.

As this report is being written, such deterioration continues. Loss reserves for many giant companies still appear to be understated by significant amounts, which means that these competitors continue to underestimate their true costs. Not only must rates be increased sufficiently to match the month-by-month increase in cost levels, but the existing expense-revenue gap must be overcome. At this time it appears that insurers must experience even more devastating underwriting results before they take appropriate pricing action.

All major areas of insurance operations, except for the "home state" companies, experienced significantly poorer results for the year.

The direct business of National Indemnity Company, our largest area of insurance activity, produced an underwriting loss of approximately 4% after several years of high profitability. Volume increased somewhat, but we are not encouraging such increases until rates are more adequate. At some point in the cycle, after major insurance companies have had their fill of red ink, history indicates that we will experience an inflow of business at compensatory rates. This operation, headed by Phil Liesche, a most able underwriter, is staffed by highly profit-oriented people and we believe it will provide excellent earnings in most future years, as it has in the past.

Intense competition in the reinsurance business has produced major losses for practically every company operating in the area. We have been no exception. Our underwriting loss was something over 12%—a horrendous figure, but probably little different from the average of the industry. What is even more frightening is that, while about the usual number of insurance catastrophes occurred during 1974, there really was no "super disaster" which might have accounted for the poor figures of the industry. Rather, a condition of inadequate rates prevails, particularly in the casualty area where we have significant exposure. Our reinsurance department is run by George Young, an exceptionally competent and hardworking manager. He has canceled a great many contracts where prices are totally inadequate, and is making no attempt to increase volume except in areas where premiums are commensurate with risk. Based upon present rate levels, it seems highly unlikely that the reinsurance industry generally, or we, specifically, will have a profitable year in 1975. While the tone of this section is pessimistic as to 1974 and 1975, we consider the insurance business to be inherently attractive. Our overall return on capital employed in this area—even including the poor results in 1974—remains high. We have made every effort to be realistic in the calculation of loss and expense reserves. Many of our competitors are in a substantially weakened financial position, and our strong capital picture leaves us prepared to grow significantly when conditions become right.

1974

The Effect of Falling Bond Prices on Insurance Companies

Several comments regarding market value of securities may be appropriate. Between the insurance group and the bank, we have approximately $140 million invested in bonds. About $20 million of this investment is in very short-term Treasury securities or commercial paper, neither of which is subject to other than negligible market fluctuation. This leaves about $120 million in bonds of longer maturities, with a very large percentage of this sum in municipal bonds with an average maturity of perhaps twelve to fifteen years. Because of our large liquid position and inherent operating characteristics of our financial businesses, it is quite unlikely that we will be required to sell any quantity of such bonds under disadvantageous conditions. Rather, it is our expectation that these bonds either will be held to maturity or sold at times believed to be advantageous.

However, on any given day the market value of our bond portfolio is determined by yields available on comparable securities. Such market values can swing dramatically. For example, during 1974 a leading index of high-grade municipals increased in yield from a level of 5.18% at the beginning of the year to 7.08% a the end of the year. In the bond market, each 1/100 of 1% change in yield is referred to as a "basis point" and thus, a change of 1% in interest levels is referred to as 100 basis points. As measured by the index bond yields increased 190 basis points during 1974. On a fifteen-year bond, an increase of 10 basis points translates to about a 1% downward change in market value. On $120 million of such bonds, it is therefore clear that a change of 10 basis points in yields (which easily can happen in one day) changes the market value of our bond portfolio by something over $1 million. Thus, in 1974 our bond portfolio, which probably had a market value roughly approximating its carrying value at the start of the year, had a market value substantially below carrying value at the end of the year. The market value of our bond portfolio will continue to move in both directions in response to changes in the general level of yields but we do not consider such movements, and the unrealized gains and losses that they produce, to be of great importance as long as adequate liquidity is maintained.

                                                                    1974

The property and casualty insurance industry had its worst year in history during 1975. We did our share—unfortunately, even somewhat more. Really disastrous results were concentrated in auto and long-tail (contracts where settlement of loss usually occurs long after the loss event) lines.

Economic inflation, with the increase in cost of repairing humans and property far outstripping the general rate of inflation, produced ultimate loss costs which soared beyond premium levels established in a different cost environment. "Social" inflation caused the liability concept to be expanded continuously, far beyond limits contemplated when rates were established—in effect, adding coverage beyond what was paid for. Such social inflation increased significantly both the propensity to sue and the possibility of collecting mammoth jury awards for events not previously considered statistically significant in the establishment of rates. Furthermore, losses to policyholders which otherwise would result from mushrooming insolvencies of companies inadequately reacting to these problems are divided through Guaranty Funds among remaining solvent insurers. These trends will continue, and should moderate any optimism which otherwise might be justified by the sharply increased rates now taking effect.

Berkshire Hathaway's insurance subsidiaries have a disproportionate concentration of business in precisely the lines which produced the worst underwriting results in 1975. Such lines produce unusually high investment income and, therefore, have been particularly attractive to us under previous underwriting conditions. However, our "mix" has been very disadvantageous during the past two years, and it well may be that we will remain positioned in the more difficult part of the insurance spectrum during the inflationary years ahead.

Overall, our insurance operation will produce a substantial gain in premium volume during 1976. Much of this will reflect increased rates rather than more policies. Under normal circumstances such a gain in volume would be welcome, but our emotions are mixed at present. Underwriting experience should improve—and we expect it to—but our confidence level is not high. While our efforts will be devoted to obtaining a combined ratio below 100, it is unlikely to be attained during 1976.

1975

Insurance Operations

We enjoyed an outstanding year for growth in our insurance business, accompanied by a somewhat poorer underwriting picture. Our traditional operation experienced a surge in volume as conventional auto insurance markets became more restricted. This is in line with our history as a nonconventional carrier which receives volume gains on a "wave" basis when standard markets are experiencing capacity or underwriting problems. Although our combined loss and expense ratio on the traditional business rose to approximately 100% during the year, our management, led by Jack Ringwalt and Phil Liesche, has the ability and determination to return it to an underwriting profit.

Our new reinsurance division, managed by George Young, made substantial progress during the year. While an evaluation of this division's underwriting will take some years, initial signs are encouraging. We are producing significant volume in diverse areas of reinsurance and developing a more complete staff in order to handle a much larger volume of business in the future.

The surety business, referred to in last year's report, operated at a significant underwriting loss during 1970. The contractor's bond field was a disappointment and we are restricting our writings to the miscellaneous bond area. This will mean much less volume but, hopefully, underwriting profits.

Our "home-state" operation—Cornhusker Casualty Company, formed in early 1970 as a 100% owned subsidiary of National Indemnity, writing standard business through Nebraska agents only—is off to a strong start. The combination of big-company capability and small-company accessibility is proving to be a strong marketing tool with first-class agents. John Ringwalt deserves credit for translating the concept into reality. Our present plans envision extension of the home-state approach and we plan to have another company in operation later this year.

1970

The Textile Business

Sales in both menswear linings and home fabrics declined significantly during the year. Thus we were continuously forced to modify production plans to prevent inventories from mounting. Such production curtailments were costly to the Company and disruptive to the lives of our employees.

Prices continue at poor levels and demand has not strengthened. Inventory levels, while reduced from a year ago through great effort, continue high in relation to current sales levels. We continue to work at making the changes required in manufacturing and marketing areas that will result in profitable operations with more stable employment.

Led by Ken Chace, the effort, attitude and enterprise manifested by management and labor in this operation have been every bit the equal of their counterparts in our much more profitable businesses. But in the past year they have been swimming against a strong tide and, at this writing, that situation still prevails.

1970

We, in common with most of the textile industry, continued to struggle throughout 1971 with inadequate gross margins. Strong efforts to hammer down costs and a continuous search for less price-sensitive fabrics produced only marginal profits. However, without these efforts we would have operated substantially in the red. Employment was more stable throughout the year as our program to improve control of inventories achieved reasonable success.

As mentioned last year, Ken Chace and his management group have been swimming against a strong industry tide. This negative environment has only caused them to intensify their efforts. Currently we are witnessing a mild industry pickup which we intend to maximize with our greatly strengthened sales force. With the improvement now seen in volume and mix of business, we would expect better profitability, although not of a dramatic nature from our textile operation in 1972.

1971

As predicted in last year's annual report, the textile industry experienced a pickup in 1972. In recent years, Ken Chace and Ralph Rigby have developed an outstanding sales organization enjoying a growing reputation for service and reliability. Manufacturing capabilities have been restructured to complement our sales strengths.

Helped by the industry recovery, we experienced some payoff from these efforts in 1972. Inventories were controlled, minimizing close-out losses in addition to minimizing capital requirements: product mix was greatly improved. While the general level of profitability of the industry will always be the primary factor in determining the level of our textile earnings, we believe that our relative position within the industry has noticeably improved. The outlook for 1973 is good.

1972

Textile demand remained unusually strong throughout 1973. Our main problems revolved around shortages of fiber, which complicated operations and resulted in something less than full utilization of loom capacity. Prices of some fibers skyrocketed during the year.

Cost of Living Council regulations prevented the pricing of many finished products at levels of some of our competitors. However, profits were reasonably commensurate with our capital investment, although below those that apparently might have been achieved had we been able to price at market levels. The textile business has been highly cyclical and price controls may have served to cut down some of the hills while still leaving us with the inevitable valleys.

Because of the extraordinary price rises in raw materials during 1973, which show signs of continuing in 1974, we have elected to adopt the "lifo" method of inventory pricing. This method more nearly matches current costs against current revenues and minimizes inventory "profits" included in reported earnings. Further information on this change is included in the footnotes to our financial statements.

1973

During the first nine months of 1974 textile demand was exceptionally strong, resulting in very firm prices. However, in the fourth quarter significant weaknesses began to appear, which have continued into 1975.

We currently are operating at about one-third of capacity. Obviously, at such levels operating losses must result. As shipments have fallen, we continuously have adjusted our level of operations downward so as to avoid building inventory.

Our products are largely in the curtain goods area. During a period of consumer uncertainty, curtains may well be high on the list of deferrable purchases. Very low levels of housing starts also serve to dampen demand. In addition, retailers have been pressing to cut inventories generally, and we probably are feeling some effect from these efforts. These negative trends should reverse in due course, and we are attempting to minimize losses until that time comes.

1974

During the first half of 1975 sales of textile products were extremely depressed, resulting in major production curtailments. Operations ran at a significant loss, with employment down as much as 53% from a year earlier.

In contrast with previous cyclical slumps, however, most textile producers quickly reduced production to match incoming orders, thus preventing massive industry-wide accumulation of inventories. Such cutbacks caused quite prompt reflection at the mill operating level when demand revived at retail. As a result, beginning about midyear business rebounded at a fairly rapid rate. This "V" shaped textile depression, while one of the sharpest on record, also became one of the shortest ones in our experience. The fourth quarter produced an excellent profit for our textile division, bringing results for the year into the black.

On April 28, 1975 we acquired Waumbec Mills Incorporated and Waumbec Dyeing and Finishing Co., Inc., located in Manchester, New Hampshire. These companies have long sold woven goods into the drapery and apparel trade. Such drapery materials complement and extend the line already marketed through the Home Fabrics Division of Berkshire Hathaway. In the period prior to our acquisition, the company had run at a very substantial loss, with only about 55% of looms in operation and the finishing plant operating at about 50% of capacity. Losses continued on a reduced basis for a few months after acquisition. Outstanding efforts by our manufacturing administrative and sales people now have produced major improvements which, coupled with the general revival in textiles, have moved Waumbec into a significant profit position.

We expect a good level of profits from textiles in 1976. Continued progress is being made in the movement of Waumbec goods into areas of traditional marketing strength of Berkshire Hathaway, productivity should improve in both the weaving and finishing areas at Manchester, and textile demand continues firm at decent prices. We have great confidence in the ability of Ken Chace and his team to maximize our strengths in textiles. Therefore, we continue to look for ways to increase further our scale of operations while avoiding major capital investment in new fixed assets which we consider unwise, considering the relatively low returns historically earned on large scale investment in new textile equipment.

1975

Our textile division was a significant disappointment during 1976. Earnings, measured either by return on sales or by return on capital employed, were inadequate. In part, this was due to industry conditions which did not measure up to expectations of a year ago. But equally important were our own shortcomings. Marketing efforts and mill capabilities were not properly matched in our new Waumbec operation. Unfavorable manufacturing cost variances were produced by improper evaluation of machinery and personnel capabilities. Ken Chace, as always, has been candid in reporting problems and has worked diligently to correct them. He is a pleasure to work with—even under difficult operating conditions.

1976

While the first quarter outlook is for red ink, our quite tentative belief is that textile earnings in 1977 will equal, or exceed modestly, those of 1976. Despite disappointing current results, we continue to look for ways to build our textile operation and presently have one moderate-size acquisition under consideration. It should be recognized that the textile business does not offer the expectation of high returns on investment. Nevertheless, we maintain a commitment to this division—a very important source of employment in New Bedford and Manchester—and believe reasonable returns on average are possible.

1976

APPENDIX IV

Principal Equity Holdings of the Sequoia Fund
(June 30, 1986)

COMMON STOCKS

No. of Shares		Cost	Market Value
	ADVERTISING (.20%)		
36,800	The Interpublic Group of Companies, Inc.	$ 94,702	$ 1,067,200
9,000	The Ogilvy Group, Inc.	47,950	317,250
		142,652	1,384,450
	BROADCASTING (7.00%)		
191,100	Capital Cities/ABC, Inc.	38,145,272	49,017,150
	CONSUMER PRODUCTS (7.87%)		
920,600	Hasbro, Inc.	41,284,750	53,394,800
42,400	Sturm, Ruger & Company, Inc.	361,700	1,749,000
		41,646,450	55,143,800
	FOOD (12.99%)		
770,000	Dart & Kraft, Inc.	14,748,080	48,798,750
600,000	Sara Lee Corporation	14,915,388	42,150,000
		29,663,468	90,948,750
	INDUSTRIAL PRODUCTS (5.36%)		
540,200	Duplex Products, Inc.	4,738,098	11,479,250
90,000	Kimball International, Inc. Class B	2,443,125	2,677,500
61,000	MacAndrews & Forbes Group, Inc.	2,766,840	3,416,000
145,300	Western Pacific Industries, Inc.	6,465,864	19,942,425
		16,413,927	37,515,175
	PAPER MANUFACTURING (13.08%)		
745,500	Consolidated Papers, Inc.	22,645,750	43,145,812
1,949,400	P. H. Glatfelter Company	12,726,070	48,491,325
		35,371,820	91,637,137

Principal Equity Holdings of the Sequoia Fund
(June 30, 1986)
(Continued)

COMMON STOCKS

	PUBLISHING (2.17%)		
200,000	Meredith Corporation	3,743,830	15,200,000
	RETAILING (2.82%)		
240,500	Melville Corporation	8,449,248	17,075,500
67,500	Weis Markets, Inc.	439,297	2,657,813
		8,888,545	19,733,313
	SERVICES (.47%)		
102,900	PHH Group, Inc.	3,178,387	3,292,800
	WARRANTS (.22%)		
28,160	Capital Cities/ABC, Inc.	$ 941,600	$ 1,576,960

APPENDIX V

Principal Equity Holdings
of Grinnell College Endowment Fund
(September 30, 1986)

Common Stocks	No. of Shares	Market Value
Allegheny Corp.	8600	894400
Allied Bancshares, Inc.	45000	849375
Applied Materials	80000	760000
Armstrong Rubber Co.	32200	466900
BAT Industries	540300	3444413
Beecham Group	60000	337500
Berkshire Hathaway, Inc.	305	800625
Burlington Northern, Inc.	105800	5898350
Cadbury Schweppes	15000	375000
Caere Corp.	1053263	368642
Capital Cities/ABC	12700	3170238
Consolidated Papers, Inc	48500	2473500
Consolidated Stores	25000	406250
Dart & Kraft Corp.	6000	324000
Des Moines Reg. & Trib. Co	31120	622400
Diasonics, Inc.	200000	675000
Duplex Products	52000	994500
Elan Corp.	20000	267500
Enterprise Systems, Inc.	311398	1245592
Federal Express Corp.	72500	4730625
First Executive Corp.	37125	658969
Fremont General Corp.	72200	1353750
General Dynamics Corp.	18500	1320438
Glatfelter, P.H. Co.	147000	3215625
Hasbro, Inc.	93400	2510125
Henly Group	28000	553000
KLM Royal Dutch Airlines	20000	405000
Kimball Int'l., Inc.	11000	291500
Lockheed Corp.	53000	2338625
MacAndrews & Forbes Grp.	9600	624000
Manitowoc Co., Inc.	34000	595000
Meredith Corp.	14700	990413
Methode Electronics 'A'	50000	306250
Mid-America Pkg., Inc.	200000	1000000
Norfolk Southern Corp.	10100	799163
Northrop Corp.	30700	1358475

Principal Equity Holdings
of Grinnell College Endowment Fund
(September 30, 1986)
(*Continued*)

Common Stocks	No. of Shares	Market Value
Old Kent Financial	15000	521250
PHH Group, Inc.	13200	415800
PNC Financial Corp.	30000	1320000
PSA, Inc.	13500	442125
Pacific Corp.	17000	584375
Philip Morris, Inc.	71300	4723625
Santa Fe So. Pacific Co.	73900	1616563
Sara Lee Corp.	36000	2160000
Sequoia Fund, Inc.	707106	31056096
Shared Medical Systems	15000	498750
Sun Co., Inc.	7224	373842
Tenneco, Inc.	22400	910000
Trinity Industries, Inc	62900	1022125
Union Pacific Corp.	25450	1444288
Western Pacific Indus, Inc	12100	2044900

APPENDIX VI

Principal Equity Holdings of
Tukman Capital Management
(September 30, 1986)

Common Stocks	No. of Shares	Market Value (in Thousands)
American Home Prods Corp	275400	20173050
Campbell Soup Co	364200	19935475
Capital Cities ABC Inc	99900	24937538
Fireman's Fund	334900	11554050
GEICO Corp	409900	39247925
International Business M	229369	30850131
Philip Morris Cos Inc	608700	40326375
Schlumberger Ltd	642600	21687750
Sears Roebuck & Co	115000	4600000
Times Mirror Co	76700	4391075

Notes

1. Bernice Kanner, "Aw, Shucks, It's Warren Buffett," *New York,* April 22, 1985, p. 65.
2. Beth Botts, et al., "The Corn-fed Capitalist," *Regardie's,* February 1986, p. 45.
3. "Corn-fed Capitalist."
4. Ibid., p. 54.
5. Richard J. Kirkland, Jr., "Should You Leave It All to the Children?" *Fortune,* September 29, 1986, p. 18.
6. "Corn-fed Capitalist."
7. "Should You Leave It All?" p. 22.
8. "Corn-fed Capitalist," pp. 45–46.
9. John Train, "Warren Buffett: The Investor's Investor," *Financial World,* December 15, 1979, p. 36.
10. "Aw Shucks," p. 55.
11. Adam Smith, *Super Money* (New York: Random House, 1972), p. 182.
12. Ibid., p. 189.
13. Ibid., p. 194.
14. "How Omaha Beats Wall Street," *Forbes,* November 1, 1969, p. 88.
15. Jonathan Laing, "Investor Who Piled up $100 Million in the '60s Piles Up Firms Today," *Wall Street Journal,* March 31, 1977, p. 27.
16. "Look at all Those Beautiful Scantily Clad Girls Out there," *Forbes,* November 1, 1974, p. 41.
17. "How Omaha Beats Wall Street," p. 82.
18. "Buffett's Complaint," *Barron's,* June 9, 1986, p. 14.
19. Warren Buffett, quoted in Columbia University Business School, "Investing in Equity Markets," transcript of a seminar held March 13, 1985, p. 23.
20. Ibid.
21. Anthony Bianco, "Why Warren Buffett Is Breaking His Own Rules," *Business Week,* April 15, 1985, p. 134.
22. "Investing in Equity Markets," pp. 16–17.
23. Ibid., pp. 11–12.
24. "Buffett's Complaint."
25. "Investing in Equity Markets," p. 19.

26. Robert T. Grieves and David Stack, "A Press Lord Comes to Buffalo," *The Nation,* December 3, 1977, p. 591.
27. "Investor Who Piled Up."
28. Warren Buffett, "Letter to the Shareholders," *Berkshire Hathaway 1984, Annual Report to the Stockholders* (Omaha: Berkshire Hathaway, Inc., 1985), p. 8.
29. "Investor Who Piled Up," p. 27.
30. "Corn-fed Capitalist," p. 50.
31. Larry van Dyne, "The Bottom Line on Katharine Graham," *The Washingtonian,* December 1985, p. 188.
32. "Corn-fed Capitalist," p. 45.
33. "Investor Who Piled Up."
34. Barry Stavro, "Grinnell College's Quantum Jumps," *Forbes,* December 31, 1984, p. 81.
35. Warren Buffett, "Oil Discovered in Hell," *Investment Decisions,* May 1985, p. 22.
36. Ibid.
37. "Why Warren Buffett Is Breaking His Own Rules," p. 134.
38. "ABC Affiliates Hear Network's Fall Strategy," *Broadcasting,* June 9, 1986, p. 126.
39. Bill Richards, "Buffett Revises His Investment Strategy," *Wall Street Journal,* April 23, 1985, p. 59.
40. "Why Warren Buffett Is Breaking His Own Rules."
41. Warren Buffett, "Letter to Shareholders, *Berkshire Hathaway 1985 Annual Report* (Omaha: Berkshire Hathaway, Inc., 1986), p. 8.
42. Ibid., p. 9.
43. Ibid.
44. "Buffett's Complaint."
45. "Words of Wisdom," *Financial World,* June 13 to 26, 1984, p. 8.
46. "Investing in Equity Markets," pp. 28–29.
47. "How Omaha Beats Wall Street."
48. Andrew Tobias, "Letters from Chairman Buffett," *Fortune,* April 22, 1983, p. 140.
49. Warren E. Buffett, "Up the Inefficient Market," *Barron's,* February 25, 1985, p. 40.
50. "Words of Wisdom."
51. "Why Warren Buffett Is Breaking His Own Rules."
52. Ibid.
53. "Aw, Shucks," p. 52.
54. Warren Buffett, "You Pay a Very High Price in the Stock Market for a Cheery Consensus," *Forbes,* August 6, 1979, pp. 25–26.
55. Ibid., p. 26.
56. "Up the Inefficient Market," p. 11.
57. Ibid., passim.
58. Ibid., p. 37.
59. "Look at All Those Beautiful," p. 41.

60. Ibid.
61. Warren Buffett, "How Inflation Swindles the Equity Investor," *Fortune,* pp. 250–60.
62. Waldemar Nielsen, *The Golden Donors* (New York: E. P. Dutton, 1984).
63. "Investing in Equity Markets," p. 10.
64. Ibid.
65. Ibid., pp. 1–2.
66. "Buffett Revises his Investment Strategy."
67. Ibid.
68. "Corn-fed Capitalist," p. 46.
69. "Investor Who Piled Up," pp. 1, 27.
70. Warren Buffett, "Berkshire Hathaway 1982 Annual Report," *Berkshire Hathaway Letters to Shareholders 1977–1984* (Omaha: Berkshire Hathaway, Inc., 1985), p. 64.
71. "Investing in Equity Markets," p. 19.
72. Anne Millett, "Mrs. B. Means Business," *USA Today,* April 1, 1986.
73. Frank E. James, "Furniture Czarina," *Wall Street Journal,* May 23, 1984, p. 23.
74. "Corn-fed Capitalist," p. 53.
75. Ibid.
76. Ibid., p. 46.
77. "Aw Shucks," p. 55.
78. Ibid., pp. 54–55.
79. "Investing in Equity Markets," p. 23.
80. "The Bottom Line on Katharine Graham," p. 204.
81. Warren Buffett, "Capital Sin," *Barron's,* April 7, 1986, p. 13.
82. Columbia Business School seminar, p. 26.
83. Warren Buffett, "Letter to Shareholders," *Berkshire Hathaway 1985 Annual Report* (Omaha: Berkshire Hathaway, Inc., 1986), p. 20.
84. Television interview, "The Money Managers," *Adam's Smith Money World,* Show No. 112, November 19, 1984.
85. John Train, *The Money Masters* (New York: Harper & Row, 1980), p. 23.
86. Warren Buffett, "Letter to Members of Buffett Partnership, Ltd., October 8, 1967.

Index

Copyright Acknowledgments

Grateful acknowledgment is made for permission to reprint the following:

Excerpts from *Street Smart Investing:* Issue 164, December 26, 1985, © 1985 Street Smart, Inc., and Issue 181, September 18, 1986, © 1986 Street Smart, Inc. Reprinted by permission of Street Smart, Inc., Yorktown Heights, N.Y.

Excerpts from Standard & Poor's New York Stock Exchange Reports: "General Foods," #972, October 7, 1985, © 1985 Standard & Poor's Corp.; "Scott & Fetzer," #1987S, November 5, 1985, © 1985 Standard & Poor's Corp.; "RJR Nabisco," #1891F, November 6, 1985, © 1985 Standard & Poor's Corp.; "American Broadcasting," #94, December 5, 1985, © 1985 Standard & Poor's Corp.; "American Express," #112L, June 6, 1986, © 1986 Standard & Poor's Corp.; "RCA Corp.," #1891, June 9, 1986, © 1986 Standard & Poor's Corp.; "Amerada Hess," #80, June 24, 1986, © 1986 Standard & Poor's Corp.; "Ogilvy Group," #4857, August 11, 1986, © 1986 Standard & Poor's Corp.; "GEICO Corp.," #932F, August 29, 1986, © 1986 Standard & Poor's Corp.; "Handy & Harman," #1093K, September 3, 1986, © 1986 Standard & Poor's Corp.; "Fireman's Fund," #887, September 8, 1986, © 1986 Standard & Poor's Corp.; "SAFECO Corp.," #514F, September 12, 1986, © 1986 Standard & Poor's Corp.; "Media General," #8508, September 23, 1986, © 1986 Standard & Poor's Corp.; "Washington Post," #9517S, September 23, 1986, © 1986 Standard & Poor's Corp.; "Affiliated Publications," #7047P, September 23, 1986, © 1986 Standard & Poor's Corp.; "Interpublic Group," #1236S, October 22, 1986, © 1986 Standard & Poor's Corp.; "Time, Inc.," #2236, November 11, 1986, © 1986 Standard & Poor's Corp.; "Times Mirror," #2237, November 17, 1986, © 1986 Standard & Poor's Corp.; "Capital Cities/ABC," #442, November 19, 1986, © 1986 Standard & Poor's Corp. Reprinted by permission of Standard & Poor's Corporation.